CONTRIBUTIONS TO AN IRISHMAN'S DIARY IN THE IRISH TIMES

ORLA KELLY PUBLISHING

HUGH ORAM

ISBN: 978-1-912328-56-7

For Bernadette

ACKNOWLEDGEMENTS

I'd like to pay particular tribute to my beloved wife, Bernadette, who has been a constant source of inspiration and encouragement in my book writing career since I began it 40 years ago. She has always had an unwavering exactitude for precisely the right approach, the right phrase and the right word, a reflection of her own dedication over the years to writing poetry.

I'm also indebted to the encouragement given by Eoin McVey, managing editor and Donncha Ó Muirithe, at The Irish Times. Donncha is editor of both the Diary and readers' letters. I'd also like to thank Dean Lochner of the Bondi Group In Ballsbridge, Dublin, for all his technical help and the publisher of this book, Orla Kelly, for all her help, advice and dedication in getting the book into print.

for Siobhan and family,
with every good wish,

[signature]

Dublin, March 6th, 2020

CONTENTS

Contributions to an Irishman's Diary 2006 Cont.

Contributions to an Irishman's Diary 2007

Contributions to an Irishman's Diary 2008

Contributions to an Irishman's Diary 2009

Contributions to an Irishman's Diary 2019

Contributions to an Irishman's Diary 2020

An Irishman's Diary

EXACTLY 40 years ago yesterday, one of Dublin's great newspapers, the Dublin *Evening Mail*, closed down. Once, it was required reading at teatime for generations of Dubliners, a surprisingly homely, almost innocent, mix of news and features. Jottings by Man About Town and cartoons, including Jiggs and Maggie and Mandrake the Magician, were very popular.

The paper carried regular listings of progress reports about people in isolation hospitals, such as the old Cork Street Fever Hospital and Cherry Orchard. Patients could be "satisfactory" or "not so well"; fortunately, they weren't listed by name, merely by number. An Óige and cycling notes, a "Lost and Found" column, limericks and even a spot for lonely hearts were also part of a time-worn tradition. If anyone had a pet dog or cat missing, they could be sure of an editorial mention in the Mail. The most widely read part of the paper was Letters to the Editor. For years, a well-known encouragement in Dublin was: "Write to the Mail about it". This unchanging formula yielded a solid circulation of some 100,000 that passed from generation to generation.

First editor

The paper started life in 1823 and its first editor was Joseph Timothy Haydn. Within a month, it had become the city's best-selling newspaper, at all of 2,500 copies an issue. Haydn's previous claim to fame was that he had been horsewhipped by the aide-de-camp to the Lord Lieutenant of Ireland for having made disparaging remarks about the ADC's parentage. But the owners of the *Mail* were so concerned that Haydn's impetuous nature could land them with big libel suits, they paid him off handsomely; he was just over 40 when he took a comfortable early retirement.

Throughout the 19th century, the *Mail* prospered against its competitors, including the *Evening Irish Times* and then the *Evening Herald*. The *Mail* was helped by such star writers as Bram Stoker, a feature writer and drama critic for the paper. It also had a claim to a big technical advance. In 1898, it became the first newspaper in the world to use wireless telegraphy for sending copy.

The yachting correspondent had found himself becalmed by heavy fog, so his copy was days late in arriving. Then he sent regatta results from what was then Kingstown by the new technology and they arrived instantly.

But the *Mail* also attracted a certain notoriety, particularly after Queen Victoria's last visit to Dublin in 1900. A compositor of nationalist hue was said to have had the august queen "pissing" instead of "passing" over O'Connell Bridge, but despite years of research, no one has been ever been able to authenticate the story by finding a copy of that particular edition, which may have

The last edition of Dublin's Evening Mail, modestly announcing its own demise on Thursday, July 19th, 1962

been changed with unusual alacrity.

Inside the *Mail*, the room for reporters and sub-editors was a genteel, clubbable kind of place, an entirely male enclave, where everyone was Mr This or Mr That. Once, a great scandal arose when Joe Anderson, editor between 1936 and 1958, a genial man, sacked a reporter for having a bottle of whiskey in his desk.

Another reporter, Ernie O'Reilly, came to a bizarre end. He had a holy horror of cars, considering them a dangerous invention, so he never drove, going everywhere instead by taxi. One night, coming back to the *Mail*'s offices at the top of Parliament Street, just opposite the old City Hall, his cab was collided with another vehicle on Capel Street Bridge. Poor Ernie O'Reilly was thrown through the windscreen and a sliver of glass sliced his jugular vein.

Saturday sports edition

Normally, the first edition of the *Mail* came out at 3 p.m. and a small crowd looking for copies gathered at the works entrance, at the back of the *Mail*'s offices. But Saturdays were special, when the *Sports Mail* came out at 7 p.m. I remember Alfie Dalton, for years overseer of the compositors, telling me how all the sports results came in handwritten on hundreds of scraps of paper. As many as 30 compositors set them in hot metal type; the air was filled with the clatter of the Linotypes, with heat and dust, yet miraculously, from this hellish but organised chaos emerged a word-perfect sports edition.

When the *Irish Times* building caught fire in 1951, the *Mail* immediately rushed to help and by 4 p.m. that day *Irish Times* sub-editors were ensconced around the subs' table in the *Mail*. The next day, the *Mail* printed a four-page emergency edition of *The Irish Times*.

For many years, the war cry of the Dublin newsboys was "Herald o' Mail". Then along came a brash interloper, the *Evening Press*, launched in 1954 with a brass band and elephants along O'Connell Street. The new paper was the death stroke of the *Mail*. Three evening newspapers

for Dublin were just too many and the old *Mail*, a venerable dowager of the Victorian era, just couldn't cope with the upstart. On the very last day of 1961 came the final blow, the opening of Telefis Eireann. These days, reflecting a worldwide trend in the newspaper business, Dublin has just one evening paper, the *Evening Herald*.

Change to tabloid

The *Irish Times* had made a last gentlemanly effort to save the *Mail*, in 1960, by buying it for £200,000 and transferring printing to its own press. Ken Gray, the former *Irish Times* deputy editor who died recently, played a big part in changing the *Mail* from broadsheet to tabloid, very revolutionary in those days. He also wrote a column for the *Mail* on that new-fangled entertainment, television.

With the takeover by *The Irish Times*, a strange daily ritual ended at the *Mail*. Since it closed the *Dublin Daily Express* in 1921, every publication day it had printed one copy of a single sheet of the *Express*, just with the masthead and date, to preserve the title.

The very last editor of the *Mail* was a young journalist with a great reputation for sniffing out news at 500 paces: John Healy. He went on to become a household name in the 1960s when he began his Backbencher column in the Saturday *Irish Times*. He was also the proud possessor of a Rolls-Royce, never a common form of transport for Dublin news workers. The last issue of the *Evening Mail*, priced at three old pence, came out on July 19th, 1962. It was signed by such luminaries as Sean Ó Ceallacháin, Paddy Downey and Peter Byrne in the sports department; Ken Gray; Jim Downey and John Healy. One of the young fellows there, Michael Hand, went on to become editor of the *Sunday Independent*.

The 1960s turned out to be a remarkably innovative decade for *The Irish Times* itself under the editorship of Douglas Gageby, who had been first editor of the *Evening Press*, the paper that had scuppered the *Evening Mail*.

An Irishman's Diary

THE BEATLES wouldn't last a year, Frank Hall predicted. When the boys came to Dublin for their famous gig at the Adelphi in 1963, Hall interviewed them about their hairstyles and sex appeal, later declaring that, as a band, they were going absolutely nowhere!

But whatever his failings as a pop pundit, Frank Hall went on to front *Hall's Pictorial Weekly*, arguably the best satirical show produced on RTÉ television. Over 250 episodes were shown from the autumn of 1971 until the spring of 1980, usually high in the ratings. Hall wrote the scripts and invented all kinds of crazy characters and among those who portrayed them were Frank Kelly and Eamon Morrissey. Terry Willers drew the cartoons. The show was often bizarre and frequently irreverent; nothing was either safe or sacred.

Much of the show's genesis came from Hall's upbringing in Newry, where he was born in 1921, troubled times indeed. The then town council was a prototype for the fictional Ballymagash Urban District Council in *Hall's Pictorial Weekly*. Further inspiration came from the strangely extended Hall family household in Newry, which included his mother's sister, otherwise known as the Great Patriot, an uncle and a great-uncle. His father, a Dubliner, had a peripatetic career that included a spell as a seaman, another as a dee-jay on a US radio station, and a stint as an unsuccessful seller of post-war army surplus.

Fear of unemployment

Frank Hall himself left school at 12 and worked in a couple of men's outfitters in Newry before heading for London. There, driven by a chronic fear of unemployment, he not only double-but quadruple-jobbed; at one stage, he was even a waiter in a Lyons Corner House café. Always in search of safe, secure work, he managed to talk himself into the art department of Independent Newspapers in Dublin, before moving into journalism on the *Evening Herald*. He wrote showbiz news under such bylines as "Frank Lee" and "Rick O'Shea"; the seeds of Hall's Pictorial Weekly were being fertilised. He also did the social diary, competing with Terry O'Sullivan on the *Evening Press*.

In time, he moved to RTÉ, working first in the newsroom, then on the *Newsbeat* programme, for which he did quirky stories from all over the country. He worked on RTÉ radio, too, and was particularly identified with the early Sunday evening

Frank Hall: pioneered political satire on RTÉ television

round-up of the provincial papers. Then RTÉ got daring and let him loose on an innocent nation with *Hall's Pictorial Weekly*.

He mocked gombeenism and political shenanigans: no rural sacred bullock was safe and neither was the Coalition government led by Liam Cosgrave that came to power in 1973. Richie Ryan, as Minister for Finance, was transformed into the "Minister for Hardship". Characters such as the two bachelor farmers – "boys, oh boys" – appealed to viewers and so too did characters that had their origins in Hall's early life.

Strong language

Cllr Parnell Mooney (played by Frank Kelly and nothing to do with a certain pub!) was based on a councillor in Newry, a man dedicated to strong and often vile language. The journalists at the press table in the council meetings could hear him very clearly, as could anyone passing up and down the street outside, but it was always reported that "the comments of Cllr ---- were inaudible". The character of Father Romulus Todd was based on a real-life parish priest from Co Tyrone, who once warned his startled congregation about the duplicity of Queen Elizabeth I. "She was the virgin queen, but she was no more a virgin than I am," he thundered.

Hall's Pictorial Weekly often homed in on issues of the day, such as the appalling phone service of the times. The programme even managed to extract humour from the new phone directory as soon as it was published annually. Hall often declared that he hated political posturing, hypocrisy and "oul' guff", so politicians were natural

targets. It was widely believed at the time that the programme helped the Coalition lose the 1977 general election. After Jack Lynch returned to power that year, Hall dubbed him the "real Taoiseach" and the critics started murmuring that the programme had gone soft, that the dog had stopped biting. This belief even surfaced in Seanad debates years later, when it was pointed out that in 1978, Hall was elevated from deputy film censor to film censor. One of his controversial decisions in that role was banning *The Life of Brian*, a Monty Python "take" on the life of Christ.

But the spirit of the series lives on even yet; subsequent satirical programmes, including *Father Ted* and *Bull Island* on television and *Scrap Saturday* on radio, owed their inspiration in many respects to Frank Hall, his dedicated team of comic artistes and the characters they created. Not long ago, John O'Connor, in his column in the *Munster Express*, noted that the *Anglo-Celt* newspaper in Co Cavan had run a headline: "Cootehill's over-run with bonking dogs". The town commission had been told that the place was awash with dogs that were "bonking in the streets night, moon and morning". One town commissioner called for an end to this disgraceful behaviour. As O'Connor commented, this would have been ideal material for *Hall's Pictorial Weekly*.

Away from the weekly television slot, Hall lived a modest enough life, bringing up a large family in Santry. He and his wife, Aideen Kearney, had eloped as teenagers in Newry. Hall was dismissive of his own fame, remarking that his face was "as well-known as a beggar's ass".

Clerical hat

When he wasn't working, he was addicted to jazz and at one time played bass with Mick Delahunty's band. He was also practised yoga and had a strong attachment to a large clerical hat that had been sold to him in 1950 by Maureen O'Hara's father, who told him that his head size was similar to that one of a one-time Bishop of Galway, Dr Browne. "The bishop and I had the two biggest heads in the country," Hall was later heard to say.

It's over 20 years since *Hall's Pictorial Weekly* ended its seminal run and seven years since Frank Hall himself died, on September 21st 1995. Just when the country is crying out for a new Minister for Hardship, all we can do is call up the mocking ghosts of the past.

An Irishman's Diary

THE recently erected Spire of Dublin has focused attention on the Corporation's ambitious plans to regenerate the capital's main street. But if an architect and town planner from Merseyside, Patrick Abercrombie, had had his way nine decades ago, the Dublin of today would bear little resemblance to what we see today. Instead of the Spire in O'Connell Street, we would have had a grand metropolitan cathedral at the top of Capel Street with a 500-foot column, a modern version of a round tower, topped by a statue of St Patrick.

Abercrombie's plan, drawn up when he was working in the school of architecture at Liverpool University, was devised with two colleagues, Arthur and Sydney Kelly. The three entered a competition to plan a revitalised city of Dublin run in conjunction with the 1913 Civics Exhibition in the city. They won the prize of £500, a substantial sum, that in those days could have bought a very decent-sized house in the city.

However, the results of the Dublin competition weren't made public until October, 1916, when the populace had other things on its mind. It was finally published, in book form, in December 1922, just as the new State was coming into being. *Dublin of the Future* described the capital as a city of magnificent possibilities, marred by the juxtaposition of incongruities and squalor.

New cathedral

Abercrombie had been much influenced by the work of Baron Georges-Eugène Haussmann and his vast improvements in 19th-century Paris. One of the key elements of his vision was a new Roman Catholic cathedral to replace the Pro-Cathedral. He sited it near what is now DIT Bolton Street and its glorious Florentine entrance would have faced down Capel Street towards the Liffey.

At the back of the cathedral, Abercrombie designed a gigantic plaza, complete with a series of cenotaphs honouring famous Irishmen. The whole edifice was to be linked to the Kings Inns, while the statue of St Patrick high above the roof would have been visible from many parts of the city, like today's Spire. Abercrombie boldly planned to have Henrietta Street, with its 18th-century houses, demolished to make way for his new cathedral.

He also designed a new national theatre for Cavendish Row, near where the present Gate Theatre stands, and he wanted the building to close off the view at the top of O'Connell Street. He planned to extend Amiens Street station down to the river, remove Butt Bridge, turn the Custom

Capel Street: would have acquired new prestige under the Abercrombie plan for Dublin

House into the new GPO and rebuild everything in the vicinity of the Custom House with new buildings in the Beaux Arts style, all taller than the Custom House. He proposed downgrading O'Connell Street to a secondary route. The plan also envisaged the old parliament buildings at College Green being turned into the new seat of government, with a new block for State administration at the corner of Westmoreland Street and Aston Quay.

Central railway station

On the north side of the river, between Capel Street and the Four Courts, he proposed a new central railway station, linked to Phoenix Park by a wide boulevard.

Nor were the suburbs spared. He planned to create radial routes across the city, widening many streets in the process, such as Northumberland Road in Ballsbridge. He also suggested that Dublin should have 14 neighbourhood parks and that 10 neighbourhood centres should be built. In other respects, too, the plan was prescient: he said that Dublin's most urgent problem was rehousing 60,000 people living in deplorable tenements and highlighted the possibilities of developing districts such as Cabra and Crumlin.

The plan extended to industry. He proposed building a "power citadel" at the Pigeon House, saying that it was pointless carting coal to every factory in Dublin when it could all be converted to power at the point where it came into Dublin port.

The report was majestically designed and printed, awash with maps and photographs, but it was destined to sit on a shelf in Dublin Corporation for years. Yet Abercrombie was invited back to remake the city again in his imagination, just as another World War was starting.

Between 1939 and 1941, he produced a second, more modest plan together with Sydney Kelly

and Manning Robertson, a Dublin-based town planner. This time, he moved the proposed new cathedral to the Ormond Quay area and placed a new civic centre to the immediate west of Parliament Street. He wanted a new central bus station on Aston Quay, and new bridges upstream and downstream from O'Connell Bridge. He proposed that satellite towns should be developed in such areas as Clondalkin, Lucan and Tallaght.

In other respects, too, he was ahead of his time, saying the city should avoid the piecemeal redevelopment of Georgian areas. He warned against the type of development that had happened in the recent past on Rathmines Road, which he described as an object lesson in chaotic building.

Distinguished career

This second report met the same neglected fate as the first. Yet despite his Dublin disappointments, Abercrombie enjoyed a very distinguished career in town planning in Britain.

He was professor of civic design at Liverpool University from 1915 until 1935, when he went to London University as professor of town planning. After the destruction of the second World War his large-scale town planning ideas were put into practice with the rebuilding of bombed-out areas of London, Plymouth and other English cities. He also did much work on the creation of new towns such as Welwyn Garden City and was greatly involved in the establishment of the London area Green Belt.

In Dublin, Abercrombie's work is merely a great historical might-have-been, just two more reports that were never translated into practical action. Yet in Britain, he is still regarded as a father of modern town planning and for his services, he was knighted in 1945, becoming Sir Patrick Abercrombie.

May 5, 2003

An Irishman's Diary

EXACTLY a century ago today, on February 13th, 1903, Georges Simenon, the creator of Inspector Maigret, was born in Liège, a dreary industrial city in eastern Belgium. Even with his date of birth, an element of make-believe crept in, as it did with so much of Simenon's life.

His domineering and religious mother, Henriette, who came from stern Dutch and Prussian stock, gave birth to Georges at 10 minutes after midnight on February 13th that year, but made a false declaration that he had been born on the 12th, so that he would not be registered with an unlucky date.

The young boy's upbringing was strict and *petit-bourgeois*. His father, Désiré was an accountant for an insurance firm and his mother worked in a store. Georges was an avid reader from about eight years of age: Balzac, Dickens, Dumas, Stevenson, anything he could get his hands on. He was educated by the Jesuits, but soon rebelled against both school and Church. For his whole life, he also found it extremely difficult to get on with his mother.

Childhood seduction

In 1915, when he was just 12. While on holiday, he was seduced by a young girl called Renée, (who was three years older then himself. He went on to become extremely promiscuous for most of his life. By his own claim, he had sex with 10,000 women. Many of them were prostitutes; as a young man, he had a penchant for the low life of Paris.

Another key moment for the young Simenon came in 1919, when he was just 16. He got a job in the office of the local weekly paper, the *Gazette de Liège*. So many of its staff had been killed in the Great War that when he asked the editor for a transfer to reporting duties, his wish was granted immediately. The young apprentice reporter covered the usual round of local events, everything from the courts to dignitaries' funerals.

This introduction to everyday city life, including its seedier elements, was seminal to his later writings. He also joined a group of artists in Liège who called themselves La Caque (The Cask). They drank, took drugs and talked endlessly about art and philosophy.

Simenon spent four years at the paper before leaving for Paris, where his first job was as secretary to a writer and politician with extreme right-wing views. Paris also saw him having his first big affair, with Josephine

Georges Simenon, enigmatic creator of the pipe-smoking detective Maigret

Baker, the wonderfully sexy black performer from Missouri, who scandalised even 1920s Paris with her nightclub act wearing nothing but a bunch of bananas.

Simenon's young wife, Régine Renchon, nicknamed "Tigy", an artist in her own right, turned an unseeing eye to his many indiscretions.

Simenon became wealthy as a result of the masses of pulp fiction he produced under many pseudonyms. He and his wife moved to an apartment in the stylish Place des Vosges, where they had a secretary, a chauffeur and a cook. He mixed socially with such artists as Picasso and Vlaminck.

During the 1930s, not only did Simenon continue his womanising with great enthusiasm, but he also became an inveterate wanderer. He and his wife lived at many addresses throughout France and travelled many of the country's canals and rivers, as well as visiting much of Europe, Turkey and Africa.

Arrival of Maigret

The publication in 1931 of the first Inspector Maigret book was astonishing for its publicity, the invention of Simenon himself. The launch took place in a nightclub in Montparnasse and guests had to come dressed either as gangsters or prostitutes. Next day, Parisian papers devoted hectares of space to this new character of detective fiction.

Over the next 40 years new investigations by the fictional French policeman appeared at an average rate of around 2.5 a year. Simenon, who started work each day at around 4 a.m., wrote a total of 450 novels and novelettes. He

never wrote the "big novel" that some critics expected, but produced more than 50 serious books, some of them profound psychological studies that had nothing to do with Maigret. After his mother died, late in his life, he wrote *Lettre à ma Mere*, an incomparable study of the mother-son relationship. However, it is for the French detective with his hat, trench coat and pipe that Simenon will always be remembered.

The archetypical on-screen Maigret was Rupert Davies, who played the detective for 51 episodes on BBC television between 1960 and 1963. Exactly 30 years later, the Dublin-born actor Michael Gambon played Maigret in 12 TV productions by Granada. Many others portrayed the detective on cinema and television screens, including Charles Laughton and Richard Harris. The character was immensely popular, with Maigret books translated into 50 languages and over 500 million copies sold.

During the second World War, when much of France was occupied, Simenon and his family lived near La Rochelle in western France, where he continued to write for publication. When the war ended, he narrowly escaped being punished as a collaborator. Then he and his family went to live in the US. He divorced his wife in Reno, Nevada and next day the same magistrate presided as Simenon wed a French Canadian woman, Denyse Ouimet, over 20 years his junior.

Return to Europe

For several years they lived in an idyllic rural setting in Connecticut, before Simenon made a disastrous decision to return to Europe. They settled in various locations in and near Lausanne in Switzerland, where his wife's mental health deteriorated sharply. Years later, when Simenon's 25-year-old daughter Marie-Jo killed herself with a gun, Simenon blamed Denyse. In 1961, Simenon took up with the last woman in his life, an Italian chambermaid called Terese Sburelin.

After Maigret was "retired" in 1972, Simenon still wrote vigorously until his health gave way in the last years of his life. He died during the night of September 3rd to 4th. He was cremated, without any religious ceremony, and his ashes were mingled with those of his beloved daughter, Marie-Jo, and scattered beneath a huge tree in the back garden of his last home in Lausanne.

February 13, 2003

An Irishman's Diary

Hugh Oram

If it hadn't been for a *Daily Express* reporter, Busáras might never have been built. Dublin's central bus station opened 50 years ago this year but behind its design and construction lay an extraordinary story of political intrigue and public controversy, beside which the recent uproar over the Spire of Dublin was feebleness personified. The story of the man who designed Busáras, Michael Scott, is just as intriguing.

Born in Drogheda of Kerry parents, the young Michael Scott was articled to an architectural practice in Dublin in the 1920s. However, Scott was just as keen on the theatre and also trained as an actor in both Dublin and the US.

In 1929 he returned from a tour in the US with the Abbey company and went on to perform in London in a play called *The New Gossoon*, by George Sheils.

He earned superlative reviews, but because he didn't want his architectural colleagues to know he was moonlighting on the stage, called himself "Wolfe Curran". He was three weeks into the run when a *Daily Express* reporter rumbled him and said in print that the leading man of such extraordinary talent was really a young architect from Dublin. Scott promptly pulled out of the play and pulled down the curtain on his acting career. He never acted again.

During the 1930s, he and a colleague designed all sorts of buildings, such as hospitals in Portlaoise and Tullamore. In 1938, he designed his own house in Sandycove in 24 hours and later remarked, "I was a quick boy in my day". His Irish pavilion at the New York Fair in 1939 was an outstanding forerunner of Busáras.

On January 1st, 1945, the State transport company, CIÉ, came into being. The initial plan was to centralise its various offices around Dublin into one new building which could also be used as a bus station. Scott was chosen to make Busáras a bold statement of the new Ireland, with the full backing of Eamon de Valera's Fianna Fáil government.

Scott had impeccable Fianna Fáil connections and was particularly friendly with Sean Lemass, later to become Taoiseach. The first chairman of CIÉ was a man called Percy Reynolds, who lived at Abbeville, Kinsealy, in north Co Dublin. For him, Scott designed alterations to the house, now the home of Charles J. Haughey.

When the inter-party government led by John A. Costello came into office in 1948, it disapproved of what it regarded as mere Fianna Fáil extravagance. It decided to downgrade Busáras and turn it into an unemployment exchange for women, which prompted the *Irish Times* columnist, Myles na Gopaleen,

Busáras at Store Street, Dublin: Scott's modernist building, now 50 years old, was a source of long-running controversies

to christen it the "Bust Station". At one stage, when much of Busáras had been built, construction work was even suspended. After Fianna Fáil returned to office in 1951, work resumed – to completion.

For years previously, Dáil debates on the topic had been marked by splendid vituperation. The site choice itself had been very controversial. Three other locations had been considered: one at Aston Quay, another beyond Christ Church cathedral and the third in Smithfield, but Store Street was the cheapest. Yet there were complaints over the cost, more than £1 million. The work on the design had been full of infighting and

intrigue and matters were made worse when a senior civil servant, Dan O'Donovan, was put in charge of the project. He and Michael Scott simply didn't get on.

Scott conceived Busáras as a work of art but the public was bemused by this first expression in Ireland of the modern architectural movement. One of the milder nicknames for Busáras was the "Glass House". Few outside the architectural profession realised that Scott was a disciple of Le Corbusier, the great Swiss modernist architect. From works of Le Corbusier, such as the Swiss Pavilion at the University of Paris, built in the early 1930s, you can trace a direct visual lineage to Busáras.

The end result created immense interest among architects all over Europe and beyond. Scott went on to leave his architectural mark on other buildings such as the Bord Fáilte building at Baggot Street Bridge, the RTÉ studios in Donnybrook, the present Abbey Theatre and the Carrolls tobacco factory in Dundalk. Donnybrook bus garage and the Charlemont Street flats also bore his imprint.

The actual Busáras bus station wasn't opened until October 1953, but before then, CIÉ had been elbowed aside and what was the Department of Social Welfare moved into the rest of the building. Civil servants had to cope with a brand new idea for Ireland: the whole building was air conditioned and the windows were designed not to be opened. Another fancy idea was a newsreel cinema in the basement, which later became a theatre. The vast, convoluted controversies about Busáras are long forgotten and while not many people, even today, would profess to love the place, it is now regarded as a classic of modern Irish architecture.

March 14, 2003

An Irishman's Diary

It seems scarcely believable now, but Sandymount Strand in Dublin once had its very own pier, the only one of its kind in Ireland and with all the jollity of Blackpool or Brighton. Today, for anyone walking along the fine, lighted promenade that runs for about a mile along the front at Sandymount, what looks like blockhouse ruins in the sand is all that's left.

Since the 18th century, Sandymount Strand has been used as a bathing beach. Until the later 19th century, a whole row of bathing huts stood along the edge of the beach. Then, the Pembroke Town Commissioners, the local authority of the time, decided to do away with them. Someone had the novel idea of a pier that stretched for three miles, to the low water mark, but nothing came of it.

But not long afterwards, the Merrion Promenade Pier and Baths Company was formed and work got under way. During 1882 and 1883, the great concrete sea baths were built; these are the ruins that can be seen today. The baths were about 150 feet square and divided into two sections, one for men, the other for women and children. The baths were replenished once a day from a seawater tank that stood 500 yards further out.

Next came the pier, linking the baths with Strand Road. It was an elegant lattice-work structure with wooden decking, the creation of Frederick Morley, the company's technical expert. Halfway along the pier, a large shelter contained a bandstand.

When the pier opened to the public for the first time in 1884, the inaugural concert was given by the band of the Highland Infantry. From that May onwards, concerts were advertised on a regular basis. For many subsequent summers, concerts were staged every week on Tuesday and Saturday evenings.

At the Strand Road entrance to the pier, there were kiosks, while further along the pier, strollers could partake of all sorts of delicacies from the food

Hugh Oram

stalls, including cockles and mussels dug up from the strand.

Sandymount Pier became immensely popular with local people, who would often sit out in summer in wicker chairs, taking refreshments, reading perhaps, in the gentle evening air, sometimes with music in the background. In an era when ladies wore long dresses and gentlemen wing collars, the pier became a place for delightfully casual relaxation.

The pier was still there when the young James Joyce frequented Sandymount Strand, but it became badly neglected

A rainy day, Sandymount Strand – in the mist the old baths, a relic of the 1880s

after only about 30 years in service. By 1920, the pier had deteriorated so much that it had to be demolished. All the ironwork was carted off to the Hammond Lane scrapyard in Ringsend and these days, no trace exists of the old pier.

While the pier disappeared, other efforts to "improve" the strand fortunately came to nothing. In the mid-1930s discussion raged about where to site the proposed new Dublin Airport. Two hot favourites were the Phoenix Park and Tallaght, but the most audacious idea came from an architect and engineer called

Desmond McAteer.

He wrote a very detailed article for *Studies* magazine in 1935, complete with extensive drawings. He suggested that one square mile of Sandymount Strand should be concreted over to form Dublin Airport. By his estimation, it would take five years to build, at a cost of £1.5 million. One big advantage was that it would be close to the railway line. Such an airport would have been fine for the small aircraft of the time, but not for today's jets.

Precedents do exist for seaside airports, like the magnificent one at Nice in the south of France. But somehow, a request from the cabin crew to "fasten your seatbelts for landing at Sandymount Strand" would have seemed just a little fanciful.

At the end of 1936, the decision was made to opt for Collinstown, the site of the present Dublin Airport and Sandymount Strand was saved. Other plans that came to nothing including a proposal in the mid-1960s from the old Dublin Port & Docks Board to redevelop part of the Strand for industrial use. Amid much controversy, that particular idea was also dropped.

In more recent times, the draft 1998 city development plan proposed an eastern bypass route running in a tunnel beneath Sandymount Strand, but over the last year or two, this brainwave has gone very quiet.

Perhaps what's needed now is some generous benefactor who will fund the rebuilding of the old pier. Gaiety would be restored to Sandymount Strand and Ireland would get back its one and only pier.

An Irishman's Diary

Hugh Oram

For sheer flying excitement, nothing has ever beaten a trip on Concorde, that droop-nosed white arrow of the skies which is soon to become extinct. Flying at just over Mach 2, or 1,350 m.p.h., was an unforgettable experience.

A lot of Concorde training was done out of Shannon, but the pencil-slim aircraft came into Dublin airport only a handful of times. On one of those occasions, a Dublin travel agent was running a weekend special to the Prix de l'Arc de Triomphe horse-race at Longchamp in Paris. My wife and I weren't remotely interested in going to the races, but we were passionate about flying on Concorde. At great risk to our bank account, we paid £1,000 just for the flight on an Air France Concorde. It was worth every penny.

The first impression on boarding Concorde was how narrow the cabin was. It was like being confined in an elongated vacuum cleaner. The aircraft can take a maximum of only 128 passengers, with the leather seats in rows of two on each side of the aisle. The sense of claustrophobia is intensified by the tiny, porthole-like windows, much smaller than in a conventional airliner.

The first surprise was take-off, a turbo-charged affair. An ordinary jet seems to take for ever to crawl into the air, but with Concorde, take-off is at 250 m.p.h. and the g-forces really push you right back in your seat. Dublin was just a blur, gone in the flash of an eye, and it seemed a mere five minutes later that the pilot's voice was telling us we were over Shannon.

To give everyone the maximum thrills for their money, the aircraft flew to Paris by a circuitous route over the Atlantic – we must have gone half-way to New York, before flying back towards Paris over the west coast of France. Then the pilot announced that we were going supersonic. With an almighty roar, the after-burners were switched on and the plane soared up to its cruising altitude of close to 60,000 feet (a commercial jet normally cruises at around 35,000 feet). The Mach display in the cabin clicked up our progress as our speed climbed ever higher. Soon, it was on Mach 2.04, the maximum, or twice the speed of sound.

At this speed and altitude, Concorde has a disconcerting little habit: it seems as if the engines cut out momentarily and the plane dips a little.

Were we going to fall to earth? The short answer was no. Out of the tiny window, we could see the curvature of the

Concorde's bold surge into the future will soon be consigned into the past

earth, with the sky a very surreal pale blue. We could vaguely make out the ocean far beneath us. However, we were unaware of the immense heat generated by this speed. At its maximum speed, the nose of Concorde heats to 127 ° Centigrade and the fuselage actually stretches a little because of the heat.

In the cabin, everyone was in a jolly mood. A meal was served and, for airline food, it was excellent. The champagne flowed with abandon – after all, this was a French Concorde. There was another little Gallic *je ne sais quoi* in the shape of an in-flight cartoonist. He was a young Italian artist who signed himself "Carlelli" and in no time at all he gone up and down the cabin doing lightning sketches of the passengers. We still have ours, together with all the other Concorde paraphernalia. For something done in about 10 seconds, its a good likeness of this pair of intrepid travellers. Perhaps every airline should employ onboard cartoonists; Ryanair please note.

We were airborne for about 90 minutes and then it was down to earth at Charles de Gaulle airport. We floated through the rest of that weekend in Paris, before coming home on a plain, ordinary jet. It was like going to work in a Porsche and coming home on the bus.

Because of its still futuristic image, it is easy to forget that Concorde has been around for a long time. Devised in the early 1960s, it was first test-flown in 1973 and went into commercial service in 1976.

For several years during the 1960s, the British and French governments squabbled like fractious children over whether or not Concorde should have an "e". The actual name had been chosen by the family of an aircraft manufacturing executive in Britain who spent an afternoon thumbing through Roget's Thesaurus. Finally, that wise old politician Tony Benn, who was then Britain's Minister of Technology, decided that Britain should use the French spelling.

Many things can be said against Concorde: that it's élitist, for example, that it's noisy, and that it guzzles enormous quantities of fuel, 25,000 litres an hour. It has also turned out to be a technological cul-de-sac and experts in the industry say that another supersonic airliner is unlikely to be developed for 20 years or more.

When a Concorde full of German tourists crashed at Roissy nearly three years ago, it was like Icarus falling to earth. Concorde did eventually return to service, but it was never the same again. Bits of the plane keep falling off in flight, but it's the sharp drop in transatlantic business travel that has spelt the end of the aircraft's commercial life.

These days, Concordes travel with only a handful of passengers on each flight – a sad last chapter for to a plane that was once such a potent image of aviation magic.

April 21, 2003

An Irishman's Diary

Hugh Oram

How holiday tastes have changed! Skerries, that agreeable seaside town in north Co Dublin, once had its very own holiday camp, Red Island. Before people started going abroad on package holidays, many families from all parts of Ireland, including the North, as well as from the north of England, made their annual holiday pilgrimage to Red Island.

The camp opened on August 1st, 1947, when it was duly blessed by the local parish priest. Looking now at photographs of the place, it seems rather like an upmarket detention centre and indeed, local people promptly christened it "Belsen". The camp was the brainchild of Eamonn Quinn, brought up in the grocery business in Newry and the pioneer of the supermarket revolution in this part of Ireland with his "Pay an' take" shops. He was also the father of Feargal Quinn of Superquinn, who has often spoken fondly in the Seanad on the subject of Red Island.

Red Island was pricey enough for the time – £7 10s a week all in for a week in peak season. For their money, however, holidaymakers got all kinds of luxuries, such as central heating and hot and cold running water in the bedrooms. But in one anomaly that seems strange now, all the accommodation for women was on the first floor, while the men were relegated to the ground floor. Most of the 250 bedrooms had two single beds. But these proper bedrooms made Red Island a little fancier than the rival Butlins just up the coast at Mosney, with its chalets.

When it came to meals, holidaymakers were positively encouraged to take second and third helpings. Eamonn Quinn said the bracing air of Red Island made for healthy appetites, even if the menus in the dining hall were decidedly stodgy – not a garlic clove nor a pasta dish in sight.

A typical Red Island lunch menu included tomato soup, boiled ham, mixed veg, mashed potatoes, steam pudding and tea, coffee or milk. Especially for people from war-deprived Britain, the big, juicy steaks were a main attraction. However, the dining hall, which doubled for dancing, looked somewhat like a works canteen.

Also very popular were the unrationed sweets and chocolates from the camp shop. Cigarettes were a mere 10d for a pack 10. Ration books weren't

Feargal Quinn: Red Island holiday camp was a key part of his business education

required. Red Island had all kinds of other delights for visitors, including a cinema, guest concerts, fancy dress contests, talent shows, a roller-skating rink, miniature golf and tennis. Guests could also enjoy the lounge, with its two open-hearth fireplaces, or the sun verandah. Refreshments came from the bar and a soda fountain.

Excursions were laid on: 13/6d to Glendalough for the day or 12/6d for a day tour of north Co Dublin and Co Meath, as far as the Hill of Tara. There were plenty of thatched cottages in those days to back up the folksy image of Red Island and some still remain in present-day Skerries.

Eamonn Quinn was a great man for publicity and through the 1950s, Red Island had a 15-minute slot all to itself on Sunday evenings on Radio Luxembourg. On one occasion, he even put out a publicity booklet headed "Britain invades Ireland". Not long after Granada television started in Manchester, a young Feargal Quinn appeared on the station

to extol the pleasures of he holiday camp. Young Feargal spent his teenage summers at Red Island, working as a waiter, a page boy or a bingo caller, whatever was needed on the day. He believes that being born into a family that runs a holiday camp is a wonderful way to grow up and get a good business education.

For his father, Eamonn, the highlight of his day was when someone came up to him and remarked: "Mr Quinn, I've had a great holiday. I'm rebooking for next year". Feargal's experiences at Red Island laid the foundations for his approach to customer service at Superquinn.

Red Island also drew local custom and the dances there were very popular with teenagers from around the Skerries district. In the 1960s, the Quinns allowed the Skerries rugby club to train on the lawns there, even though it couldn't have done the grass much good.

Changing patterns in the holiday market put paid to Red Island. In the early 1960s, package tours to Spain started and suddenly it was just as cheap to go to Spain as to a holiday camp in Skerries. The final blow came in 1972, when the troubles in the North were at their worst.

That year saw Bloody Sunday in Derry; then, as part of the widespread protests that followed, the old British Embassy in Merrion Square was burned down. The cross-channel holiday trade collapsed and so did Red Island, which shut its doors for the last time.

In 1980, the whole complex was demolished, so that these days, there isn't a single memento left of the old Red Island holiday camp, once so integral to an old-fashioned holiday tradition that's vanished forever, along with the meat and two-veg meals.

May 6, 2003

An Irishman's Diary

When the River Liffey ferry made its last trip, on October 20th., 1984, the day before the East Link toll bridge opened, it was the end of a tradition that dated back to the late 14th century. However, the last captain of the ferry, Peter Murray, is alive and well and enjoying his retirement, still full of river lore, looking every inch the old salt. When he goes for a pint, he's still called "Captain".

He lives in Kilmainham, Dublin, not far from where he was brought up, in Marrowbone Lane. Peter says that working on the river for so long was a good means of keeping fit. Once you were properly togged out, you never got a cold. He started on the ferry in 1952, when he was 18, collecting the fare, one old penny, and three years later, was made a captain in the old Dublin Corporation's very own "fleet".

The main ferry crossing started at Ringsend slipway and ended across the river, near where the Point Theatre stands today. The trip took about five minutes. Another, earlier, service ran from near the old gasometer across to near Spencer Dock. The boats plying from Ringsend were licensed to carry 60 passengers and a crew of two. The passengers were mostly dockers and people who worked in factories on the north side of the port.

They were a great bunch of hard working men, recalls Peter, who never caused any trouble. When they crossed the river, they were open to the elements because only in the latter years of the ferry did the Corporation put up canopies on the boats. The fleet was made up of five boats, numbered One to Six, but for some unknown reason, always missing Number Three.

Wooden hulled boats were far safer than the steel ones, he says, in the event of an accident. A wooden one would fill to the gunwales, but the steel one would sink.

The first ferry of the day left Ringsend at 7.30 am and it want backwards and forwards all day, until the last sailing at 7pm. The service operated Mondays to Saturdays, but rarely, if ever, on a Sunday. In the old days, when dock work was casual, hundreds of men turned up twice a morning, once at 8am, then again at 10am, to see if they would be picked for a day's

Hugh Oram

work..

These days, only a fraction of the number of dockers work in Dublin Port; containerisation has brought automation. The old fleets, too, have gone, including the Gas Company, Guinness, Irish Shipping and Palgrave Murphy.

All the dockers had nicknames; Peter recollects one man who was called "God Save You". He also remembers another docker, up in court over maintenance payments to his estranged wife. When he told the judge that he earned £80 a week, the judge said: "I'll give

Ferry crossing started at Ringsend slipway and ended near where the Point now is.

her £20 a week", to which the docker replied, "I'll try and give her something myself, too".

Peter is eloquent about the difficulties of working on the river. When a strong easterly wind was blowing, it was difficult getting across. Tide surges, as the tide went in or out, had to be taken into account and always, Peter had his tide book with him. The seagulls gave the most accurate forecasts of changes in the weather. At night, the ferry boats had to be taken upstream, to be moored on the river, near the former Irish Press building on Burgh Quay.

On one infamous occasion, about 30 years ago, a very fast cross-channel cargo ship was going astern up the river when it managed to run down the ferry, which Peter had been on just five minutes previously. The ferry sank in a couple of minutes, but fortunately, the skipper of the boat and the lone passenger were rescued.

The dark side of the river is the number of bodies Peter fished out of the water. In his early days, it was mostly lonely

old people who threw themselves in, but later, it was young people. On one occasion, he rescued a woman twice from the Liffey on the one day. One man was known to have disappeared in the river, but there was no sign of him for five years. Then, one day, his car was found on the river bed, with a skeleton at the wheel, dressed only in a tie. Another man tried to jump into the ferry after it had left the quayside, but fell in and drowned.

Peter remembers vividly when Jack Smyth, news editor of the old *Evening Press* and his wife Eileen took the wrong turning and drove into the river one dark Saturday night. It was in 1956, and he was needed back in the office to help make up the front page of the next day's *Sunday Press* with the story of Ronnie Delany's win in the Melbourne Olympics. Almost two years later, a relative who was looking after two young orphaned Smyth children also drove into the river accidentally, just 50 yards away.

The ferry service that ran until 1984 dated back to the lease granted to one Nathaniel Fowkes, in 1669, but in fact ferries had started running on the Liffey in the late 14th century, in the time of Richard II.

Peter's favourite boat, the wooden hulled No 4, was sold after the ferry closure, to someone who used it for fishing. Peter himself was put on other duties by the Corporation, collecting money from parking meters, which he hated. He finally retired five years ago.

A river taxi service did run in the mid-1990s, between City Quay and the Point Theatre. Now, the Dublin Docklands Development Authority is trying to get a fast river "taxi" service running up river as far as Heuston Station.

Peter believes that it will be very difficult to start such a service, but perhaps, despite all the obstacles, a ferry service on the Liffey will once again become an everyday reality.

June 12, 2003

An Irishman's Diary

Hugh Oram

I was in Prague in August, 1968, 35 years ago this week, just a day or two before tanks from the Soviet Union and other Warsaw Pact countries rolled into the city, crushing the so-called "Prague Spring" of liberalisation swiftly and brutally. It was my first foreign assignment and I was working on a business story there, nothing whatever to do with the great political events of that summer.

During the week I spent in Prague, the atmosphere was electrifying. Everyone was on a high over the liberating reforms of the Czech premier Alexander Dubcek, but people knew that invasion was imminent and that the relative freedoms introduced over the previous six months would soon be swept away. One day, I went into a jazz club just off Václavské námesti (Wenceslas Square) and joined the throngs of people listening to a radio, tuned to a French long-wave station, full of crackling from interference, which could just be heard reporting the rumours of tanks being massed close to the Czechoslovak borders.

Despite the situation, I met everyone I needed to meet in Prague and, amazingly, everything I needed to get organised was dealt with efficiently by various government departments. At the offices of *Hospodarske Noviny*, still going today as the Czech Republic's daily business newspaper. I got into conversation with a middle-aged journalist there, who told me that he and some of his colleagues had done time in the coal mines during the early 1950s because they had fallen foul of the regime over some minor criticism. One taxi driver told me that in a previous existence he had been a university professor.

Yet in many ways, Prague that August was remarkably normal. I stayed in a bed and breakfast place on Národni, a main street in the city centre leading up to Wenceslas Square. My room was vast, big enough

for a family of a dozen, and the landlady was very friendly, even though we only had one or two words in common.

In between all my work, I went around like an ordinary tourist, seeing all the great sights of Prague. Nowhere in Europe had more architectural splendours, including St Vitus's cathedral, the castle, the Charles Bridge, the Tyn church, the Betramka villa

Alexander Dubcek, the leader who ushered in the short-lived "Czech Spring"

where Mozart stayed when he was in Prague, and the Child of Prague. I explored Mala Straná, an old quarter near the cathedral and Staré Mesto, the old town. All the sights of Prague, then hardly known in Western Europe, were wonderful. I took in at some exceptionally colourful and melodic folk dance performances, which were truly intoxicating.

But in restaurants and banks, you could wait hours for service. The busiest people in Prague were the illegal moneylenders, who seemed to be at every street corner. One I spotted must have been a juggler in his previous occupation: he was busy changing money and at the same time, keeping a procession of black balls in the air – quite a dramatic performance! For anyone who was willing to take the risk, a fistful of US dollars meant a very cheap holiday.

On the last night I spent in Prague, I went to see a performance of Jánacek's opera *Jenufa* in the late 19th-century National Theatre, just across

the street from where I was staying. The sheer emotional charge among cast and audience flooded out like the last outpouring of hope before the curtain came down on the brief period of reforms.

The next morning, I took the plane from Ruzyne airport; the weather was grey and rainy and the flight to Brussels was extremely turbulent and unsettling. I had no sooner got home to Dublin than the TV and newspaper images of the invasion started coming through.

A protest meeting was held in the old Jurys hotel in Dame Street. Hundreds of people attended, but what could we do except pass totally ineffectual resolutions? I had been quite friendly with Miroslav Hudec, who had been the Czechoslovak representative here, and I had often enjoyed great hospitality with him and his family at their home in Raheny. I told him I was very sorry for what had just happened to his country, but in best diplomatic style, he just shrugged his shoulders and said nothing. Soon afterwards, he was recalled to Prague and I never heard what happened to him.

The following year, 1969, I managed to get a visa to return, this time on holiday with a friend. The Czech hospitality was still evident; I remember vividly the stuffed goose, a typically Czech dish, that the family we stayed with served up for Sunday lunch.

But Prague itself was sullen and quiet, with soldiers plentiful on the streets. All the life had been drained out of the place and the country had to wait another 20 years before freedom returned.

These days, Prague is a totally different city, due to become an EU capital next year. Czech people themselves tend not to remember too much about August, 1968, but for one journalist at least, young at the time, it was an assignment I've never been able to get out of my head.

August 23, 2003

10

An Irishman's Diary

Hugh Oram

Paddy Linehan, a retired publican in Youghal, Co Cork, remembers with total clarity the summer of 1954, when Hollywood arrived in all its triumphalism.

That year, nearly 50 years ago, many scenes from John Huston's film *Moby Dick*, based on the eponymous Herman Melville novel, were shot in Youghal, where the waterfront was turned into the busy 19th century whaling port of New Bedford, Massachusetts, complete with the whaling ship *Pequod*.

Captain Ahab, the lead part, was played by Gregory Peck, who died recently. Others in an outstanding cast included Orson Welles, Noel Purcell and Seamus Kelly, who was one time Quidnunc in *An Irishman's Diary* in *The Irish Times*, as well as its drama critic. He was also keenly interested in ballet and in sailing and he had the nickname of "Commodore of the Royal Bog of Allen Yacht Club".

Seamus Kelly had met up with Huston and it was said that over three nights and three bottles of poitín, Seamus had been induced to sign up for the part of Flask, the third mate on the whaling ship. He duly took seven months' leave of absence from his newspaper work but he was badly injured during the making of the film. In one scene, he was being filmed in a small boat that was supposedly being towed at 40 knots by a harpooned whale. The turbulence caused an old surgical wound to open up and he had to be rushed off to hospital in Cork for an emergency operation.

Paddy Linehan remembers that the first inkling he had of the film was when a whole lot of people descended on the town with measuring tapes and cameras. The advance contingent arrived in two Dublin taxis. The quays were derelict, but were soon transformed with a little magic from the set designers and decorators.

Local people did well out of the filming, which went on for about three months. The Linehans rented two rooms in their house to film people for the then extraordinary sum of £5 a week. They also got their house painted for free, which Paddy reckons saved them about £60.

Takings in the bar shot up from around £7 or £8 a day to £100 a day.

Filming was thirsty work; an early opening licence also helped. One day, the crew were shooting a scene where local women were kissing goodbye to the sailors on the quayside. Many young women were encouraged to take part,

Gregory Peck: played Captain Ahab in John Huston's film of *Moby Dick*, shot in Youghal

including one of the staff from the Linehans' pub. For 10 minutes' work, she was paid 10/6d and as Paddy Linehan recalls now, she thought that she was on her way to Hollywood! But like all good things, the filming eventually ended and Youghal reverted to its then usual state of poverty-stricken somnolence.

When the film was released, about 18 months later, the reviews were generally good and one perceptive reviewer, Paul Rotha, said that "Kelly, the Dublin drama critic, was the only true Melville man in the cast".

Today, the Linehans' pub, now called the Moby Dick, in Market Square, in the centre of Youghal, is an unofficial showplace for the film. There's even a video of *Moby Dick*, put on from time to time. Photographs taken at the time of the film hang on the walls and the pub, which is now run by Paddy Linehan's son, Kevin, has many press cuttings and brochures in 11 languages.

A steady stream of visitors from all over the world seems keen to follow the film trail; just the other week, the Linehans had a whole group of *Moby Dick* fans from Denmark, as well as their first visitor from Belarus.

Youghal had another connection with *The Irish Times*: the writer Claud Cockburn, a great chevalier of the left, lived in the town from 1947 until 1978, when he moved to the nearby seaside town of Ardmore. In 1979, he ran into a spot of financial bother, when he was declared bankrupt, owing five creditors around £6,000. Cockburn, a vitriolic but far-seeing commentator on world affairs, died at the end of 1981 and is buried in the graveyard of St Mary's Collegiate church in Youghal, beneath the town's walls.

When Claud Cockburn was writing a regular column for this paper, he usually posted his copy. In those pre-electronic days, Youghal seemed as far distant from Dublin as if it were on another continent.

For many years, the town languished, poor, undeveloped and well off the tourist trail. Until about a decade ago, Youghal preserved more potently than anywhere else in Ireland, the faded, dusty feeling of the 1950s.

Recent years have seen much tourism and other business development, apartments, restaurants and shops, as well as its own official heritage and tourist information centre centre.

Yet all the old buildings remain, including the clock tower spanning the main street, where two centuries ago, rebels were hung from the windows. One of its museums, the Fox's Lane folk museum, shows gadgets used by bygone generations, such as a cucumber straightener, a moustache cup, a wasp trap and an egg topper. Youghal's history is never far away.

UCC's history department is organising a major conference on the subject in the town towards the end of September. And the spirit of *Moby Dick* remains ever-present.

July 26, 2003

11

On the set of recent hit movie, *Veronica Guerin*, which starred Cate Blanchett and was directed by Joel Schumacher and produced by Jerry Bruckheimer. Photo: Jonathan Hession

A quick take, and you'll reel

HUGH ORAM

If you've got an interesting car, make some interesting money – in front of the cameras

Hiring out your car, especially if it's vintage or a specialised model, for use in TV productions, films and commercials made in Ireland, can be a nice little earner. John Wilkinson, who lives in Bagenalstown, in Co Carlow, an expert on the subject, says that car owners can make up to €350 a day.

However, most owners are too close to their cars to simply hand them over to some junior hired hand on the set. Many owners of rare cars won't lend them out for TV or film work unless they can be on set themselves.

Sometimes, production companies can be tight and won't pay extra for the driver, while others are more flaithiúlach and will pay more for the driver.

On one recent occasion, relates Wilkinson, he looked unsuccessfully for a long wheelbase Land Rover in a particular colour. Just before shooting started, he was standing in a car park in Bray, Co Wicklow, not far from Ardmore film studios, the heart of the industry in Ireland, when someone drove in.

He was at the wheel of exactly the Land Rover Wilkinson was seeking, and a deal was struck on the spot. The Land Rover was needed for eight days, but the schedule went on much longer than planned and the vehicle was used for 22 days, which netted the Land Rover owner almost €6,500.

Here in Ireland, matching car owners to film makers is a much more ad hoc business than in Britain. But if someone wants to hire out his or her car for this kind of work, it helps if they are immediately available, perhaps self-employed or retired.

It can be very tedious work. Filming usually starts early in the morning and often goes on well into the night. John Wilkinson says: "It's just like being an extra, except that car owners are paid more."

One production that used lots of vehicles was the 1995 film of Maeve Binchy's *Circle of Friends*. Some 35 vehicles were hired – cars, buses and trucks – as well as 50 to 60 bicycles. On the other hand, when the *Michael Collins* epic was being made at around the same time, many of the period vehicles used were in fact reconstructions.

Period cars have been less in demand over the past few years, but "Garda" cars are always much needed.

Liam Kelly, who runs his eponymous film company at Kilmacanogue, Co Wicklow, just minutes from Ardmore studios, says that he is busy at the moment, but adds "the work is very up and down. It comes in splashes".

During the boom years of the 1990s, many international films and TV series were shot in Ireland and there's no doubt about it, business now is much quieter. Possible changes to the tax incentives for the film industry are hanging over the industry like a dark cloud.

Kelly himself has diversified, into the weddings and limousine business.

He worked on many top TV productions, supplying vehicles for *Ballykissangel*, *Glenroe* and *Father Ted* but he says that all this type of TV work has now dried up.

Besides TV series, movies for TV and cinema films, commercials for TV and cinema use are big business. Liam Kelly has worked on many commercials, including ones for Nissan, Opel, Renault and Toyota. Production is getting under way on a new, big budget road safety commercial that needs all types of vehicles, from cars to lorries and tankers.

In addition to all the vehicles needed on camera, the "backstage" demand is for tracking, heavy terrain recovery and other vehicles. Standby ambulances are needed for stunt work.

For anyone who wants to get their car into films, much depends on being in the right place at the right time, preferably Bray, early in the morning.

September 3, 2003

An Irishman's Diary

The village of Roundstone, Co Galway, is Shangri-La for many people in Ireland, if they daydream for a moment or two of the perfect getaway place. From the pinnacle of its steep main street, you can see across the harbour and the bay to the Maamturk mountains in the heart of Connemara.

The man responsible for creating Roundstone was a Scottish engineer, Alexander Nimmo, who also left us the harbour and lighthouse at Dunmore East, Co Waterford – and many other less celebrated works.

Born in Kirkcaldy, Scotland, in 1783, the son of a watchmaker, he excelled at school and went on to become a pupil of Thomas Telford, the leading engineer of the time. When he was a mere 19, Nimmo was appointed rector of Inverness Academy and during the holidays, he was employed by Telford to determine the boundaries of the Scottish counties – all of them.

When he was 25, work was just beginning on the *Edinburgh Encylopaedia*, which eventually ran to 32 volumes. The young engineer wrote hundreds of entries. By 29, he was a Fellow of the Royal Society of Edinburgh.

Then he discovered Ireland and in 1811 he began mapping the boglands of south Kerry and building new roads. His truly magnificent Kerry maps are in the National Library of Ireland; they were drawn years before the Ordnance Survey started work. In 1813 that Nimmo went to Connemara for the first time, beginning a lifelong devotion to the place. He started by examining in detail what he reckoned were the 560,000 acres of Connemara and looking at improvements.

Altogether, he built some 30 harbours and piers around the coast of Ireland and many of them were in Connemara. In the early 1820s he decided that what Roundstone needed was a brand new harbour, so he built one, with a daring cliff face at the back, rising up to the level of the road. For ever after, it was called the "New Harbour". Not content with that, he added to

Hugh Oram

the few sparse buildings by constructing a whole new village, present-day Roundstone. Barna, too, was his creation, on the road from Galway to Spiddal.

The harbour and lighthouse at Dunmore East were completed around 1821. Costs rocketed during construction; what had begun as a £20,000 project ended up costing

Nimmo's legacy: the pier in Roundstone, with the Twelve Bens in the background

£108,000. It was designed for the mail boats that came from Milford Haven in South Wales, but within about 10 years it had silted up and the mail service was transferred to nearby Waterford. In recent decades, Dunmore East has been a major fishing port and it has another claim to fame. In 1980, Frances Glody became the first woman to be officially part of an RNLI lifeboat crew in Ireland and she is still part of the Dunmore East crew today.

Back in Connemara, Nimmo continued the good works, including new roads. He made one from Oughterard to Clifden and another from Roundstone to Clifden.

He also found time to be on good terms with the landed families of the West, including the Martins of Ballynahinch, in Recess. At their home, which is now an hotel, he instructed the teenage Mary Martin, the heiress to the family fortunes, in engineering and she became the first woman engineer in Co Galway and one of the very first in Ireland. Nimmo also built himself a house near Maam Cross.

Alexander Nimmo was

self-taught in engineering, because this was years before any formal university education on the subject. He was proficient in Greek and Latin, as well as Dutch, French, German and Italian. He was also greatly interested in astronomy, chemistry and geography.His friends included William Wordsworth.

Nimmo did other bridge building in Ireland. The unique arch-shaped bridge at Poulaphouca, near Blessington, was his and the famous Spectacle Bridge in Co Clare was inspired by him, though he didn't design and build it. His most ambitious bridge was Sarsfield Bridge across the River Shannon in Limerick, which he modelled on the Pont de Neuilly in Paris. Again, he went way over budget, but fortunately for posterity, elegance overcame economy.

As a sideline, Nimmo also designed and built the docks in Limerick.

Quick in his work and visionary, he did all kinds of other things too, such as surveying Dublin Bay and then the whole coast of Ireland, writing a navigation book about the Irish Sea and making the initial plans for the first railway in Ireland, from Westland Row to what was then Kingstown.

For such a proficient engineer, little is known of Nimmo the person. J.W. de Courcy, an associate professor of civil engineering at UCD until his retirement in 1988, discovered that even though much is known about Nimmo's work, nothing much ever came to light about his private life. It is not even known whether he was married, although it seems unlikely.

He died at his town house, in the then fashionable Marlborough Street in Dublin, in 1832, aged just 49. It is believed that he was buried in what was then the Presbyterian graveyard in Roundstone, but again, no one is quite sure.

The man who left such a legacy in stone remains an enigma.

September 22, 2003

An Irishman's Diary

Maps have an eternal fascination for many people and few are more intriguing than old maps of Dublin.

It's not just the cartographic and illustrative excellence that makes them so interesting, but the way in which they show the city expanding over the years. After all, it's only two centuries since Dublin ended at St Stephen's Green on the southside and Bolton Street on the northside and Donnybrook, Drumcondra, Fairview and Glasnevin were all open country.

The first recognisable map of Dublin, still frequently reproduced, was published by John Speed in 1610. Little is known about Speed, except that he was born in Cheshire, spent most of his life in London and was father to 12 sons and six daughters. He began as a tailor but switched to map-making. His highly ornamented and stylised "Dublin" map was part of an exercise called "The Theatre of the Empire of Great Britaine".

This was still medieval Dublin, stretching from Trinity College up to St James's Gate. Much of Speed's information came from other sources, some of which have never been identified. Speed's map-making deficiencies were offset by his engraving and lettering.

This map and the other maps of Dublin done before the Ordnance Survey have a home in the Glucksman map library in Trinity College, Dublin, which is the only dedicated map library in Ireland. However, there are other significant map collections in such places as the National Archive, the National Library of Ireland and UCD. Lewis Glucksman, benefactor to Trinity, the University of Limerick and most recently, University College, Cork, is a retired New York banker who lives near Cobh, Co Cork and has a particular interest in early maps. His Irish-American wife Loretta chairs the America-Ireland Fund.

After Speed came Bernard de Gomme, with his 1673 map of Dublin. It showed Lazy Hill, close to the route of the present day Pearse Street, then all open country. What is now D'Olier Street and Burgh Quay remained to be reclaimed from the sea. One city centre thoroughfare was well named in de Gomme's map: Dirty Lane in

Hugh Oram

Temple Bar.

The next significant cartographer of Dublin was Charles Brooking, whose map was published in 1728. This was an "upside down" map of the city, with the south at the top, which had a magnificent panorama of Dublin and all its churches. The spaces between the streets were shaded in,

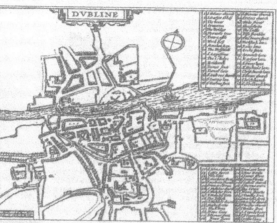

Putting Dublin on the map: John Speed's depiction of the city, drawn in 1610

giving no detail, though the streets were finely delineated. This map shows Bolton Street at the very northern edge of the city.

Paul Ferguson, the Trinity mapping librarian, who showed me these and other mapping treasures, hugely detailed maps of many major European cities were produced around this time. Nothing similar was ever produced for Dublin, probably because its medieval heart was so small.

But Dublin made up for this deficiency with John Rocque's 1756 map of Dublin. This is not just fantastic, but spectacular, in Paul Ferguson's opinion. Rocque was of French Huguenot extraction, had made his career in London and had also mapped Paris and Rome. He came to Dublin late in his career, not just to make his map of Dublin but to map the estates of the Earl of Kildare.

Rocque was as much a businessman as a map-maker and he set up shop at Bachelors Walk to sell copies of his Dublin map, in which every house and garden was included. He must have gone behind every house to get the details of the garden and in nearly every case, archaeologists have verified his accuracy.

He calculated that Dublin had 12,060 dwelling houses with a population of 96,480, which was

probably an under-estimate. But Dublin was still very small. The street that led from St Stephen's Green was almost entirely devoid of houses and was known simply as "the road to Donnybrook", running through open countryside. It is now Leeson Street. As late as 1780, only two sides to Merrion Square had been built, while in 1798, what is now Haddington Road was still Watery Lane.

One fascinating aspect of these early maps is that often they showed features that were planned but never built. At the end of the 18th century, the Royal Circle was planned just off the North Circular Road, Dublin's answer to the Crescent in Bath. It was never built, but showed up on maps for the next 20 or 30 years, getting more ghostly each time. In an 1820 map, the faint outline of the Royal Circle that never was can still be seen.

Map-making changed dramatically with the arrival in 1824 of the Ordnance Survey, equipped with vast manpower resources. Within little more than 20 years, its men had finished their basic mapping of Ireland.

The Ordnance Survey's six-inches-to-the-mile map of Dublin in 1843, its first on this scale, showed Rathmines and Rathgar just beginning to take off as two of Dublin's new residential districts. The 1876 OS map showed the start of the city's sprawl into suburbia.

But even an OS map of Dublin published as late as 1947 showed a city still compact by today's standards. In south-west Dublin, the countryside began at Drimnagh, while what is now the Naas Road area and the infamous Red Cow roundabout was still farmland.

On the north of the city, the countryside began just beyond Drumcondra and Marino. Tallaght was a delightful little country village.

These old maps are also a priceless barometer of social change, as Dublin changed from village to town to capital city. Now the greater Dublin area is home to half the population of the State and today the suburbs of Dublin extend into counties Wicklow, Kildare and Meath.

Speed would have been astonished by the speed of change over the past 20 years.

November 17, 2003

An Irishman's Diary

No one is more familiar with Dublin and its history than Pat Liddy, who has made a second career for himself out of drawing the city. During the 1980s, his weekly series,"Dublin Today", beautifully executed line drawings complete with admirable potted histories, were staple reading in this newspaper.

Since then, he has gone on to do nearly a dozen books about Dublin. His latest title, *Pat Liddy and the Changing Landscapes of Dublin*, strikes me as an immeasurable achievement. It is also an engrossing sweep across the history of the city from prehistoric times into the imagined future city of 2050.

The book is a judicious mix of black-and-white ink drawings, done with exquisite penmanship, and full colour illustrations, some in oil, others in watercolour.One good example among many comes from Liddy's two drawings, side by side, of the facade of Trinity College, facing onto College Green. In the coloured one, every stone block is lovingly delineated. One big full colour plate I particularly liked shows what the Dublin area might have looked like 12,000 years ago, when it was all open land going down to the sea.

Elsewhere, Liddy colours the Speed and Rocque maps of 17th- and 18th-century Dublin, making them so vivid that they are almost three-dimensional. All the changes in the city's landscapes are well marked out, showing for instance, the peninsula or spit of land on which Ringsend village once stood.

Pat Liddy has drawn many individual properties for the book, including the four remaining "Dutch Billies", the Dutch-style houses with unusual front gables that were so prevalent in 17th- and 18th-century Dublin. Thousands of them were built. He has also included the Jewish cemetery in

Hugh Oram

Ballybough, built in the Jewish year 5618 (1857 AD). The last interment took place there in 1908.By way of contrast, he includes the old St Fintan's church at Sutton, dating from the 9th century.

Producing a book of this quality is enormously expensive.The print run was limited to 2,000 copies and substantial but non-intrusive sponsorship was led by CRH. The book follows on from an exhibition held in City Hall,

The new-look George's Quay in Dublin, as painted by Pat Liddy

Dublin, last autumn.

While the book is so informative on the visual aspects of the developing city from Norse times onwards, the present is not neglected. Lots of recent and planned developments are given the Liddy treatment, from the Westin Hotel in Westmoreland Street to Ongar village in Clonsilla and the proposed redevelopment of Tara Street railway station. Liddy goes into such detail that for the St Stephen's Green shopping centre, he lists many of the businesses that stood on the site until nearly 20 years ago, including Rice's pub.

The human touch is there, too. Liddy has included a colour plate, done in 1982,of an old man who used to walk up and down Grafton Street ceaselessly in the late 1970s. The image serves as a reminder of the battalions of

street characters who once graced Dublin, such as the woman who played her harpsichord in Wicklow Street; "Bang Bang", who pretended to shoot everyone; the photographer on O'Connell Bridge; and the Hickey brothers, who wandered round all day, rearranging the city centre buildings in their imaginations with constant gesticulation.

Changing social patterns are highlighted. Pat Liddy includes a drawing of the mosque in Clonskeagh and notes that he was made to feel welcome there.

While so much of the historical and current material is so fascinating, what is most intriguing is Liddy's vision of the future. Perhaps surprisingly, he believes Dublin will be a safer city. Not only will there be Luas lines and a Metro system criss-crossing the city, but everything will be inter-connected. The city will also have more tunnels; clearly,the Dublin Port tunnel is just the first.

Buses,however,will still have a pivotal role in public transport. As for Dublin airport, he predicts new runways and 50 million passengers a year; what will the check-in queues or the car parking look like?

Liddy forecasts that the historic villages in Dublin will have rediscovered their identity, but at the same time, the city will have spread out to embrace Naas and Greystones. Skerries and Balbriggan will have coalesced into one vast conurbation.

In fewer than 150 pages, Pat Liddy has encompassed a vast amount of information, besides countless illustrations. For anyone who loves the history of Dublin, where the city has come from and where it's going, this is a priceless production. It is also a fine complement to his new website all about – you guessed it – Dublin,its history and people (www.patliddy.com).

February 2, 2004

An Irishman's Diary

Dublin once had a grand total of over 60 streams and rivers that flowed entirely above ground. Today, most of those rivers and streams have disappeared from view, forced underground as the city has expanded, so that they have largely vanished from the public consciousness. The Liffey, the Dodder, the Santry River and the Tolka are among the few that remain uncovered.

One person with a lifelong knowledge of Dublin watercourses is Michael Corcoran, who still works part-time, for the drainage department in Dublin City Council. He has worked in Dublin local government since 1947 and claims, with a knowing smile, to have been the oldest person in the Corporation to have become computer literate. His great knowledge of the city's rivers gives an unusual perspective on Dublin's history and buildings.

His book on the subject, *Your Good Health*, is being published by the city council in time for Christmas. Next month, he will give the last in a series of talks in City Hall examining the epidemics that once plagued the city. The development of the city's drainage system did much to make the city a healthier place in which to live.

Michael Corcoran explains that Dublin's very first water supply came from the River Poddle, back in the mid-13th century. In the late 18th century, much of the city's drinking water was drawn from the canals, until they became too polluted. By the 19th century, the Poddle had become an open sewer, although it is not in such a bad state nowadays.

The Poddle rises at Cookstown in Tallaght and eventually flows into the Liffey near Grattan bridge. Upstream of Kimmage, it is known as the Tymon River.

About 15 watercourses are connected with the Poddle, including the wonderfully named Glib River and the Tenter Water in the Tenters' district.

The Poddle flows underground beside Dublin Castle, and a branch of it rushes beneath the Olympia Theatre in

Hugh Oram

Dame Street. Another river that was much cleaned up is the Camac, to the west of the city; once, it was heavily polluted by the old paper mills in the Clondalkin area.

These days, you can still see parts of the Poddle in places such as Kimmage, while the Camac is also visible in parts of Inchicore.

Periodic flooding in Dublin is a reminder that many rivers and streams flow beneath the city's streets

But one well-known river on the southside has totally disappeared from view – the Swan, which drains Terenure, Rathmines and Ballsbridge. These days, the only remembrance of the Swan is in name of the local shopping centre in Rathmines. The Swan flows underground beneath Morehampton Road and Clyde Road and eventually falls into the River Dodder near Londonbridge Road. One branch of it flowed into the Dodder near the bridge at Ballsbridge after passing through what is now Herbert Park. For generations of schoolchildren going up to Muckross convent school, it was known as the "Swanee".

Other streams on the southside can still be seen, however, such as the Elm Park stream and the Nutley stream. The underground part of the Nutley stream runs beneath the RTÉ studios in Donnybrook.

The northside has an abundance of rivers and streams, such as the Tolka, still a surface river. Its numerous tributaries include the Finglas River, the Wad River in Donnycarney, the Grace Park Stream and the Hampstead

Stream. Some of the northside rivers have vanished from view, such as the Naniken in Beaumont, which drains to the sea near North Bull Island. It took its name from the Nanny River, which flows into the sea at Laytown, Co Meath and which is three times bigger than the river in Dublin. The suffix "iken" means small.

The hill of Howth has a whole complex of streams while the Phoenix Park has three main ones, the Magazine Stream, the Vice-Regal Stream and the Furry Glen Stream.

Underneath the city centre, several streams and rivers run in channels far below the surface. The Stein River starts near Charlemont Mall canal bridge, flows beneath the south side of St Stephen's Green, then under Clarendon Street and eventually empties into the Liffey.

The Gallows Stream, which flows close to Government Buildings, is a modest affair, starting near Leeson Lane. It drew its name from Gallows Road, which was the forerunner of Baggot Street. Some 250 years ago, the Gallows River flowed through largely open countryside that became built up only in the 19th century, when the river disappeared from view.

The Liffey itself is a much cleaner river nowadays. Fortunately, the plans hatched in the late 1970s to build a barrage across the river were abandoned.

The subject attracts a certain kind of humour. The Creosote Stream, in its various branches, flows beneath the railway works in Inchicore and many decades ago the outdoor lavatories were placed directly above one of these watercourses. There was concern about the amount of time the men were spending there, studying racing form in the day's newspapers. A foreman had the bright idea of dousing balls of paper in oil and setting them alight before sending them downstream beneath the lavatories. It's said that the occupants emerged like greyhounds from the traps.

October 22, 2004

An Irishman's Diary

Hugh Oram

Dublin Airport's original terminal building was once a place of elegance and practicality for people using the airport. Air travel then was vastly different from what it is today; budget class air fares and airlines just didn't exist.

The whole story of Dublin Airport had begun back in 1937, when the government bought 100 acres of land at Cloghran in north Co Dublin for the proposed new airport at Collinstown. The runway was built over the next couple of years and work got under way on the design of the terminal building. It was the first significant new building in the modern Ireland.

The man entrusted with the design was Desmond FitzGerald, who headed a team of architects on the project at the Office of Public Works. He came up with an immensely stylish Art Deco design based on the bridge of a luxury ocean-going liner, just as that type of travel was just starting to go out of fashion. It was an age of elegant airline travel; the terminal at Le Bourget airport in Paris, opened shortly before, had been designed in similar style.

The new Washington Airport in the US had equally splendid lines.

He had a younger brother to help him with plenty of advice, Garret, then a teenager, who later revealed how reluctant the powers that be were to sanction a full-scale airport terminal. They thought that a couple of rooms would be sufficient and there was little expectation that there would ever be enough traffic to justify the construction.

But work went ahead and the terminal was eventually completed in early 1942. Features included a verandah viewing point, an aero club lounge, banking facilities and loudspeakers for passenger information, announcing arrivals and departures. FitzGerald also designed covered walkways from the terminal building to the aircraft, but these weren't implemented for another 20 years.

The design of the four-storey building with the control tower perched on top, avant-garde in so many ways, was the pinnacle of Desmond FitzGerald's career. Today, the building is still regarded as a classic, a rare Art Deco-style building in Ireland. Aviation experts of the time said that Dublin Airport was one of the finest in the world.

The very first Aer Lingus flight from the new airport took off on January 19th, 1940 and since the second World War was well under way at that stage, traffic at the new airport was almost non-existent for the next five years. One flight a day was usual and two a day was considered busy. Often, sheep were let graze on the runway.

The new airport terminal didn't come to life until the war ended and it took until 1946 for coverage of the new building to begin in the national newspapers. Local people promptly christened it the "White Elephant".

The old Terminal at Dublin Airport: an immensely stylish Art Deco design based on a luxury liner

The setting was still very rural and unspoiled and at harvest time, passengers in the terminal could see workers with horse-drawn carts bringing in the hay that had been saved from the airport grounds, close to the terminal.

Slowly, the momentum was stepped up. Aer Lingus started increasing its services and people grew accustomed to air travel. The first service to mainland Europe, by KLM to Amsterdam, began in 1947. Flights were slow by today's standards; Lourdes in a DC3 took five hours.

Air travel was also very expensive and only the better off could afford it, so the passengers then were very different from the complete cross-section of people one sees today. In those far-off days, a complement of passengers for a flight resembled a fashion plate from a glossy society magazine. Travel was very elitist and people thought nothing of bringing 30 or 40 kilos of luggage with them. But the whole place was so different that for many Dubliners, a trip out to the airport was an exciting day out.

The old terminal had a great "institution", the restaurant run by Johnny Oppermann, which had clear views out over the airfield. The head chef was Jimmy Flahive, who made a great name for himself in the early days of Telefís Éireann. Dinner at the airport was mandatory for many gourmets and the gala events, like New Year's Eve, became legendary.

This restaurant had been included by Desmond FitzGerald in his original design, complete with room for an orchestra and space for dancing. By today's standards the prices were incredibly modest. A 1962 menu shows steak priced at 10 shillings and a bottle of Beaujolais for 14 shillings, but at the time, those prices were way beyond the means of ordinary working people.

On the ground floor, with its large foyer, people using the check-in desks were signed in for their flights and their baggage weighed all in a matter of minutes. Arriving on a flight, collecting luggage and going through customs were equally fast.

The glory days for the old terminal were really in the 1960s, culminating in the arrival of John F. Kennedy, the then president of the US, in June, 1963. The arrival of the Beatles that same year created almost as much excitement at the airport, but when US President Nixon arrived seven years later, it was a complete let-down.

However, by the mid-1960s, the terminal was already beginning to creak at the seams with the numbers of passengers, so planning began for a new one.

This very utilitarian terminal was opened in 1972, with the expectation of handling five million passengers a year. Today, with numbers heading towards 20 million, that terminal, much expanded, is still in use.

The old terminal was decommissioned and turned into offices by the organisation then responsible, the old Aer Rianta company. These days, the original terminal is almost lost amid the surrounding buildings and it's hard to imagine the impact it had in its early days.

It's equally hard not to become a little nostalgic for those earlier days of flying, slower, elegant, devoid of any hassle and not a security check in sight.

November 1, 2004

An Irishman's Diary

Hugh Oram

It's the charity with the very odd name, the Sick & Indigent Roomkeepers' Society, but in fact it's the oldest charity in Dublin, still helping the sick and the destitute in the inner city. It was founded in 1790 by a group of eleven concerned citizens, all of whom came from what might be politely called the middle class of society.

One was a wholesale linen draper, another a pawnbroker and a third a schoolmaster. All were deeply troubled by the appalling deprivation so widespread in the city then. Often, people in the poorest areas of the city lived 16 or more, several families in fact, in a single room. In those days, Dublin had a vast array of charities, but somehow, the Sick & Indigent Roomkeepers' Society has managed to outlast them all.

In its early years, its work was confined to a very limited area around Ormond Quay and the relief it gave was itself small, confined to potatoes, fuel and a few other essentials of life. Three years after its establishment, the society had expanded so much that four divisions were set up to cover the city, including one for the St Stephen's Green area.

Income built up, from such sources as subscriptions, investments and charity sermons, which were a compelling feature of Dublin social life in those days. They created enormous interest and raised considerable sums of money. Charity balls also became big fundraising events.

By the middle of the 19th century, despite the fact that the nobility, who often donated to charities like this one, had largely moved from Dublin, either to London or down the country, the society had become one of the leading organisations of its kind in Dublin.

In 1855, it moved into new premises at Palace Street, just off Dame Street and right beside Dublin Castle. The tall house, with the letters of the society's name prominent on the facade, became a Dublin landmark. Over 30 years ago, the then City Council wanted to compulsorily purchase the building, but the society eventually saw that threat fade away. Then, when it discovered that equipping the building to comply with new legislation on access for disabled people would cost a small fortune, it could no longer afford Palace Street.

About 10 years ago, it moved out, to its present location, a one-room office in Lower Leeson Street. After the society left Palace Street, Peter Pearson, the architectural historian, made it his family home for a number of years.

Inevitably, the society had its scandals. After the secretary of the time, Mark Casey, died in 1861, it was discovered that just over £2,000, an enormous sum

for the times, had disappeared from the accounts. The matter was hushed up, for fear that it could dissuade donors.

Towards the end of the 19th century, Dublin was overwhelmed by regular outbreaks of disease, including typhoid fever. The need for the society was greater than ever and in November, 1896, *The*

A tour group at the former home of the Sick and Indigent Roomkeepers' Society

Weekly Irish Times praised it for its work in " seeking out the honest poor to offer them charity in their own homes" .

In the aftermath of the 1916 Easter Rising and the following years, more suffering by the poor people of the city had to be looked after. In 1921, the British military commandeered the Palace Street building, occupying it for a year. Around 1930, a further challenge came when the city' s boundaries were extended to take in such townships as Pembroke and Rathmines. The society decided not to follow suit, but to continue helping people within the "old city" , the space between the two canals.

A new form of fundraising began in 1935, when the then Lord Mayor of Dublin, the renowned Alfie Byrne, gave the first appeal for the society on Radio Eireann, now RTÉ. These radio appeals continued for over 30 years. The Earl of Wicklow gave the talk in 1954, while in 1966, it was the turn of Richie Ryan, later to become a Minister for Finance. In the 1940s, one of the big benefactors of the Society was Joe McGrath, of Hospitals Sweepstakes and Waterford Glass fame.

These days, the fundraising is just as assiduous as ever. The society circularises many commercial firms in the city for contributions. People are generous with their donations, from €5 upwards, sometimes very much more. Bequests are another source of income and church collections are still done. Last year, the society gave out assistance to the tune of €235,000 and it says that its

work is as much needed as ever. It's not just the urban poor who need its help; sometimes, middle class families can fall on hard times, through illness or other misfortunes.

The society has been through its own revolution; these days, for the first time in its existence, women play a much more prominent role.

Back in 1988, Dr Geraldine O'Brien of Aer Lingus was appointed a trustee, the first woman appointed by a society that she noted had been seen until then as "rather quaint and male dominated".

The first woman secretary, Ina Ryan, had been appointed four years previously . She served for 20 years and today, Thelma Tutty continues in that role. 1990 saw the society mark its bicentenary with its history written by Deirdre Lindsay.

In 1995, Tona O'Brien became the first woman chairperson in the society' s history and that year also, Bernadette Madden, the artist, became a trustee, a position she held until recently. This past summer, Tona O'Brien was succeeded in the chair by her daughter, Aphria, who runs her own concierge company. This gives her the flexibility to devote time to the society as and when it' s needed.

Many of the problems remain resolutely the same, although in modern times, drug addiction has had a devastating effect on many families. Some families, Aphria points out, will never have employment. Then families spend vast amounts of money they can't afford on first communions and funerals. They pile up huge debts at Christmas.

People are helped on a case by case basis. Sick children can be helped in hospital with presents, such as a Walkman. Some families that haven't been away on holidays for years are helped, modestly. In one recent case, such a family was helped to go on holiday in Tramore. Applications for help usually come through social workers.

Not all requests are granted. One woman whose husband had died went to great expense to get him embalmed. She didn' t like the end result so decided on cremation and asked the society for the necessary funding, which it had to turn down. Council rent arrears, or ESB or gas bills that can' t be paid, are all considered to be much more deserving of help. The basic needs of the less well off sections of society really haven't changed all that much in the past 214 years.

November 8, 2004

An Irishman's Diary

Hugh Oram

A verdant woodland corner of Donnybrook, close to the centre of Dublin, is destined to stay like that for ever: it can never be built on. The Grove occupies a fifth of a hectare of land at the corner of Morehampton Road and Wellington Place, close to the underground Swan river. Thousands of motorists drive past it every day, yet few know what an oasis of natural tranquillity and wildlife lies behind the gate and the high walls.

The Grove is owned in perpetuity by An Taisce. Together with the Upper Leeson Street Residents' Association, it is responsible for maintaining the area, with its many trees, plants, birds, other wildlife and pond.

Open days are held from time to time and schools also pay visits there; by its very nature, the Grove cannot be opened to the public on a regular basis, but anyone who is really interested can borrow a key to the gates of Donnybrook's little paradise.

How and why The Grove came to be bequeathed to An Taisce by a local resident, Kathleen Goodfellow, is a fascinating story. Her father George was a builder, who constructed and owned six properties in adjoining Morehampton Road in the late 19th century. Kathleen herself, who was known to her friends as either "Goodfellow" or "Michael", was born at Number 4, Morehampton Road. A student at Alexandra College in the days when it stood in Earlsfort Terrace, she went on to gain an Arts degree from Trinity College. She was in the fortunate position of never having had to go to work, so she was able to devote her time to developing her interests in literature and writing stories and poems. Translating into French had a particular appeal.

During the 1916 Easter Rising, a chance meeting with another young woman, Estella Solomons, who was sheltering from snipers' bullets, led to a lifelong friendship. Together, they enlisted in Cumann na mBán, where they were taught first aid, drilling and signalling by Phyllis Ryan, later to become the wife of President Sean T. O'Kelly.

Kathleen also became friends with Seumas O'Sullivan, the Abbey actor, writer and publisher, and the man behind the *Dublin Magazine*, a noted literary publication of its time.

Gateway to The Grove, Donnybrook, an oasis of greenery near the city centre

Seumas later married Estella and Kathleen played a substantial financial and editorial role in the *Dublin Magazine*, from its foundation founded in 1923 until it ceased publication with the death of Seumas in 1958. Estella became an outstanding portrait and landscape painter; she and Kathleen loved painting The Grove. The two of them were often described as Bohemian characters.

Goodfellow, a Quaker, Estella, a Jew, and Seumas, a Methodist, were all well-known in Dublin artistic and literary circles. After they married, Seumas and Estella lived in Rathfarnham, until damp threatened to overwhelm Seumas's collection of 10,000 books. Kathleen, who continued to live at 4, Morehampton Road, offered No 2 to Estella and Seumas at a modest rent. Weekend hospitality at No 2 was enjoyed by many in Dublin's artistic community.

In 1939, when she was 48, Kathleen fell off a tram and broke her leg. The resultant lameness meant she had to give up her great love of gardening, but she never lost her enthusiasm for nature.

Eventually, she decided to leave the woodland area of The Grove in perpetuity, so that it couldn't be touched. She had been concerned that the then Dublin Corporation wanted to place a compulsory purchase order on the place to build a fire station. Kathleen talked with the Upper Leeson Street Residents' Association; then The Grove came into the ownership of An Taisce, one of around a dozen properties it owns in the State. Kathleen died in 1980, the year after her bequest, and is buried in the family grave at Mount Jerome.

In the years after it was handed over, this little patch of woodland became quite derelict and overgrown, a place of refuge for urban foxes. In the past few years, a substantial management programme has been put in place, so that these days, the woodland area is maintained in an excellent state. Bird nesting boxes have been built and new trees and wild flowers planted. Once again, the flora and fauna have flourished; birdlife has increased.

The Upper Leeson Street Residents' Association has paid for some of the maintenance. Bodies such as Conservation Volunteers Ireland and Birdwatch Ireland have helped in the work of looking after The Grove.

Such areas of urban conservation are rare in Ireland, although more common in other European countries. Kathleen Goodfellow may have got her idea for preserving The Grove from similar schemes elsewhere in Europe.

For Dublin, The Grove is a unique area that is destined to remain for ever green, a priceless oasis, almost in the city centre, on which developers can never lay their hands.

April 29, 2005

An Irishman's Diary

Eddie MacSweeney, better known to generations of RTÉ radio listeners as Maxwell Sweeney, was a genteel figure by today's media standards, but enjoyed a career that was very modern in its scope and diversity.

He was born in England to an Irish father and an English mother. His father, Dominic, worked for the Royal Mint before coming home to work for the Currency Commission when it was set up in the new Irish Free State.

Dominic also had a close connection with the Holborn Empire in London, one of that city' s great variety theatres. He passed on his love of theatre to his son, who subsequently wrote and broadcast frequently on the subject.

Eddie himself started work as a junior reporter with *The Irish Times* and spent the whole of the 1930s with this newspaper. One of his early "bloodings" came when he was sent to cover a story in Roscommon town, where it had been reported that IRA members were drilling in the castle. Eddie got his story – the reports had been accurate – but not before Jasper Tully, the tempestuous editor of the *Roscommon Herald*, had been thoroughly abusive in print to the young reporter from Dublin with what he described as an "Oxford accent" . Tully himself earned further notoriety after his wife died and he readdressed letters sent to her, "Not known at this address. Try Hell".

That wasn't the only excitement at the time for the young reporter. Aviation was one of his lifelong passions and when Sir Alan Cobham brought his flying circus of a dozen stunt planes on a tour of Ireland in 1933, Eddie helped with the publicity.

His next big newspaper job came in 1941, when *The Irish Times* decided to relaunch its weekly newspaper as the *Times Pictorial*, inspired by *Picture Post* in Britain. Eddie was made art editor of the paper and, along with his colleague George Burrows, devised and ran a very modern newspaper that broke with tradition and was also a useful training ground for many journalists.

He wasn't without a sense of humour, though he was an essentially serious, urbane man. Eddie and George Burrows devised a wartime photograph showing two men getting a fill-up in a tankard from a petrol

Hugh Oram

pump at the Guinness brewery. Petrol rationing was at its height and the picture was never published because of wartime censorship.

Immediately after the second World War, Eddie decided on a change of career and became

Eddie MacSweeney, alias Maxwell Sweeney: man behind *Sunday Miscellany*

publicity manager for Metropole and Allied Cinemas in Dublin. This led to an even more stimulating job in the early 1950s with Rank Films at their film studios in Denham, Buckinghamshire. It must have been fun: the Rank starlets were in their heyday.

Eventually, he returned home to Ireland and developed many other interests. For many years, he edited a magazine about the hotel trade. For about 20 years, he wrote for Fodor's, the American travel guide. He also contributed for many years for the American show-business magazine *Variety*. He wrote features for *Cara*, the Aer Lingus magazine, and for *Ireland of the Welcomes*. He worked for the Law Society.

But his real claim to fame came at RTÉ. He had started freelancing for the old Radio Éireann in the 1950s, contributing many of the *Topical Talks* that ran after the lunchtime news. Shortly after Teleifís Éireann started on the last day of 1961, he hosted a religious discussion programme called *Enquiring Minds*. When he was put in charge of *Sunday Miscellany*, which started on RTÉ Radio in 1968, he flourished.

He was its producer for the

best part of 20 years, assembling an impressive array of talent, the likes of Agnes Bernelle, John Fleetwood, Shevaun Lynam, John Jordan, Ben Kiely, F.S.L. Lyons of Trinity, Val Mulkerns, Sam McAughtry, Sean MacCarthy, Michael Mulvihill, John Ryan and Bernard Share. The programme was introduced by Ronnie Walsh, the noted actor. It became an unmissable mix of music and musings, mandatory listening for many people on Sunday morning.

It had a wonderfully clubby atmosphere – so much so that many people thought that after each programme had been completed, all the participants repaired to some literary club, where they exchanged *bon mots* over generous libations. The reality was totally different, of course: there was no "club", as each of the contributors usually came in, recorded his or her piece, then left the Radio Centre in Donnybrook to go quietly about their business. Eddie was a very courteous and calm man, but like all good producers he knew exactly what he wanted, getting quite impatient if it wasn't delivered.

During his time in RTÉ, Eddie MacSweeney, aka Maxwell Sweeney, was legendary. Colleagues often said that he started full-time work at the station at an age when everyone else would have been thinking of retiring. He was working on *Sunday Miscellany* scripts in his hospital bed until just before his death on June 1st, 1991, just over 14 years ago. He had almost reached his 82nd birthday.

He is survived by two daughters, Anne and Colette. His wife and their mother, Maura, had died many years before, in 1974. She had accompanied him on many of his trips abroad and to the many social functions in the hospitality industry in Ireland.

It is largely a tribute to his theatrical and broadcasting skills that *Sunday Miscellany*, one of the longest-running of all radio programmes on RTÉ, is still going strong today. But there was only one Eddie MacSweeney.

June 9, 2005

An Irishman's Diary

Hugh Oram

A century ago this year, an 18-year-old from Durrus in west Cork arrived in China. Over the next few years, he played an inestimable role in the first great revolution of the 20th century. Sean Hurley was one of the first Irish people to have had a detailed knowledge of China and he was the first Irish person to hold a Chinese passport.

From a farming background in Durrus, Hurley started travelling in his teens, first to the United States. Then in 1905, he was appointed to a job in the British customs office in Shanghai, a move that began a lifelong obsession with China. Shanghai was then a colonised city, controlled by Britain, France, Japan and the US, but already a vast port.

For the next 10 years Hurley travelled widely throughout China, at a time when the sedan chair was still one of the main means of transport. He was one of the very few Westerners to visit the troubled Sino-Russian border region.

During his first few years in China, the Qing dynasty was starting to collapse after the failed Boxer Rebellion of 1900. A man called Sun Yat-sen, later known as the "father of the revolution" and "father of the republic", was fomenting dissent against the Qing dynasty, which finally crumpled in 1911. The young Sean Hurley, who became a fluent speaker of Chinese, was active in helping to train activists loyal to Sun Yat-sen, as he sought to overthrow the corrupt and feeble old ruling order. It was a time of great turmoil and uncertainty as the old framework of dynastic rule in China, dating back over two millenia, began to collapse.

On January 1st 1912, the new Republic of China came into being, with Sun Yat-sen as its president. (It was eventually replaced in mainland China by the Communist regime, which came to power in 1949.) The young Hurley later received a gift of many items of armoury, including cannon shells and guns, as well as Chinese porcelain, from the new Chinese president, who also honoured him with the first Chinese passport given to an Irish person.

In 1915 Hurley returned home to Ireland, where intense nationalist activity was in full flow, just as it had been in China a few years previously. One of

his great political friends was Michael Collins and a still extant photograph shows the two of them in obviously serious conversation as they walked across O'Connell Bridge in Dublin.

Hurley's time in China had encouraged his artistic instincts – he loved drawing and photography – and eventually he opened two photographic studios in Dublin city centre, one in Henry Street, the other in Grafton Street.

Left: Sean Hurley, political activist, photographer and film producer. Above: Micheál MacLiammóir and Phyllis Wakely in a scene from Hurley's ill-fated film *Land of Her Fathers*, which featured many of the leading Abbey actors of the day

Then he poured much of his savings and income into an ill-fated film venture, a production called *Land of her Fathers*, with a storyline of a traditional Irish romance. His production company was called Transatlantic Pictures.

Hurley and his director, an American called Frank Winslow, lined up what was starry cast of Abbey actors. Included were Barry Fitzgerald, Arthur Shields, FJ McCormick, Gabriel Fallon, Maureen Delany and Eileen Crowe. The female lead was played by a young Trinity graduate, Phyllis Wakely, daughter of a judge in Dublin, while the male lead was played by the up-and-coming Micheál MacLiammóir, then aged 26.

The exteriors sequences were shot on the Powerscourt estate in Enniskerry, Co Wicklow and at Garinish Island, in west Cork. Most of the interiors were filmed in and around Dublin. Locations used included what was then Lady Ardilaun's residence, St Anne's in Raheny. Lady Ardilaun, one of the Guinness clan, died the year the film was made and the house itself was burned down in

1943. Its name is today remembered in the surrounding park.

Another location used was "Westbury" in Dundrum, the home of the family of Denis Devlin, the diplomat and poet, while Sean Hurley also used his own large house in Stillorgan, then still a rural part of south Co Dublin.

Duly passed by Ireland's first film censor, the film had a private screening at the old Grafton Cinema, Grafton Street, October 1st, 1925. Hurley's eye was on the American market and he hired two people recommended to him to work as distributors for the film in the US. They attended the various locations in Ireland during the shoot, then returned to the US with Hurley to screen the film there.

However, the morning after their arrival in New York, the two agents disappeared with their copy of the film. Hurley never caught up with them, despite hiring a private detective. The two men succeeded in organising clandestine showings of the film in various US cities, but Hurley never showed it publicly there or in Ireland. Hurley never made another film, though the few critics who had seen the film on its only showing, were very favourably impressed. One evening newspaper critic described it as the most ambitious Irish-made film yet attempted.

In 1960, the year before he died, Hurley presented his copy of the film to the National Library. It was last seen there in the early 1970s by Peter Kennerly, who was making a film for RTÉ television about Micheál MacLiammóir and Hilton Edwards. In subsequent years, the film vanished, though some offcuts and still prints still survive.

Sean Hurley himself later became involved in the setting up of Aer Lingus and what is now IDA Ireland, but for the past 15 or 20 years of his life, he was crippled by asthma. However, he remained a fluent Chinese linguist until the very end.

His family went on to successes of their own, including a daughter, Maureen, a noted singer and harpist who worked for RTÉ for many years. She was first Irish harpist to appear on Russian television

August 20, 2005

An Irishman's Diary

Hugh Oram

The Liddy family, steeped in aviation lore with the Air Corps for three generations, have lived with danger for so many decades that they appear totally nonchalant about the risks of flying.

Captain Mick Liddy, 28, has just completed a remarkable single-handed sailing circumnavigation of Ireland in record time, but he has also performed many aviation feats. His father, Graham, and his grandfather, Seamus or Jim Liddy, did likewise before him.

Dangerous living began with Mick's great-grandfather, Sean Joseph Liddy, who had been the o/c of the Old IRA in West Clare during the War of Independence. He was elected to the Dáil in 1921 and he was one of the first recruits to the Garda Síochána. Not long afterwards, the Dáil decided that guards could no longer remain sitting TDs, so his career in national politics was brief.

For the rest of his career, he rose through the ranks in the Garda, retiring as a chief superintendent. He had many narrow escapes, including falling down a cliff and having a bomb put in his car, fortunately found in time. During the Emergency years, he was stationed in the then Sligo-Donegal district and by this time, was vehemently opposed to the IRA; hence the bomb in his car. After he retired, he was knocked down and killed after getting off a bus in Dublin.

Jim Liddy's mother, Nan Breen, had been Ireland's first female dentist and wanted her son to follow in her footsteps. He had no such interest and served in the Army during the Emergency, transferring to the Air Corps in 1945. Jim flew such planes as Spitfires and Hurricanes and for a short time in the early 1950s was a pilot for Aer Lingus, when Air Corps pilots were seconded to the national airline. However, the daily tedium of being a civilian pilot didn't appeal and he returned to the Air Corps.

When the Air Corps got its first jets, Vampires, in 1956, he flew those, then flew operationally with the UN in Lebanon. He had his lucky escapes - notably when his plane crashed into a hillside near Shannon. Lucky Jim, who was trapped by his shoes in the wreckage, managed to escape before the aircraft blew up, although he was caught in the blast. The sole survivor of the crash, he was badly burned in

the explosion and had to have 165 stitches in his head. But he was back flying within three months.

He was addicted to flying; it must run in the family, because Jim's brother Jack joined the RAF. When Jack was based in north Wales, flying jets, the two brothers met at 7,500 metres (about 25,000 ft) over the

Captain Mick Liddy, pilot and yachtsman: risk-taking runs in his family

middle of the Irish Sea, for mock dog-fights. That wasn't in the rule books! However, his luck ran out in 1970, when aerial scenes for a film called *Zeppelin* were being filmed off Wicklow Head. A helicopter being used in filming the aerial sequences collided with Jim's plane and all crew were lost.

Long before that, Graham Liddy, father of our present hero, claims to have flown with the Air Corps at the age of two. He explains that around 1949, when the Inter-Party government was in power, it was quite keen on joining Nato. Graham's father was flying an Anson over Donegal one weekend and as Graham's mother was in hospital at the time and no babysitter was available, he was taken along for the flight.

Graham made his first solo glider flight just after his 16th birthday and by 19, he was the youngest gliding instructor in Ireland, and probably in Europe. At one stage, he set a brief Irish altitude record for a glider – 5,486 metres (18,000 ft), without oxygen. In the late 1970s and early 1980s, he put on many dazzling displays at air-shows around the country.

As he wears glasses, he couldn't join the Air Corps as a pilot, but instead joined in 1973 as an aeronautical engineer. But having been responsible for maintaining so many aircraft, he managed to fly in practically everything in the Air Corps fleet, retiring as a commandant officer in charge

of helicopter maintenance. For the past 10 years, he has been working with the air accident investigation unit in the Department of Transport. It's a bit like doing jigsaws, putting all the pieces together, he explains.

Mick Liddy's first memories are of a glider wing being built in the house where they were living at the time. The family lived and breathed flying, including the fumes from the wing construction. When he was six, he started sailing, an enthusiasm he has retained. He says that the skills you need for sailing helped him get into the Air Corps. He started training in the Air Corps in 1996 and won the much coveted trophy for best pilot in his class. By the end of the 1990s, he was flying government ministers around Europe.

In late 1999, he transferred to helicopters and went on to spend nearly five years flying on over 150 rescue missions, including SAR (Search and Rescue), air ambulance and neo-natal transfer work. He logged over 1,000 flying hours on the Dauphins. He is full of stories about SAR, such as one about a colleague who was returning from a rescue mission far out in the Atlantic. This man managed to land his helicopter at Castletownbere, when all that was left in the fuel tank was fumes.

Mick has had his own narrow escapes. On one occasion, when he was training, he put the helicopter into a spin. Normally, it should be a straightforward manoeuvre to bring a helicopter out of a deliberately induced spin, but Mick found that his foot had become trapped in a bar on the floor of the cockpit. He just managed to free his foot and operate the foot controls, with 10 seconds to spare before the helicopter plummeted to earth.

At the moment, he is doing all kinds of helicopter work, everything from formation flying to transporting VIPs around the country. Next year, when the Air Corps starts taking delivery of its new Bell Augusta helicopters, he is due to start training on them in Italy.

In line with his long family tradition, Mick is addicted to flying, and completely relaxed about his near misses. If you say to him that they sound really scary, he merely replies: "Interesting".

October 10, 2005

An Irishman's Diary

You'd never imagine it now but Capel Street was once Dublin's most fashionable commercial street, the Grafton Street of its day. These days, Capel Street, often clogged with traffic, is better known for having probably more charity shops and more sex shops than any other street in Dublin.

It all began way back in the late 17th century, when it was named after the lord lieutenant of Ireland, Lord Arthur Capel, Earl of Essex. A friend of his, Sir Humphrey Jervis, Dublin's first property "improver", or developer, built the street on the lands of St Mary's Abbey, which he had bought around 1674. Sir Humphrey named the new street as a little "thank you" for favours granted to him by the lord lieutenant, who came to a bloody end.

In 1682, he was accused of conspiring against King Charles II and ended up in the Tower of London, where he was later found with his throat cut.

After the first Essex bridge had been opened in 1676 (Grattan Bridge wasn't opened until two centuries later), the first houses were built in Capel Street. During the early 18th century, Capel Street became incredibly fashionable, *the* place to live in Dublin, well before Georgian Dublin was developed.

William Connolly, who commissioned Castletown House in Celbridge, Co Kildare, had his town house in Capel Street. Margaret "Peg" Woffington, one of the great acting personalities of the 18th century, lived in Capel Street, where her house was the setting for many outstanding parties. She moved to London in 1740 and even greater fame on the stage. Peg's father had been a bricklayer, while her mother had taken in washing.

One of Ireland's first mints was set up in Capel Street – the other was in Cork – and shopkeepers were under threat of being sent to the gallows if they didn't use the new money made in Capel Street. Later, King James's Mint became Sheridan's School; its principal, Thomas Sheridan, was a great friend of Swift, who often visited him in Capel Street.

The lavish Capel Street linen hall was opened in 1702 and thrived for that century. Dublin also had a busy lottery culture in the 18th century and the draws for it were done in a hall in Capel Street, by boys from the Blue Coat School. A well-known late 18th century

Hugh Oram

Malton print shows two lottery shops at the bridge end of the street. In those days, Dublin was a very small city, with a population of not much more than 150,000.

Two events conspired to downgrade the street. In 1791, the Custom House was opened and shipping, which had sailed up as far as Essex Bridge,

Capel Street: days when it was Dublin's most fashionable thoroughfare are long gone

gravitated downstream. Then the Wide Streets Commission decided to widen what is now O'Connell Street, and as soon as this work was ready, Dublin's centre of gravity swung away from Capel Street.

During the 19th century, Capel Street became a mecca of shops and craft workshops, a pungent mixture of commercial outlets and tenements. It saw some of Ireland's first immigrants from Europe arrive, including Engelbert Shirtsinger, a German Jew, who ran a clockmaking business at Number 48.

The Italian connection has long been important. At Number 85, Dominick Farrara, the first Italian to live in the street, had a curious combination of business interests: he ran a boarding house and made religious statues.

The Cafollas once had an ice cream shop in the street. The Italian links are continued by the present day Fusciardi fish and chip shop, which opened in 1937. The street even once had an Italian grocery shop, run by one John Halliday, long, long ago.

About 150 years ago, Rosanna Ennis, baker by appointment to the lord lieutenant, had her premises at Number 133, while a few doors up the street, at Number 141, Richard Coyne was bookseller and publisher to the Roman Catholic bishops of Ireland.

During the 19th century and well into the 20th, the retail mix in Capel Street was truly eclectic, everything from hardware to pram shops.

Capel Street used to have a

gin palace, a theatre and St Patrick's music hall, a rowdy place indeed. Solicitors liked the river end of the street, because it was so near the courts. At one stage, one building on Capel Street, near the Liffey, housed no fewer than 27 solicitors. One of Dublin's first two public libraries was opened here in 1884, lasting for just over a century, until its closure in 1986. Its successor was the new central library in the nearby Ilac centre.

James Joyce, who mentioned the street and its library in *Ulysses*, (Bloom borrows a book from there) was an aficionado. He said that places he knew in Paris had the same joy and excitement as Capel Street, where bargaining on Saturday nights for Sunday's dinner was a "holiday". The Joycean connection continued until very recently. One of Capel Street's great characters of recent decades, Gerald Davis, artist, gallery owner, writer, raconteur and jazz enthusiast, liked to impersonate Leopold Bloom. Sadly, Davis died this past June.

In the earlier 20th century, as part of the Abercrombie plan to redevelop central Dublin, a great metropolitan cathedral was proposed for the top of Capel Street, to replace the pro-Cathedral in Marlborough Street.

It would have made a fantastic architectural vista, stretching from the old City Hall, down the length of Parliament Street and Capel Street to the new cathedral, but it was not to be. This was yet another great plan, a vision for the future, that got shelved.

Capel Street has also long been a great musical street. One of the last of the great Irish violin makers, John O'Neill, set up shop at Number 140 Capel Street about 1830; the last of his children died as recently as 1929.

Music shops and music-making have long been part of Capel Street, a tradition continued by Slattery's pub.

Now, it's very rare to find someone who was born and reared in Capel Street actually living there, although Michael Walsh, the manager of Halston Street credit union in Capel Street, is a native of the street. These days, it's a one-way street, the wooden cobblestones long gone and the Luas line from Tallaght cutting across it. Dublin City Council hopes to rejuvenate it, but Capel Street has far to go before it can be restored to even some of the fashionable prestige it enjoyed in the 18th century.

July 2, 2006

An Irishman's Diary

Hugh Oram

Dundalk people have been keeping a lovely little secret to themselves for years – the seaside village of Blackrock, which is just five kilometres down the road. Generations of Dundalk folk have enjoyed strolling along the promenade in Blackrock, or just sitting on the sea wall and whiling away the time.

Despite a burst of new house and apartment building in recent years, Blackrock still retains much of its traditional charm.

Yet in the more southerly parts of the country, if you mention Blackrock, people will think automatically of a suburban village in south Co Dublin, or perhaps in Cork, but rarely of Co Louth. Three decades of the Troubles also helped push the place off the map, but these days it is really coming into its own, as is Dundalk itself, whatever the *Lonely Planet* guide might say.

Blackrock has been a place for Dundalk's well-to-do to live for well over a century, but it also became a holiday haven. A century ago, crowds of Scottish holidaymakers used to come over during the summer, while the highlight of the calendar was always August 15th, the Feast of the Assumption, when vast crowds would come from all over counties Louth, Armagh, Down and beyond. Photographs taken in the early 1960s, when it always seemed to be summer, show shoals of cars parked along the Main Street, which is the seafront promenade, and hordes of people on the beach.

One of the seafront shops in those days was that of Herman Richter, who ran the "Pork and Continental" shop, specialising in German hamburgers. He was also the man who set up the German Salami Company in Dundalk, still trading today. The German immigrant tradition in the Dundalk area has long been strong.

But Blackrock always had a certain cosmopolitan aura. Photographs from the early years of the 20th century show a man with a performing bear. It turns out that a husband and wife circus team from Budapest, for whom the dancing bear was their livelihood, used to travel

to Ireland every summer. They began their annual tour in Wexford and worked their way up the east coast, until they got to Blackrock.

In those days, the main street was separated from the sea wall by a tree-lined walk, which survived until about 50 years ago, when the dividing wall between street and promenade was demolished, in the interests of "progress". But walking along the seafront these days, it is still easy to see just why the village

Blackrock's beach and promenade in the town's heyday as a holiday resort

has long been billed as having the purest air in Ireland. The great views of Dundalk Bay and of the mountains of the Cooley peninsula are an added bonus.

In the old days, Blackrock had an array of about six hotels and 40 boarding houses along or close to the front. Often, the prime attraction of these boarding houses was their well-sprung beds. Indeed, practically every house within easy reach of the seafront took in lodgers during the summer. One of the truly delightful old-time buildings in Blackrock was the old post office, Caseys, which sold almost everything. It had an agency for W & A Gilbey, the wine importers and distillers, which meant you could go to the post office for a bottle of wine or whiskey as well as a stamp.

Other attractions included Callan's hot salt-water baths, where elderly people from all over north Leinster and south Ulster would come in search of a cure for their rheumatism. Behind the baths stood the Lifeboat Tearooms, a testimony to the lifeboat stationed in Blackrock for close on 80 years, up to 1935.

The seawater baths themselves were demolished in

1975, five years after the tea-rooms closed down. Blackrock also had an Olympic-sized, open-air swimming pool, opened in 1962, which was demolished just 10 years ago to make way for an apartment development. However, the bay in Blackrock is still used for swimming and board sailing.

For many years, Dundalk people had an easy way of getting to and from Blackrock in McGeough's horse-drawn brake, which started its journey in Roden Place in the centre of Dundalk. Fares were 4d for a single, 6d for a return ticket. Each of the brakes, pulled by two horses, could seat 10 people, and carry their luggage. In the early 1920s, McGeough's was replaced by various bus services. One of them, the Violet, run by the Halpenny family, is still running today. The name of the old horse-drawn service is remembered today in the Brake restaurant, one of a number of good restaurants in the area.

Blackrock always had a name for entertainment, with the old Pavilion ballroom and the Skating Hall. In the mid-1980s, the town also had its own pirate radio station, Telstar community radio.

Blackrock is fortunate to have people who are committed to preserving its history, despite all the inevitable new building. Danny Hughes is Blackrock's unofficial historian and he has a wealth of stories going back for decades. He has also written several books on the place he loves so well.

The immediate district also produced a noted playwright, Paul Vincent Carroll (1900-1968), who was born at Haggardstown, between Dundalk and Blackrock. Carroll often used to say that gazing out over Dundalk Bay from Blackrock, was a great inspiration to him.

One distinguished contemporary citizen of Blackrock is Dermot Ahern, Minister for Foreign Affairs. He says that in almost 20 years in the Dáil, he reckons he has never overnighted in Dublin: he always prefers to get home to Blackrock – and who can blame him?

February 18, 2006

An Irishman's Diary

It's one of those little signs that summer is on the way. The ferry service between the east pier in Howth and Ireland's Eye, a mile-and-a-quarter offshore, will soon be starting its summer runs, which will continue until the end of October.

The ferry service dates from 1947, when Cyril Doyle, a Howth fisherman on holiday in Limerick, noticed a converted lifeboat being used for fishing, which he promptly bought. The boat had been built in London in 1909 for the RNLI at a cost of £892, expensive for its day. The wooden open craft depended on the rowing skills of its crew, as it had no engine. It was named the *General R. Dudley Blake*, after an RNLI benefactor, and went new to the lifeboat station at Blackrock, Co Louth. It served there until 1935, when the lifeboat station was closed down.

From then until 1947, its history was obscure, but after Cyril Doyle bought the boat, he piloted it up the Shannon and along the Grand Canal to Dublin. He promptly renamed the boat the *St Therese* and put in a diesel engine. It is still in service today, in excellent condition, licensed to carry up to 32 people across the narrow channel to Ireland's Eye between April 1st and October 31st.

The boat is now run by Mark Doyle, Cyril's grandson, together with his brother Greg. They also operate a sister boat, the *Little Flower*, which was bought by their father, Frank Doyle, father of Mark and Greg, back in 1960. The *Little Flower* was built in Dun Laoghaire in 1921. It can carry up to 30 people at a time across to Ireland's Eye. Frank Doyle was also the pilot in Howth Harbour which, in the days before smokeless fuels, used to take in shipments of coal as well as steel for the Parsons factory near the harbour.

This is the last season for the *St Therese*; even though the boat is perfectly sturdy and seaworthy, Mark Doyle has decided to replace it. So he is selling the vessel through Nelson's boatyard in Donaghadee, Co Down, which specialises in selling old lifeboats.

Mark Doyle also has another maritime life. When he not in Howth, he works as chief engineer on a ferry that plies

Hugh Oram

between Rossaveal, Co Galway and the Aran Islands. When I caught up with him the other day, he was on Inisheer.

During the summer season,

The Stack – the rocky outcrop off Ireland's Eye, near Howth, is home to a large colony of gannets

when the weather is calm enough for landing on Ireland's Eye, the Doyle brothers run frequent daily trips out to the island. It is a place of unspoiled beauty and peace, with just two buildings. In the centre of the island, there is a church, St Nessan's, whose origins go back to about 700 AD. Close to the landing stage, the island has a Martello tower, built in the early 19th century, when a Napoleonic invasion of these islands was feared. The rocky outcrop near this point of the island is called the Steer. The island's outstanding feature is a large free-standing rock called the Stack, just off its eastern side.

The island stretches for only about a quarter-mile in each direction. Its only inhabitants are thousands of sea birds and seals. Ireland's Eye currently has a big colony of gannets, on the rocky outcrops to the east of the island. About a dozen other species of sea birds can be seen, including cormorants and puffins; the noise and the smell from the shags is quite phenomenal.

Just offshore from the island, between it and the entrance to Howth Harbour, is a rocky outcrop called Thulla, home to numerous cormorants. It can be reached at low tide from Ireland's Eye, but getting there is very dangerous and not to be recommended. The channel between the island and Howth Harbour can also have strong currents.

Often, says Mark Doyle, sees considerable numbers of seals on the Rowan Rocks, which face Howth Harbour. For anyone not interested in bird-watching, the big attraction of the island, he adds, is simply its solitude. It is one of the few places in Ireland never to have seen any development.

Many families like to take the boat over in summer to picnic on Carrigeen beach. It's also a popular place for courting couples. People who like rock climbing can enjoy some steep challenges, but everyone must make sure to catch the boat back in the evening: there isn't even any fresh water on the island.

As for the name Ireland's Eye, it is a corruption of the original name of Eria's Island. One explanation is that Eria, a woman's name, became confused with Erin. Newfoundland in Canada also has an Ireland's Eye, once a thriving fishing settlement, abandoned in the early 1960s.

Like any good seafarer, Mark Doyle has his own host of stories. In 1957, a whale and her two young offspring were stranded on the island, where they died. Keeffes the Knackers from Blackpitts in Dublin had to be called in.

Mark recalls one result of that episode: for weeks afterwards, his father and grandfather were pumping whale blood out of the boat.

It may be just a short boat trip from Howth Harbour to Ireland's Eye, but it's a journey into a different world, aloof from the frenzy of mainland life.

April 5, 2006

An Irishman's Diary

Hugh Oram

Every time I walk along the south side of St Stephen's Green in Dublin, my heart sinks when I get to the corner of Harcourt Street. The bleak office building at that corner of the Green, surely one of the ugliest of the modern blocks in Dublin city centre, replaced the old Russell Hotel, the epitome of elegant hospitality that once occupied the site.

The origins of the old Russell Hotel dated back to the earlier 18th century and by 1910, three houses on that side of the Green – Numbers 102, 103 and 104 – were occupied by the Russell. The hotel was bought in 1947 by Ken Besson of the Royal Hibernian Hotel and he added a fourth house, Number 101.

The facade of the old Russell may have been rather plain, but the hotel excelled with its culinary delights, including in the Robert Emmet Grill.

For many years, what was then the Department of External Affairs, now the Department of Foreign Affairs, just along that side of the Green, had the food for State banquets in Iveagh House supplied by the Russell kitchens.

The grand old hotels of Dublin city centre also attracted many celebrities.

Close on 50 years ago, one famous film star who stayed at the Russell, together with her first husband, Mel Ferrer, was Audrey Hepburn.

Just over 30 years ago, the Russell closed down and was then demolished, to be replaced by the present ghastly office block.

The following decade, Besson's other hotel, the Royal Hibernian Hotel in Dawson Street, suffered a similar fate. It closed down in 1983 and was demolished to make way for a shopping mall and offices.

The Royal Hibernian Hotel had been there for two centuries, beginning life as a coaching inn. In the earlier 19th century, Bianconi, the coaching man from Clonmel, had his Dublin headquarters there. In its later years, when the Royal Hibernian had a certain discreet but fading charm, it was managed by that most genial of hosts, Michael Governey, who went on to manage the Berkeley Court Hotel when it opened and who completed his career at the Conrad on Earlsfort Terrace, from where he is now retired.

When you went up the steps to the old Royal Hibernian, you were greeted by an always blazing coal fire in the small lobby. Downstairs, the hotel had a profusion of public rooms, including a ballroom. Fresh flowers were everywhere.

The Lafayette restaurant was renowned in its heyday, three small but different rooms combined into one restaurant. One of those rooms mirrored the decor of Maxim's in Paris. The hotel also had a basement level grill bar, the Bianconi, that was open all day, until about 11pm. One guidebook published just a few years before the hotel closed for the last time noted that its restaurant was still

Audrey Hepburn: famous frequenter of the old Russell Hotel on Stephen's Green

serving classic dishes from its august menus, with the occasional short cuts and lapses. But it had a superb wine list, mostly French. In its final years, the hotel suffered the indignity of having three changes of ownership in just eight years.

The old Jurys hotel, at the corner of College Green and Anglesea Street, lasted from 1839 until 1973.

When it closed, the Victorian Long Bar was shipped intact to Zurich, where it still forms the centrepiece of the James Joyce Pub.

The old Jurys hotel building was demolished in 1980, by which time the hotel had moved out to Ballsbridge, to what had been the modern Inter-Continental hotel. Ironically, Jurys in Ballsbridge is now under threat of demolition and redevelopment.

Other hotels, too, in the city centre, are also long gone, but are still well remembered, like the Moira in Trinity Street. The Temple Bar district once had the popular Dolphin, which closed in 1966, but which lingered on for another 13 years as a pub.

The Harcourt Street area once had a profusion of sedate residential hotels, like the Standard.

Dublin's most famous old restaurant was Jammets, which for years regarded itself as the only authentic French restaurant in Dublin, long before the restaurant explosion of recent years. The original Jammets was in St Andrew Street; it was bought in 1900 by two brothers from France, Michel and François Jammet. When the lease expired in 1926, they moved the restaurant to Nassau Street.

For another 40 years, Jammets was a haven to many of Dublin's literati, artists and theatrical figures, as well as business people around town. It closed in 1967 and today, on part of the site, Lillie's Bordello in Adam Court is located, just at the back of where Jammets used to be. Another long gone but fondly remembered city centre restaurant was the Red Bank, famed for its oysters and fish, in D'Olier Street. The building is now occupied by budget tourist accommodation, having been a chapel for many years after the restaurant closed.

The Red Bank was a great meeting place for its time and a favourite lunching spot in the days when working lunches were seriously vinous affairs that went on until late in the afternoon. When McConnell's Advertising Agency was in Pearse Street, the Red Bank was the "local" for many of its staff and some of its best creative campaigns were dreamed up amid the hedonistic splendours of the Red Bank.

Its heritage has been preserved in the name of the eponymous present-day restaurant in Skerries.

It's symptomatic of the times we live in that what was once Mitchell's cafe in Grafton Street, which included a coffee shop and a superb gourmet restaurant, is now occupied by the first McDonald's fast food place to have opened in Ireland, back in 1977.

The Robert Roberts cafe is another famous but vanished name from Grafton Street in the old days, as was the original Bailey in Duke Street, just a few paces off Grafton Street.

Restaurants and hotels by their very nature, tend to be ephemeral, but it's still a litany of loss: the magic was carted off in skips.

Regrettably, the Parisian approach to hospitality heritage has never been adopted in Dublin.

Imagine the uproar in Paris if it was suggested that the Ritz or Crillon hotels should be pulled down for redevelopment.

And in Paris, what is claimed to be the world's oldest restaurant, Le Procope, founded in 1686, is still going strong in the sixth arrondissement.

When SNCF, the French state-owned railway company, once proposed that the Belle Époque Train Bleu restaurant in the Gare de Lyon should be demolished in the interests of modernity, the cries of indignation could be heard from one side of Paris to the other and the Train Bleu is still there today.

Sadly, here in Dublin, you won't even find a plaque where the Russell, the Royal Hibernian, Jammets or the Red Bank once stood.

May 11, 2006

An Irishman's Diary

Just the other day, I talked with one of that select group of Dublin residents, the people who live on Bull Island on the city's northside.

Louis Barton is a member of one of the three families who still live in the cottages on the island, just past the century-old wooden bridge, as you head towards the Royal Dublin Golf Club. He reckons that about 16 people in all live in that cluster of homes and he says he is the only one to have been born and reared on Bull Island.

Louis worked for the *Irish Press* until it closed in 1995. He spent nearly 40 years at Burgh Quay, first as a compositor then as a journalist. He says he's quite happy living on Bull Island, a seaside oasis just three kilometres from the city centre. The only problem is one common in Dublin these days: the sheer volume of traffic passing to and fro across the bridge. The only other way on to the island is by the main causeway, built in the early 1960s.

Earlier, in glorious summer sunshine, I had walked along Dollymount beach, which runs the length of the seaward side of the island. The sand was white and the beach was clean; the setting could have been a blue-seas island in the Caribbean, far away from any big conurbation. The island wasn't always as clean as this; a serious litter problem prompted action and every third Saturday, the Bull Island Action Group does a clean-up.

Rubbish could have been a much more bigger feature of the island. Back in 1971, incredible as it now sounds, the then Dublin Corporation proposed that the island be used as a dump for household waste. Fortunately, that plan never materialised. The corporation had bought the island, apart from the Royal Dublin golf course and the land owned by the old Dublin Port and Docks Board, back in 1955.

There was an earlier and even more bizarre plan for Bull Island. In 1944, the then Irish Tourist Board announced that it had taken control of the island

Hugh Oram

and was preparing to develop a holiday camp there. At the end of the following year, the plans were unveiled, showing a proposed cinema, dance hall and restaurant. But they never got off the drawing-board.

During the first World War, the island had been taken over by the British military as a firing range. Afterwards the place needed considerable rehabilitation. Many of the Royal Dublin's tees and greens

Brent Geese at Bull Island, with Clontarf in the background

had disappeared, while the clubhouse was almost derelict. The course was redesigned and rebuilt.

Today, Bull Island is a specially protected area, renowned for its flora and fauna. In 1981, it was designated by Unesco as a biosphere reserve, the only one of its kind in the world so near the centre of a capital city. In 1988, the island got further protection, as a nature reserve. Dublin Corporation built a visitor and interpretative centre, though it was padlocked on my recent visit.

Other attractions include the statue of Our Lady of Dublin Port, which is down the causeway, past the entrance to the Royal Dublin Golf Club. The statue was unveiled and blessed in 1972 by the then Archbishop of Dublin, Dermot Ryan. A breakwater runs from the statue down to the North Bull lighthouse.

The island is, of course, an artificial creation; just over 200 years ago, it didn't exist. The South Bull Wall was built during the 18th century to improve navigation into the

port of Dublin. It didn't bring the expected improvements, so in 1800, the Royal Navy's Capt William Bligh (yes, he of the *Bounty*) carried out a survey of Dublin Bay and proposed the building of the North Bull Wall, which was completed by 1823.

After the building of the South Bull Wall, tidal patterns in the bay had started changing. In 1800, a new sandbank was seen off Dollymount and over the succeeding two centuries, the tides have swept in sand to build up Bull Island, which is now over 5 km long and 800m wide. What is properly called North Bull Island now covers over 350 hectares and is still growing, year by year.

In 1889, the Royal Dublin Golf Course got the permission of Col Edward Vernon of Clontarf Castle, who then owned most of the island, and of the then Dublin Port and Docks Board, to lay out a golf course, which has been there ever since.

The Royal Dublin is Ireland's second oldest golf club; it started in the Phoenix Park, then flitted to Sutton, before settling on Bull Island in 1889. The other course on the island, St Anne's, opened in 1921. The links on both courses are superbly maintained, while their club houses offer a high standard of services and comforts for golfers, but both clubs are highly respectful of the wonderful island paradise that is their home.

Bull Island boasts habitats ranging from salt marshes to dunes. It has a vast array of plant species and is noted for its wild flowers, especially orchids. Many bird species live on the island, including the Brent geese from northern Canada which winter here each year. There may be up to about 30,000 birds at any one time. The island is noted also for its hares and its mice.

As for the name of the island, it derives from the Irish name for Clontarf, Cluain Tairbh, or Meadow of the Bull. Before the harbour walls were built, the sound of the waves crashing on the shoreline was said to have resembled a bull bellowing.

May 22, 2006

An Irishman's Diary

On a sweltering Saturday afternoon recently, I visited the St Mary's Graveyard in Donnybrook, in company with about 20 other people, all interested in finding out more about this hidden corner of Dublin. The old graveyard, next to the Garda station in the main street, is normally kept locked, so this was a rare chance to explore the place in the company of like-minded historical enthusiasts. We had the benefit of a splendidly detailed commentary by David Neary, who retired recently as a community officer with Dublin City Council's south-east area.

Disused for many decades, the graveyard was tidied up in the 1980s with the help of a community employment scheme and the good offices of a local politician, Dermot Lacey, later a Lord Mayor of Dublin. The place is now in the care of the City Council. During the course of that clean-up, the granite base for a wooden cross dating from the 8th or 9th century was found – a remnant of the ancient St Broc's convent. This is where Donnybrook began, around 1,200 years ago.

The Garda station next door was built in 1931, replacing the older Dublin Metropolitan Police barracks. When the station was built, this part of the main street was widened. A portion of the front of the graveyard was removed and some graves disturbed. Within a year, the three foremen working on the scheme had all died.

The entrance to the graveyard is through a modest ornamental archway built in the late 19th century by members of the Dublin Stock Exchange to commemorate a registrar, Thomas Chamney Seawright. Within the graveyard itself, perhaps 7,000 people were buried over the centuries.

The earliest burial records in parish registers date from 1712, but the graveyard had been in use for several centuries before that.

Many of the gravestones are no longer legible; the passing of time has worn them smooth. But many others can still be read. Some are of ordinary folk, such "Jane Wheeler, died June 9th, 1873, aged 58". No other details are given.

Another tombstone records the passing of James Tobin, grocer, late of Kevin Street, who died in 1793.

David Neary pointed out that in those days, the mortality rate for young mothers and their infants was very high. It is fitting , then, that Dr Bartholomew Mosse, who opened the Rotunda, the

Hugh Oram

world's first maternity hospital, in 1745 – originally in what is now South Great George's Street – is buried here. A

The entrance to St Mary's Graveyard, Donnybrook. Photograph: Matt Kavanagh

memorial was put up in 1995, on the 250th anniversary of the founding of the Rotunda, close to his reputed burial spot.

Another grave of great historical interest is that of Richard Madden, author, historian and politician, and a benefactor of Anne Devlin, who helped in the planning of the abortive 1803 rising.

The time of the United Irishmen is also recalled in a plain grave that says simply, "Leonard McNally". He was the barrister who defended the United Irishmen, but after his death, it turned out that he also been in the pay of Dublin Castle, as an informer.

Another notable figure buried here was the architect Sir Edward Lovett Pearce, who was only 34 when he died in 1733. His great work was the Irish Parliament Building in College Green, today owned by the Bank of Ireland.

Someone else interred here who also made a great contribution to Dublin's architectural legacy in the 18th century was Bishop Robert Clayton, who was Church of Ireland bishop of Cork and Ross when he built Number 80, St Stephen's Green in 1736 as his town house.

It was acquired in 1856 by Benjamin Lee Guinness, who added Number 81. In 1939, the second Earl of Iveagh donated

the mansion to the State. The government of the day made it the headquarters of the Department of External Affairs, now Foreign Affairs.

Literary connections also abound, as with the vault of the Graves family, where at least six ancestors of the poet, critic and novelist Robert Graves are buried. One of them was John Crosbie Graves, the first commissioner of police in Dublin, who was great-grandfather of the writer.

The graveyard was closed for burials in 1880, except for 45 families named in the closure order. The very last burial, of Amy Ryder, daughter of a clergyman, took place in 1936.

Recently, some cemeteries in Dublin and Belfast, including that in Donnybrook, were opened up for guided tours, as part of European Cemetery Week.

Up to the end of August, Ray Bateson, an expert on the subject, who gave part of the commentary during the Donnybrook graveyard tour, hopes to organise one cemetery tour a week in Dublin.

He can be contacted through his website, www.deadireland.com or by phone at 086-8104359.

You can borrow the key to Donnybrook graveyard from Donnybrook Garda station.

Danny Parkinson, who lives just round the corner in Donnybrook Manor, is keenly interested in local history and is the author of a comprehensive book on the graveyard, first published in 1993, which has sold more than 2,000 copies.

Once, on a visit to Rome, I went to see the graves of Keats and Shelley in the Protestant cemetery there. More properly, it's called the Cimitero Acattolica, or non-Catholic cemetery. Although currently afflicted by a financial and conservation crisis, it remains a deeply elegiac spot, full of cypress trees.

Several years before he died, Shelley wrote of this graveyard: "It is a spot so beautiful it might make one in love with death, to be buried in so sweet a place." The same could be said of the graveyard in Donnybrook.

An Irishman's Diary

For a brief period during the late 1940s and through the 1950s, lovers of classical music in Dublin enjoyed a venue that is today almost forgotten, the Phoenix Hall. For those who attended concerts there, the name has assumed an almost magical aura. It was a simple, austere place where the quality of music making was superb.

In 1947, Radio Éireann decided to split its orchestra into two separate orchestras, the symphony and the light. At the beginning of the following year, the radio station opened the Phoenix Hall in Dame Court, between Exchequer Street and Dame Street in Dublin city centre. As Richard Pine recalls in his recently published book, *Music and Broadcasting in Ireland*, the hall had previously been used by the Irish Hospital Sweepstakes organisation.

The Phoenix Hall was a radio studio with room for an audience, rather than a concert hall as such. It replaced the Round Room of the Mansion House, and the Capitol Theatre in O'Connell Street, where public concerts had been held previously, while Michael Bowles was Radio Éireann's first director of music; he also conducted the radio orchestra.

This new hall was decidedly spartan and as a now retired RTÉ conductor, Eimear Ó Broin, recalls, the acoustics were a little dry and some more reverberation would have been welcome. But the hall had room for 400 hard wooden seats and one of the advantages of concerts there was that the audience was seated close to the orchestra, in a very intimate music-making atmosphere. A series of guest and principal conductors appeared regularly in the Phoenix Hall, including Jean Martinon from France, Milan Horvat, who was Croatian, and Hans Schmidt-Isserstedt, from Germany. Great Irish artists, such as the pianist Charles Lynch, also performed there.

Eimear Ó Broin recalls that usually three concerts were staged each week. On Tuesdays, the programme would include new pieces, while the Friday symphony concerts had more popular works from the classical repertoire. On Saturday nights, the Radio Éireann Light Orchestra performed. From 1952 onwards, children's concerts were staged at the Phoenix Hall, which also

Hugh Oram

served as the venue for a summer school of music.

Eimear Ó Broin says that the classical programmes were surprisingly adventurous and

Hans Schmidt-Isserstedt, one of the international musicians who performed in Dublin's Phoenix Hall

were a good outlet for new works, some Irish, some international. He remembers a Shostakovich symphony being played not long after it had had received its first performance in the USSR.

Often, new international works were performed in the Phoenix Hall long before they were first performed in London and at one stage in the late 1950s, a delegation from the BBC arrived at Radio Éireann – then based at the top of the General Post Office in O'Connell Street – to find out just how the station was managing to broadcast such a wide classical music repertoire on such a limited budget.

In those far-off days in radio music, a time of great financial austerity, a certain creative inventiveness was in the air, recalls Eimear Ó Broin.

From an audience perspective, the Phoenix Hall had another great advantage – the concerts were free. People simply collected their tickets from Radio Éireann in advance. On the way into the concerts in the hall, groups of classical music enthusiasts would chat away about the programme they were about to hear, without any

of the social one-upmanship that seems to beset so much modern concert going. Once inside the hall and seated on those hard wooden seats, the audience could enjoy the *hors d'oeuvres* of the orchestra tuning up.

Such was the excitement generated by those concerts that when Milan Horvat gave his final concert in Ireland, at the Phoenix Hall in the mid-1950s, the excitement rivalled and even excelled what would have been seen at a Beatles concert.

The Phoenix Hall survived as a music radio studio only for about 12 years, before being superseded by the much larger St Francis Xavier Hall in Upper Sherrard Street. For most of the 1960s, the Budapest-born conductor Tibor Paul was principal conductor of the Radio Éireann Symphony Orchestra and the radio station's director of music. The St Francis Xavier Hall was used for concerts through the 1960s, 1970s and into the 1980s; the free Friday evening classical concerts there were very popular. Another venue, the Gaiety Theatre, had begun to be used for Sunday orchestral concerts in 1953 and these continued for many years.

A couple of fruitless attempts were made to build a proper concert hall in Dublin. In 1960, work started on clearing at site at the junction of Nicholas Street and High Street, close to Christ Church Cathedral, but the project got no further. Then in 1964, the saga of the planned John F. Kennedy Memorial Hall began. This was also the first attempt at a national conference centre – which we are still awaiting, more than 40 years later.

First the was to be sited at Beggar's Bush, then in the Phoenix Park. Government dithering on the project lasted for a full decade before the plug was pulled and the government of the day finally decided to convert the Great Hall at UCD in Earlsfort Terrace into what is now the National Concert Hall.

September 9, 2006

29

An Irishman's Diary

If you walk along Fitzwilliam Place in Dublin, you'll pass a rather decrepit building at number 13, part of a long Victorian terrace close to Fitzwilliam Square. Nothing in its appearance gives the slightest clue as to the extraordinary goings on in the cellars here over 50 years ago, when the Catacombs were at the hub of Dublin's wild artistic life.

Around 1950, many young artists and writers, some later to become well-known, gathered for all-night drinking sessions and worse. The Catacombs owed their origins to a tall, rather effeminate Englishman called Dickie Wyman, whose officer boyfriend had been killed during the second World War. Wyman subsequently became a night-club manager in London, before mysteriously turning up in Dublin. He was often infused with laudanum, to soften the pain of losing his boyfriend, whom he called "the Faithful Heart". Brendan Behan liked to annoy him by referring to "the Sacred Heart".

Wyman rented the basement at number 13, Fitzwilliam Place and turned it into a hotbed of artistic discussion and more. After McDaid's pub, off Grafton Street – then a second home to much of Dublin's literary set – had closed for the night, many of the patrons set off for the Catacombs. A second group of artistic people would also make their way there, people who had been at salons held by a writer, sculptor and artist called Des MacNamara, whose studio was at Number 39, Grafton Street. (Today, the thought of an artist having a studio or organising salons in Grafton Street is simply unthinkable.)

Once the gang of literary and artistic layabouts had arrived at the Catacombs, around midnight, the serious drinking began. The only passport for entry was a brown paper bag, filled with bottles of Guinness or a bottle or two of gin. The habitués included writers such as JP Donleavy, Anthony Cronin, John Jordan and Patrick Kavanagh. Tom Nisbet, an artist and Dan O'Herlihy and Godfrey Quigley, who both later became noted actors, were also part of the Catacombs congregation .

Hugh Oram

Another regular was Gainor Crist, who was at Trinity College with his fellow American Donleavy and who became the model for Sebastian Dangerfield in Donleavy's novel *The Ginger Man*, which evidently derived much of its inspiration from the goings-on in the Catacombs.

One of the women who

JP Donleavy and Brendan Behan were among the set who frequented Dublin's Catacombs

attended the Catacombs was Irene Broe, a sculptor. While she relished the below-stairs Bohemian life, she was also a creator of religious statues, including that of St Valentine in Whitefriars Street church.

More than drinking went on in the Catacombs, which were in fact a series of cellars and pantries. The place became renowned for its sexual licence. Brendan Behan, who was as prolifigate in his bisexual activities as in his consumption of alcohol, once remarked of the Catacombs that it was a place where "men had women, men had men and women had women". It was a fair field and no favour, he added.

While the cellars had plenty of mattresses, others who were there at the time consider that Behan was exaggerating. Everyone was so drunk and the place was so dark that no one was quite sure what was going on.

But if the stories of sexual activity were even partially correct, they showed that the Catacombs was somewhere gay men and lesbians could meet without fear of the law. More than 40 years were to pass before homosexuality became decriminalised.

The nocturnal happenings of the Catacombs took place at a

time when Dublin was an impoverished city, though it had a thriving artistic life. But many up-and-coming artists had literally to beg on the streets for the price of a drink or a meal. It was also a very conservative city in a deeply reactionary country; after all, John Charles McQuaid was the Archbishop of Dublin.

Yet somehow, for about three years, the nightly activities in the Catacombs went on without interference. So much drink was consumed that a large part of Dickie Wyman's income derived from getting money back on all the empties the following day. Come dawn, and the inhabitants of the Catacombs staggered up the steps into the daylight, just as more respectable citizens were starting to come into work.

Some people actually lived in the Catacombs for a while, including a young Anthony Cronin. He noted the smell of damp, decaying plaster, as well as remarking that the room he had was so small that it barely had space for a bed. It had once been used as a wine cellar. Cronin himself described the Dublin of that era as being a city suffocated by sexual frustration, where people took refuge in strong drink. He wondered how anything actually got written.

When MJ MacManus, the literary editor of the *Irish Press*, died in 1951, Brendan Behan was among the congregation at the funeral. He noticed the recently painted Stations of the Cross in the church and saw that none other than Dickie Wyman, the landlord of the Catacombs, had been the model for Christ. Behan collapsed into fits of laughter and the late Ben Kiely, who was sitting next to him, had to nudge him in the ribs and tell him to behave himself in church.

These days, Number 13 Fitzwilliam Place is occupied by an insurance company – all very staid and sedate, with not a hint of the Rabelasian frolics that once went on in the cellars.

March 12, 2007

An Irishman's Diary

Well over a century before the first whispers about global warming and changing weather patterns caused by human activities, Ireland had its worst ever storm. It happened on the night of January 6th, 1839, which promptly went down in history as the night of the Big Wind, or An Ghaoth Mhór.

On the previous night, January 5th, there had been heavy snow right across the country. Then, as morning broke, an Atlantic warm front moved in, bringing a period of complete calm, with dense cloud cover. Temperatures rose rapidly throughout the day, melting all the snow. Then a deep Atlantic depression moved towards Ireland, bringing a cold front which collided with the warmer air, creating strong winds and heavy rain.

The first signs of the big wind came on the coast of Co Mayo around midday and the storm slowly moved across the country. By midnight, the wind had reached hurricane force and remained at that strength for about five hours. It swept across Ireland, doing tremendous damage in the north, the west, the midlands and all along the east coast. Munster was the only province to escape widespread damage.

In Dublin, about a quarter of all houses in the city were either badly damaged or destroyed and this pattern was repeated across the country. In Carlow town, the chimney that had been on one of the towers of the castle for the previous six centuries blew down. Some of the worst damage was in Co Mayo, where the storm first landed. In Castlebar, practically every house was wrecked and the town provided one of the most tragic stories of the storm. The Mooney family lived in a roadside cabin in the town; after it was wrecked, they had to live under a hedge. The parents then died from fever, leaving five children orphaned.

On the Westport House estate, 1,500 trees were blown down. Scarcely a house in Westport itself escaped severe damage, while the town's one

Hugh Oram

hotel (the Olde Railway) was badly damaged. Two ships were completely wrecked in Killala harbour.

The ferocity of the storm was such that seawater was swept inland for miles along the west coast, and seaweed and fish were later found far inland. For weeks afterwards, many people

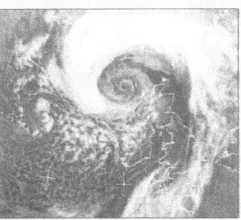

Satellite image of a severe storm over Ireland: but no tempest in living memory compares to the Big Wind of 1839

living well inland were still trying to clear the salty smell of the sea out of their houses.

Up to 300 people lost their lives, in the the storm. When dawn broke the following day, January 7th, the landscape across much of the country was devastated and many familiar landmarks had simply been swept away. People were dazed by the scale of the destruction.

In those days, insurance was almost unknown, so most people had to pay for their own repairs. For poorer families, it was a huge burden. Building workers did well, however, as did all the merchants supplying materials. For months afterwards, armies of bricklayers, carpenters, slaters and thatchers enjoyed an unprecedented demand for work.

The storm left its legacy to the landscape: for years afterwards, if someone in the country was building a new house, they chose a sheltered spot at the foot of a hill, in case another such storm should blow

up. More people were left homeless by the Big Wind of 1839 than by evictions between 1850 and 1880.

At the time of the Big Wind, many theories were advanced as to its cause, some of them outlandish. Some people believed Freemasons had caused it by unleashing the devil from hell and failing to persuade him to return. Many thought that the following day, January 7th, was going to be Judgment Day.

The great storm was so well remembered that it came in useful when the British old-age pension was introduced to Ireland in 1909. People of 70 years and more became entitled to a state pension of up to five shillings a week. In those far-off days, birth certificates were quite rare and for many people to qualify for the pension, it was enough for them to say that they could remember stories of the Big Wind when they were very small children.

Curiously enough, although the Big Wind loomed large in folklore, not much has been written in more modern times about the phenomenon. A Northern writer, Peter Carr, did write a book called *The Night of the Big Wind*, published in Belfast in 1993, while Beatrice Coogan used the storm as the title of a novel. She used the events of January, 1839 as the backdrop for *The Big Wind*.

But more recent weather events of almost similar severity have been largely forgotten. How many people still remember the big snow of February, 1933, which was the biggest snowfall since 1867, or the big snow of 1947, which lasted for three months, from January until March? A more vivid memory, thanks not least to the name, is Hurricane Charlie, when over 12 cm of rain fell in a couple of hours.

It caused £25 millions worth of damage, considered an enormous amount at the time.

April 9, 2007

An Irishman's Diary

Hugh Oram

Sometimes, when I've an idle moment, I click on to the live webcam on the beach at Collioure, a magical French fishing village on the Mediterranean coast, on the edge of the Pyrenees and close to the Spanish frontier.

Somehow, the sun almost always seems to be shining in Collioure. Across the bay, I see the iconic image of Notre Dame des Anges, the tall church tower topped with the strange cupola, and built right into the sea. The church began as a primitive lighthouse in the Middle Ages.

Collioure is quite a small place, with about 3,000 people living there, and until Henri Matisse and some of his friends discovered it in 1905, it was merely a sleepy little fishing village where little happened. The arrival of Matisse and company changed all that. He and his fellow painters were enchanted by the colours of the Mediterranean and of the skies here, the brilliant light and the turquoise, pink and yellow of the anchovy fishermen's cottages. An artists' colony soon sprung up.

Georges Braque, Charles Rennie Macintosh (the great Scottish exponent of Art Nouveau) and Picasso were among the many painters inspired by Collioure. Matisse and Braque stayed in Les Templiers, an hotel on the quayside of the river, and they paid for their keep in paintings. Today, this same hotel is packed with more than 2,000 works of art collected over the years. Indeed art is everywhere in the town and you can follow the Fauvism "footpath", where reproductions of 20 well-known works are displayed at the very places where the originals were painted. The town also has a fine museum of modern art.

A more recent famous resident was the novelist Patrick O'Brian, who wrote 20 tremendous novels about seafaring life 200 years ago. These were all written in longhand – he shunned even a typewriter. But at the end of his life, an illusion was shattered, when it was revealed that he wasn't Irish at all and had created a mythical identity for himself. orn Patrick Russ in England, he had changed his name in 1945 to make it sound Irish. In 1949, with his second wife, Mary Tolstoy, who had been married previously to a prominent divorce lawyer, he came to live in Collioure. His wife died in 1998 and that year it was also revealed by the *Daily Telegraph* that his Irish identity was a complete fabrication. He then left Collioure and came to live in rooms at Trinity College, Dublin, which had made him an honorary doctorate of letters in 1997. Patrick O'Brian died in the Fitzwilliam Hotel, Dublin, at the beginning of 2000, aged 86. He is buried in the town cemetery in Collioure, alongside his wife.

Collioure is particularly busy during the main French holiday months of July and August and, above all, during the three-day festival centred on August 15th, the Feast of the Assumption. But the town has changed little since the days of Matisse. Its narrow medieval streets are still the same, the balconies of the houses lined with flowers. The main historic building, apart from the church, is the great castle, the Chateau Royal, built by the Templars in the 12th century.

The motto promoted by the current Mayor, Michel Moly, is "*Collioure sera toujours Collioure*" (Collioure will always be same"), which is a take-off of the Maurice Chevalier song Paris sera toujours Paris.

The market, held in a central square of the town every Wednesday and Sunday, is a cornucopia of food, including cheeses, meats, fruits and vegetables. You'll also find some of Collioure's own wines, which have become better known in recent years. The vineyards in the hills above the village have long produced red wines, but in recent years whites and rosés have been added to the repertoire.

The best time to sample Collioure is in the evening, when the restaurants along the riverside and facing out on to the beach, are full of conversational buzz and the scents of cooking. The food on offer reflects the political history of the place, with a mix of French, Catalan and Spanish dishes.

I know most of the French seaside towns and cities all along the coast, from Calais in the north-east, right round the Atlantic coast and on to Menton on the Italian frontier. Few if any can equal Collioure, in my opinion. That webcam on the beach at Collioure is a constant reminder of the paradise that the town is, if one ever needed reminding.

But every earthly paradise has its darker moments. One trip to Collioure very nearly ended in disaster for my wife and me. One afternoon, we went to a small harbour on the far side of the bay and, on the spur of the moment, decided to accept the offer of a trip on an open-deck boat going out to sea with a party of sub-aqua divers. It was a fine enough day, in early summer, and the sea was calm, so we had no apprehensions. But when we were a few kilometres out to sea, the weather changed abruptly and a raging storm blew up.

The waves became enormous and the spray was washing over the little boat as it tossed up and down in the violent seas. We had to cling on for our lives, soaked to the skin, and convinced the boat was going to sink. But after a harrowing couple of hours, when everyone on board was too sick to get sick, the boat eventually made the safety of the harbour where we had started the voyage in such innocence.

Once ashore, there was only one option: head for the nearest beachside bar and order two large cognacs.

The harbour at Collioure, made famous by Matisse and his friends

An Irishman's Diary

The story of Constance Smith, an Irish actress who once sparked high hopes in Hollywood, is salutary. She began in rags, briefly tasted riches, then returned to rags. She died in London a few years ago, by which time she was an alcoholic down-and-out.

She was born in Limerick, her mother's home town, in 1928, one of a large family. Her father, who had served in the British army during the first World War, was working at the time as a labourer on the building of the Ardnacrusha hydro-electric scheme on the River Shannon.

Within a year of her birth, the family moved to Mount Pleasant Buildings in Ranelagh, Dublin, a now demolished slum immortalised by Lee Dunne in his novel *Goodbye to the Hill*.

Constance began her working life young and modestly, including spells in chip shops, one of them in Charleston Road, Ranelagh. Then the family in Rathmines for whom she worked as a maid encouraged her to enter a look-alike competition being run in 1945 by a Dublin film magazine, *The Screen*. She won the section for women, dressed up as Hedy Lamarr.

As a result, Constance went to England, to be groomed in the Rank Organisation's charm school for budding starlets. She made few if any films for Rank, though she had a seven-year contract with the company, but she did show up in several films made by independent producers in the late 1940s. If you look closely at the 1947 film *Brighton Rock*, based on the Graham Greene novel, you'll see her as a singer on the pier. In 1950, she was fired by Ranks; she said it was because she was always objecting to their complaints about her Irish accent.

But she was soon talent-spotted by Darryl Zanuck, the Hollywood producer and director, a long-time power in Hollywood and a co-founder of 20th Century Fox. Zanuck whisked her off to Hollywood; he took a special interest in her, a euphemism for the infamous Hollywood casting-couch.

Constance signed a seven-year contract with 20th Century Fox. The following year, 1951, she married Bryan Forbes, a well-known figure in the English film business. At the end of that year, 20th Century

Hugh Oram

Fox lent her $3,000 to pay for an abortion. The marriage to Forbes was brief, lasting just two years.

The ill-fated Irish actress Constance Smith, pictured on the cover of a 1951 issue of *Picturegoer* magazine

But once in Hollywood, with her talent largely undeveloped, and a temperamental and difficult actress to boot, she failed to make the progress predicted for her. At the time, many in the film business thought Constance would emulate Maureen O'Sullivan. She did make about six films in Hollywood, none of them memorable, but with such leading stars as Anne Bancroft, Charles Boyer and Jack Palance. In 1952, she had been sufficiently well-known to host the annual Academy Awards ceremony in Hollywood. She also got married for a second time, in 1956, to an Italian photographer called Araldo di Crollolanza, whose father had been a Fascist senator in Mussolini's time.

While she was living in Italy, she made several more films, but her last major feature was released in 1958. Intriguingly, the Italian film publicity machine described Constance Smith as being descended from Irish aristocrats. As her career faltered in Italy, she took the first of several overdoses and

her husband, unable to cope, left her.

Constance returned to England but was unable to revive her career. She met Paul Rotha, one of the most distinguished names in English documentary film-making; they were lovers for many years, an unlikely pair.

In 1961, she returned to Ireland with Rotha, who planned to write a book about her life and then film it, but it never happened. But Constance did pose for pictures outside the house in Wolfe Tone Street, Limerick, where she was said to have been born. On several occasions, she stabbed Rotha during the frequent and monumental rows they had; they were both heavy drinkers. Once, in 1975, she ended up in Pentonville Prison in London. Somehow, however, they managed to reunite; in the end, it was she who left a heartbroken Rotha.

At the end of her life, Constance Smith was cleaning hospital wards and doing childcare jobs. She was in and out of hospital and by the time she died at Islington in north London, in June 2003, she had been reduced to a homeless wreck, moving between hospitals and hostels.

Today, she is sometimes put forward as one of the great "might-have-beens" of the cinema industry. Perhaps, with proper training and a calmer temperament, she could have gone much further.

The academic Ruth Barton probably knows more than anyone else about Constance Smith. She has been connected with the film studies centre in UCD, has written much on Irish film history and will be lecturing in film studies at Trinity College, Dublin, from September. She wrote a book last year about the Irish who made it in Hollywood, from Barry FitzGerald to Colin Farrell. Constance Smith was included, as a near miss.

August 7, 2007

33

An Irishman's Diary

Carlingford is underrated. It's one of the most striking medieval towns in Ireland, in a magical setting on the southern shores of Carlingford Lough, backed by Slieve Foye and facing across the water to the Mountains of Mourne; yet somehow it doesn't have the same tourist rating as somewhere like Kinsale, which it deserves.

The largest of its historic buildings is King John's Castle, which dates from around 1200, while the town also still has its medieval Tholsel and some of its old walls. Yet another ancient building is Taaffe's Castle, built in the 16th century. Carlingford Mint dates back to the 15th century, but even though the town was given the right to mint its own coinage in 1467, the mint was never used for this purpose.

The ruins of the Dominican friary another important part of the town's heritage. The former Holy Trinity Church in the town, again with medieval origins, was turned into the local heritage centre in the early 1990s and is a splendid repository of local history.

The town also features a memorial to one of its most famous sons, Thomas D'Arcy McGee, who achieved much fame as a journalist and poet, then as a politician in Canada in the 19th century. Another key historical figure was Fr Laurence Murray, who was largely responsible for starting the Gaelic revival movement. He once described Carlingford as a "gold mine to the antiquarian".

But while the historic buildings of Carlingford survive, many other aspects of life in the town have changed dramatically. Much of the town's commercial life centres around the ancient Market Square, but many of the old shops there have vanished, places where you could buy groceries, hardware and drapery.

Chequins was one of those stores, selling groceries in one part, drapery in the other; eventually, the building became a high-class boutique. What was

Hugh Oram

a newsagent's shop, once a popular gathering place in Newry Street, is now home to an ATM machine.

Carlingford's ancient edifices are surrounded by new buildings, among them the Four Seasons Hotel, which has the local nickname of "the wedding warehouse" because of the number of receptions held there. One of the big local issues is the rezoning of more land for housing development. Yet many

Pony-trekkers in the Cooley Mountains above Carlingford, Co Louth

of the new houses being built are second homes for owners from Belfast and Dublin.

It's a familiar story all over the country – conservation versus progress – yet in few other Irish towns is the conflict so acute. In the past few years, the pressure of development has become ever more insistent.

When the railway came here in the 1870s, linking Greenore, Carlingford and Omeath with Dundalk and Newry, Carlingford started to blossom as a Victorian holiday resort. One of the results of that first flush of tourism was the imposing Carlingford Hotel, which traded for years as a temperance hotel, but closed after the tourist trade faded in the 1920s. The place was taken over by the Sisters of Mercy, who used it as a holiday home for its nuns. In those far-off days, the bathing places for men and women on the seashore were over a mile apart. A few years ago, the building was demolished and replaced by an apartment block.

Some old traditions have been revived, such as the annual Carlingford Oyster Festival.

Carlingford Lough once had a great store of native oysters, whose decline led eventually to restocking with foreign oysters, so that the trade has made something of a comeback. The town also once had a great fishing tradition – in the late 19th century, the then new harbour often had up to 100 fishing boats from as far away as Arklow and the Isle of Man. In those days, Carlingford could claim three hotels, 13 pubs, eight grocery shops, two draperies, two shoemakers, two blacksmiths and a photographer, all for a population that was then around 500.

Certain families continue to play a key role in the town, such as the McKevitts, of Village Hotel renown, right in the centre of town. Ghan House, an early 18th-century house, has become noted for its luxurious accommodation, fine restaurant and cookery school, run by the Carroll family. In recent years, tourism has been much revived, with bistros and restaurants galore.

Carlingford and the Cooley peninsula have had to contend with many difficulties over the year, not least the partition of Ireland, which cut it off economically from Newry, the closure of its railway service in 1952, and in latter years the dark effects of the Troubles. But now the area is rightly claiming its place at tourism's top table and another scheme that's on the cards could help.

After years of haggling and pleading, it finally looks as if a bridge is going to be built across Narrow Water, which will link the northern and southern sides of Carlingford Lough, to the benefit of both areas.

The famous Fr Murray said, nearly a century ago, that Carlingford wasn't a handsome town because it was "narrow, hilly, angular and gloomy" – but that it had a medieval suggestiveness that could carry one back many centuries and fill the mind with vague dreamings.

Despite the rash of recent developments, you can still dream there, but in much more comfort these days.

September 22, 2007

34

An Irishman's Diary

Hugh Oram

Two of the brightest Irish stars ever produced in the entertainment firmament were both top of the pops 50 years ago, but are largely and undeservedly forgotten today, namely Ruby Murray the singer and Stephen Boyd the film actor.

Both were from the Belfast area.

By today's standards, Ruby Murray's songs were decidedly saccharine and sentimental, but in the 1950s, audiences couldn't get enough: they adored the young singer from Belfast. At one stage, in 1955, she had five hits in the Top 20 in Britain all at the same time; subsequently, she was only bettered by Elvis Presley and Madonna.

She owed much of her fame to her unusual voice, acquired accidentally, the result of an operation she had had for swollen glands in her throat. Ruby Murray was just six weeks old; that was in 1935. A permanent effect of that operation was to give her a unique-sounding husky voice, which became her trademark.

Born in Belfast, she won her first talent competition there, at the age of 11. The following year, 1947, she made her first television appearance, with the BBC in London. By the time she was 14, she was on the road in Scotland, doing her first ever tour. Then she came home and spent two years touring the length and breadth of Ireland.

Her big break was when she was still a teenager, appearing in a variety show at the Metropolitan Theatre in London. The BBC was looking for a singer/presenter for a show called *Quite Contrary* and signed up Ruby Murray. Murray's gentle ways and her soft singing voice were an instant hit with viewers.

She went on to do many more programmes over the years with the BBC. When the BBC in Belfast started a new television series in 1968 called *Rinnce Mór*, she and the Dundalk-born tenor Brendan O'Dowda, that great interpreter of Percy French songs, were the two stars.

Ruby Murray's theatrical work blossomed as well in the 1950s and for an incredible seven months, she topped the bill at the London Palladium. But she also did over 40 single records, starting with *Heartbeat*, when she was 19. Her last chart success was in 1959 with *Goodbye Jimmy, Goodbye*. Of all her songs, her most famous was *Softly, Softly*, which became her signature tune.

But by the end of the 1950s, her days as a chart-topper were over.

These days, her style of singing is totally at odds with current musical trends; perhaps

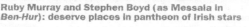

Ruby Murray and Stephen Boyd (as Messala in *Ben-Hur*): deserve places in pantheon of Irish stars

one of these fine days, she might find favour once again, if the tide ever turns back to the simpler musical tastes of the old days.

Married twice, she carried on performing right into the 1980s, touring the cabaret circuit. For many years, she lived in Torquay, Devon, a genteel seaside resort that was a complete antithesis to her native Belfast. Despite her fondness for her native city, she had made England her permanent home since 1957. She died in December, 1996, from liver cancer. Incongruously, her name survives as Cockney slang for curry.

While Ruby Murray was climbing the hit charts, a Belfast-born actor called Stephen Boyd was making it big in Hollywood. Born in 1931 as William Millar into a very poor family, with nine children altogether, in Glengormley, he began acting in Belfast, then moved to stage work in Canada and the US, where had some success.

He then broke into films in Britain, without making much impact. Boyd's lucky chance came in 1957. He appeared in a

French film, *The Night Heaven Fell*, playing opposite Brigitte Bardot. Immediately, Hollywood sat up and took notice.

Soon, he was starring in a couple of epics, *Ben-Hur* and *The Fall of the Roman Empire*. His duel to the death with Charlton Heston in *Ben-Hur* is considered one of the classic American film scenes, but after that performance, he was virtually typecast for life as a spear-carrying Roman.

Stephen Boyd nearly played opposite Elizabeth Taylor in the epic *Cleopatra*, but he couldn't because of other contractual commitments.

The part went instead to Richard Burton and Boyd always used to say later in life that it was he who was responsible for introducing Taylor and Burton to each other.

He also missed out on the James Bond films. Boyd had been the original choice to play Bond in *Dr No*, but in the end, Sean Connery got the part.

Boyd made many other films and considered that the sci-fi adventure that he starred in, *Fantastic Voyage* (1966) was his best performance apart from *Ben-Hur*.

Also in the 1960s, he starred in an epic about Ghenghis Khan, filmed in what was then Yugoslavia.

He also appeared in another French film, a story of Napoleon, *Imperial Venus*, in which he played opposite Gina Lollobrigida.

But in the 1970s, his career nosedived and Boyd descended into appearances in several mediocre European potboilers. He was all set for a comeback in a 1977 British-made gangster film, *The Squeeze*, but at the comparatively young age of 45, dropped dead from a heart attack when playing golf in California.

Stephen Boyd and Ruby Murray were two extraordinary entertainment talents from Ireland, both from very modest backgrounds, yet such is the ephemeral nature of the business that neither is much remembered these days.

But they deserve their places in the pantheon of Irish stars who really made it on the international circuit.

November 3, 2007

An Irishman's Diary

Hugh Oram

The chic of Audrey Hepburn is once again much in vogue, an antidote perhaps to the endless displays of crass vulgarity on so-called "reality" TV shows. She had a remarkable film career, including the film of *My Fair Lady* and before that, *Breakfast at Tiffanys*. Her own life story was equally amazing and while she had very little if any Irish ancestry through her parents, she did have a lot of connections with Dublin.

Her mother, Baroness Ella van Heemstra, was a Dutch aristocrat and she was a descendant of King Edward III of England. Her father was English, originally a wealthy banker. But later in life, through her father, she established many links with Dublin.

Audrey's father, Joseph Hepburn-Ruston, had an extraordinary career, that began in banking and ended up, via a second World War internment camp, in the insurance business in Dublin. In the early 1920s, he was the honorary British consul in what was then Java, now part of Indonesia. In those far-off days, this was part of the Dutch empire in Asia and it was in Java that he and the Dutch baroness met. Subsequently, the pair married; it was the second time round for both of them.

Audrey Hepburn herself was born in Brussels on May 4th, 1929. In 1939, her parents divorced. She herself said that the day that her father walked out of the family home was the most traumatic moment of her life. During the second World War, the future film star managed to survive horrendous conditions in her mother's native country, mainly in Arnhem. The young girl was exactly the same age as Anne Frank.

Before the war, her father had become firmly devoted to the Nazi cause. With his strong pro-fascist leanings, it was inevitable that he would spend much of the second World War interned in the Isle of Man. Later, her father's extreme right-wing views were a cause of severe shame to Audrey Hepburn and she was also terrified that the unpleasant truth might surface to damage her movie career.

While he was interned in the Isle of Man, Hepburn-Ruston spent much of his time writing a history of the Celtic peoples and when he was released in 1945 at the conclusion of the war, he came to Dublin, where

Audrey Hepburn: fascist sympathiser father was a long-time Dublin resident

he spent the rest of his life.

With the help of the Carmelite order in Dublin, he was able to get work in the insurance business in the city. The order here helped many people with fascist sympathies at the end of the war, people who would have been otherwise unable to find employment, particularly in Britain. In 1947, Hepburn-Ruston met a model called Fidelma Walshe at a dinner in the Shelbourne Hotel and they subsequently got married, in May, 1950.

The insurance man about town quickly got to know the right people, including members of the Guinness family and Sir Alfred Beit, the founder of the Chester Beatty Library, who had arrived in Ireland as a tax exile from Britain. Hepburn-Ruston also became very friendly with Lord Dunsany and often went horse riding on his lordship's estate in Co Meath.

After Hepburn-Ruston got married, he and his new wife moved into a smart flat in Fitzwilliam Square, eventually moving to another flat, this time just off Merrion Square. Not having seen her father for 20 years, Audrey Hepburn made the big decision to come to Dublin and meet up with him once again, having discovered his whereabouts through the Red Cross.

Accompanied by her first husband, Mel Ferrer, also a film star of note, she came to Dublin and they stayed in style at the old Russell Hotel on St Stephen's Green. Audrey Hepburn duly met up with her father and subsequently, they kept in touch on an intermittent basis. She was to support him financially for the rest of his life but he never reciprocated the love that Audrey always showed towards him.

By the early 1960s, the health of Joseph Hepburn-Ruston was very frail, so he and his wife moved to a ground floor flat at Sydenham Road in Ballsbridge, a cul de sac off the Merrion Road, directly opposite the RDS.

He spent the rest of his life in that flat and one of the last times that Audrey Hepburn met u⸺

⸺ ⸺ ⸺ere of *My Fair Lady*. Quite a number of people in the Ballsbridge area still remember Joseph Hepburn-Ruston. Ironically, he was known in some quarters in the district as "Colonel Hepburn".

He died in 1980, at the age of 91 and after his death, Audrey Hepburn never visited Dublin again. Fidelma herself subsequently remarried, to Harry Donnelly.

As for Audrey, the beloved elfin-like film star, she died in Switzerland, where she had lived for many years, on January 20th, 1993, at the age of 63, from cancer of the colon. In her last years, she had been an active goodwill ambassador in Africa for Unicef, spurred on by her own wartime experiences, and this hadn't helped her health.

November 27, 2007

36

An Irishman's Diary

The first Irish-born woman writer to sell copies of her books by the millions, Ethel Lilian Voynich, is largely forgotten today, but her's is a truly extraordinary story.

Her English father, George Boole, was a man of remarkable achievement. He had been appointed professor of mathematics at what was then Queen's College, Cork (now University College Cork) in 1849. It was he who invented Boolean alegbra. In his day, the idea of computers was theoretical, but without his work in creating this algebra, modern computers couldn't work. The life of George Boole and his family has been well chronicled by Desmond MacHale, a present-day academic at UCC, who enjoys a second career as a prolific humorous writer.

Ethel was the fifth daughter of Boole and his wife, Mary Everest,an ardent avant-garde feminist. She was related to the man who discovered Mount Everest.

Ethel was born just six months before her father died, in 1864. After her father's death, the young girl grew up mainly in London.

Her childhood was tough, including spells staying with Boole's brother, Charles, who was manager of a coal mine in Lancashire. But she spent frequent holidays in her native Ireland and in Cornwall.

When she was 18, she came into a small legacy that enabled her to study music. This led to a spell in Berlin, where she first became interested in revolutionary causes in Russia and eastern Europe, an interest that led her to Warsaw. One day, standing outside the Warsaw Citadel, she saw prisoners being paraded. One who caught her eye was a Polish-American count, Wilfred Voynich, who was both a bibliophile and a revolutionary. At one stage, he had been imprisoned in a camp in Siberia.

In 1890, Voynich and Ethel Boole managed to meet after he had been released from prison. The ensuing marriage didn't last long, but the count provided the inspiration for Ethel Voynich's great novel, *The Gadfly*. After her marriage broke up, Ethel had a passionate affair with a man called Sigmund Rosenblum, a Polish/Russian Jew who was also known as Sidney Reilly, the first super-spy of the 20th century.

Hugh Oram

While Ethel was deeply involved with him, it is often suggested that Rosenblum was interested in her mainly

Ethel Voynich: her book *The Gadfly* had extraordinary sales in Russia and China

because of her connections with Russian emigrants and their political plottings. However, her great affair did provide some further material for *The Gadfly*, which came out in 1897, shortly after her liaison with the spy ended.

Published first in New York, then shortly afterwards in London, it was a revolutionary and anti-clerical story set against the background of the Young Italy movement of 1848. Although it was set in various European cities, principally Rome, it was also infused with the culture of Irish Fenianism.

The novel became an instant success, selling many millions of copies and making Ethel Voynich a comparatively wealthy woman. It had an extraordinary vogue in Russia, where it became almost a bible of the revolution. Over five million copies were sold in Russia and a similar number in China. Even today, in those two countries Voynich is still considered a Western writer on a par with Shakespeare and Dickens.

The Gadfly formed the first part of a trilogy, whose final part, written 50 years later, dealt with Ethel's early days in

Cornwall. Published in 1945, it attracted little attention. Indeed, none of her other work attracted the public interest or the sales that *The Gadfly* enjoyed.

Later still, in the USSR, a film of *The Gadfly* was made and Dmitri Shostakovich was commissioned to write the score, which became known as *The Gadfly Suite*. A subsequent 1980s TV series, *Reilly, Ace of Spies*, used the *Romance* from this suite as its theme tune. It is still very popular today, and is frequently requested on Lyric FM.

Eventually, Ethel moved to New York and spent the rest of her life there.

Her estranged husband, Wilfrid, also moved there in 1914. He became one of the world's greatest experts on rare books and a leading dealer in them. Ethel rediscovered him in New York in 1920, but they weren't reconciled and he died there a decade later, in 1930.

As for Rosenblum, he went on to play a key role in the failed attempt to overthrow the Bolshevik revolution in Russia. Much later, when Ian Fleming started writing the James Bond novels, Rosenblum was the model for Bond.

Ethel devoted the rest of her life to music and to her devoted companion, Anne Nill and her adopted daughter, Winifred. Ethel herself knew little of the success of *The Gadfly* in Russia and subsequently in the USSR until a Soviet delegation arrived in New York in 1955, determined to find her. Not only did she make a big story for *Pravda*, which landed a huge scoop, but in an unprecedented step, the USSR paid her $15,000 in royalties.

Ethel Voynich died in New York in 1960 at the grand age of 96. Her life had been as amazing as the story of her most popular book and the current generation of Irish female writers will find it hard to match the publishing success she chalked up over a century ago.

An Irishman's Diary

Hugh Oram

ST NICHOLAS of Myra church in Francis Street, in the centre of Dublin's Liberties, is in some ways no different from many public places today, with its 24-hour closed circuit television and video recording as well as a request to switch off your mobile phone before you go in. But in other ways it is unique, with its richly ornamented interior and its beautifully restored Harry Clarke stained glass window.

As I walked in the door the other day, the choral singing sounded almost too good to be real, and in a sense it was: it was coming from the church's audio system. But it induced a suitably reverential tone in the church, whose building was begun in the year of Catholic Emancipation, 1829, completed in 1834 and finally dedicated in 1854.

There has been a church on this site since at least the 12th century, when a Franciscan monastery stood here; it is indeed part of the most historic area in Dublin. As for St Nicholas of Myra himself, there's a long story attached, that brings in Turkey and includes the claim that he was the original Santa Claus.

The parish itself was also the smallest in Dublin, a little over two hectares. When the Coombe Women's Hospital was in its original location in this immediate area, all the births there were registered in this church. At one time, it was even the parish church for the Isle of Man, so its early registers contain baptismal entries for that island. A Manx emblem can be seen in the ceiling panels. A modern plaque commemorates Very Rev Conleth Curley, parish priest here from 1993 to 2005, the year he died; he is interred in the crypt.

On the other side of the road, at 100 Francis Street, a battered plaque announces that a room in the Myra Hall there was where Frank Duff founded the Legion of Mary on the evening of September 7th, 1921.

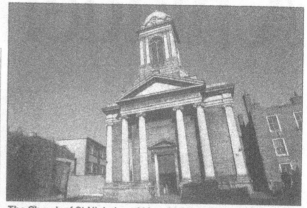

The Church of St Nicholas of Myra in Francis Street, Dublin: focal point of one of Dublin's most historic areas

Francis Street is steeped in history. Towards the end of the 17th century, many of the houses were the so-called "Dutch Billys", the tall, narrow, gable-fronted houses then so popular in Dublin. By the middle of the 19th century the street was full of small shops, including nearly 20 groceries shops and several dairies. Slightly more exotically, John Doherty, a brogue maker, lived and worked at Number 11, while at Number 46 was Daniel Murphy, a literary teacher.

By 1900 the street had turned into a Liberties slum. No fewer than 45 houses had been turned into multi-occupancy tenements, although one M.M. Maugham, a surgeon, was ensconced at Number 108. By the middle of the 20th century, Francis Street had become more workaday and housed many manufacturers of beds, cabinets, sheet metal and shirts. These have now gone, as have some more recent fixtures, such as the Old Dublin restaurant, which in its heyday was a much-loved place in which to dine on Russian and Scandinavian food.

About 20 years ago, the antiques trade began drifting towards Francis Street from the quays, and today the street has the highest concentration of antique dealers in Ireland. The most spectacular shopfront is that of O'Sullivan Antiques, founded in 1991, close to the church; the shop has a black grand piano hanging off its upper front wall. Some stylish modern shops have opened up, such as those of Michael Connell and Niall Mullen, both opened recently. Other personalities in the trade here include the Johnston brothers, Kevin Jones and Esther Sexton. Several art galleries also have their home in Francis Street.

Up at the top of the street, close to Thomas Street, is the Tivoli Theatre, with O'Reilly's auction rooms, founded in 1948, close by. Also nearby is the MABS (Money Advice and Budgeting Service) centre, for people with pressing financial problems. For despite the upmarket trade of the antique shops, Francis Street remains rooted in the working class realities of life in the Liberties.

Much of the street's future depends on the planned development of the derelict Iveagh Market, which has been closed for just over a decade now. It had been a thriving market since 1906. If elaborate plans work out as intended, the site will become Dublin's equivalent of Covent Garden, complete with a luxury hotel, cafés and restaurants and a myriad of arts and crafts. If that happens, it may lift the down-at-heel air that still pervades much of Francis Street. But gentrification would dispel that air of workaday scruffiness that seems part of the real spirit of the street.

April 18, 2008

An Irishman's Diary

Hugh Oram

DURING one of those gloriously sunny days we enjoyed recently, I climbed to the top of a small hill in Howth to reach the radio museum housed in a Martello tower. The view of Ireland's Eye, Lambay and the great strand at Portmarnock equalled anything you'd see around Sorrento. Rhododendrons in full bloom heightened the vista.

Inside, the objects on view were equally astonishing. Ye Olde Hurdy-Gurdy Museum of Vintage Radio has been open for four years now. It is the creation of Pat Herbert, whose knowledge of radio is encyclopedic. His small museum presents not just the history of radio over the last century, but a social history of the country.

Pat Herbert grew up in a small village outside Crossmolina, Co Mayo. He remembers vividly the impact on village life of the first local radio set, immediately after the Emergency days of the second World War. He has been hooked on radio ever since. During his working life, he was a supervisor in the construction industry, but now has been able to turn his hobby into a second career, the fruits of more than 40 years of collecting.

The Martello tower, which is up a steep path opposite the Abbey Tavern in the centre of Howth, dates from the early 19th century. When the first undersea cable was laid between Britain and Ireland late in that century, its Irish landfall was this selfsame tower. In 1903, Lee de Forest, the pioneer of American radio, ran transmissions from here to Holyhead, while two years later Marconi had a wireless station in the tower. So radio seems embedded in the very stones of the old tower, making it the perfect place for such a museum.

Pat Herbert has assembled a vast collection of old radio sets, all superbly restored and labelled. They begin with crystal sets, then move into the next generation of sets, which had external horn speakers. He has one very rare example of a set of "parrot" speakers, made in porcelain by Royal Doulton in 1927. From crystal sets, radios developed further into valve sets and the museum has some fine examples from the 1930s. In those days radios depended on wet and dry batteries, including those supplied by the old Exide

One of the many old posters on display at the Ye Olde Hurdy-gurdy Museum of Vintage Radio in Howth

factory at Portobello in Dublin.

All kinds of oddities are on show, such as the radios disguised as picture frames, used in occupied France during the second World War. Later, during the hippy days of the late 1960s, radios in the shape of spice-racks enjoyed a brief vogue; only about 1,000 were made and one of them is in the museum. Another eye-catching piece is an American car radio styled like a miniature juke-box.

Transistor radios flooded on to the market in the 1960s. Nowadays young women often go out equipped with a mobile phone and a bottle of water. Then, they often had a transistor radio shaped like a small handbag. On a recent trip to London Pat unearthed a contemporary equivalent of a handbag radio, one of the latest exhibits in the museum.

Some early TV sets, dating back up to 60 years, are on show. In those days, a 14-inch television cost around 60 guineas. Ireland once had a thriving industry assembling radio and TV sets, including the old Pye factory in Dundrum, close to the present-day Dundrum Town Centre.

Publicity material on the early stars of radio and television are featured, including a poster of a young Audrey Hepburn advertising Pilot portable radios and Eamonn Andrews promoting GEC television sets.

The museum also houses an amateur radio station, manned by Tony Breathnach – the Irish Radio Transmitters Society has been going for over 75 years. On most Sundays, the amateur radio station in the tower crackles into action, using wireless telegraphy, with its call sign EIOMAR. On the museum's website, the call sign is included, in Morse.

Radio recordings are included in the museum's inventory.

When the US *Columbia* space shuttle passed over Ireland in 1983, a group of enthusiasts set up an amateur radio station in Dublin and communicated with it. You can listen to some of the conversations in the museum.

Other recordings include old 78rpm discs issued by the Gramophone Shop that used to be in Johnson's Court off Grafton Street. One features Eamon de Valera's famous 1943 speech about the comely maidens at the crossroads. Another 78rpm disc carries a recording by an actor of Pearse's celebrated oration at the grave of O'Donovan Rossa, also issued by the Gramophone Shop. The museum also has some old wind-up gramophones, which used needles to reproduce the sound.

Apart from all the radio, TV and recording memorabilia, Pat Herbert has packed many other items of social interest into just two small areas, the ground floor space and the basement. Items include a photograph of Foley's tourist bus outside Clerys in O'Connell Street in 1923; tourists were still coming to Dublin in the midst of the Civil War. He has some late 19th-century sugar bags that carried advertising for politicians such as Isaac Butt; many country households in those times didn't get daily newspapers, so sugar bags were a more effective advertising medium. He has a copy of the Irish telephone directory for 1940, just 12mm thick, covering the whole State.

Even though Pat Herbert himself is such a treasure-house of information on radio, there are always new stories and, as he says himself, he is always learning from the visitors from all over the world who come to visit and be intrigued by what lies within this old Martello tower.

June 9, 2008

An Irishman's Diary

Hugh Oram

The old terminal building at Dublin airport: flying has been transformed since it was inaugurated

FLYING in the old days was great fun, for the lucky few who could afford an air ticket. But in return, they got no hassle over parking and no elaborate security checks when they checked in. The flights were leisurely, devoid of any inflight entertainment or sales pitches. Flying then was elitist, almost like an exclusive gentleman's club, to which ladies were admitted in certain favourable circumstances.

In many ways, the 1950s was the golden era of this old-style flying, when stepping on to a plane at Dublin or Shannon was a real novelty. Few people could afford to fly; as an example, a return ticket from Dublin to Frankfurt cost £30, which was almost a month's wages for many people. As a result, flying was a preserve of the middle classes and the aristocracy and quite a number of people turned up at Dublin Airport in their own chauffeur-driven cars. People dressed up to fly and some of the women passengers looked as if they had stepped from a fashion photograph.

Some people went one better; the Aly Khan, who owned a stud in Co Kildare, was a glamorous racing car driver who exuded the air of pre-second World War European sophistication. He happened to own his own plane, then virtually unheard of in Ireland.

For the people who did fly, it meant turning up at Dublin airport with mountains of luggage, which created no great problem when they presented their paper tickets at the check-in desk. Security checks and baggage restrictions were unknown and if you arrived at the right time, the concourse was almost deserted. The big drawback was the time it took to fly anywhere.

Until 1964, Aer Lingus was still using that old workhorse of the skies, the DC3. This aircraft was launched way back in 1935 and amazingly, 400 of them are still in service in various offbeat parts of the world. But the DC3's cruising speed was a mere 130 knots, or 240 km/h, which meant that a flight from Dublin to the old Le Bourget airport near central Paris took a mind and seat-numbing three hours. The arrival of the Viscounts in 1965 was a big advance; Aer Lingus had got into jets when the Boeing 720 came into use in 1960 on the transatlantic service started two years previously.

Apart from flying, Dublin airport itself was still a big novelty in the 1950s. Many people went out there at the weekends, just to breathe in an exotic whiff of aviation; in those days, if you asked someone what they were going to be doing for the weekend, they would quite often reply: "I'm going out to Aer Lingus". Celebrity-watching was a popular pastime at the airport.

A regular double-deck bus service ran from the city centre out to the airport, while there was plenty of car parking at the airport, as well as ample bicycle parks for the people who worked there.

The first departure bar had opened at Dublin airport in 1948, while the first newsagent's shop opened in 1953. The big attraction was the restaurant run by Johnny Oppermann, with Jimmy Flahive the head chef, who went on to become Ireland's first TV chef. Lunch or dinner at the airport was always a great treat and dinners there on a Saturday night were always booked out.

The menu and wine list prices, too, were tempting indeed by today's standards, although dear enough for the time, with a sirloin steak for 10 shillings or a bottle of Chablis for 21/6d. Some of the dishes had flying connotations, such as the Veal Viscount, while Jerry Dempsey, then the head of Aer Lingus, had a steak named in his honour. The Aer Lingus inflight menus, too, were tasty and innovative.

The old Dublin airport terminal was the creation of Desmond FitzGerald, brother of Garret FitzGerald. It had opened for business in 1940 and exactly 50 years later, the then transport minister, a youthful looking Seamus Brennan, unveiled a plaque to this effect at the airport.

It was Garret FitzGerald who, while working for Aer Lingus and engaged in what was for him, the absorbing task of devising timetables, came up with one of the very first marketing ideas for the industry – reduced prices for midweek flights.

Launched in 1949, the Dawnflights and Starflights to London became very popular, but strangely enough, those cheap flights to Paris didn't catch on as much. But for anyone willing to travel at some ungodly hour of the early morning or late evening, the savings were considerable. The first package holidays started at the very end of the 1950s and they began the popularisation of air travel.

When Desmond FitzGerald and his architectural team designed the first Dublin airport terminal, it was meant to cater for 100,000 passengers a year.

By the time it closed for passenger use in 1972, when the new terminal was opened, the throughput was two million.

Technical innovations continued apace, like the new radar system that was inaugurated in 1956. This newspaper said at the time that it would make Dublin airport one of the most modern in the world. Six years later, in 1962, Aer Lingus became the first organisation in the country to use a computer. Behind the scenes, one of the people who worked assiduously in the 1950s and 1960s to develop civil aviation in Ireland was Dr Thekla Beere, the first woman to be secretary of a government department; hers was the old Department of Transport and Power. A spirit of aviation pioneering was very much in the air, long before Ryanair came along.

If comings and goings at Dublin airport were free and easy in the 1950s, it was the same at Shannon airport, where the man behind all its innovations, Dr Brendan O'Regan, was a ferment of new ideas.

In May, 1947, a small kiosk was opened in the terminal to sell Irish souvenirs and transatlantic passengers could avail of the world's first duty-free shop. During the 1950s, the restaurant in the terminal was a model of white linen tablecloth elegance.

After Cork airport opened in October, 1961, it had 10,000 passengers in its first year. These days, more than that number travel on a single day, using Cork's impressive new terminal, opened two years ago.

As the 1960s developed, more and more people developed a taste for flying and what had once been a minority preserve moved much more into the mainstream.

Along the way, flying was democratised and the exclusive tag was ditched. In retrospect, the 1950s and 1960s, when flying was great fun, easily done, without many complications, were a wonderful time in aviation, compared to the rigours and restrictions of modern day flying.

An Irishman's Diary

Hugh Oram

TO MY mind, Ardmore, Co Waterford is almost the perfect seaside village: a main street, plenty of beaches, a cliff walk and that's just about it – or is it? I first became aware of Ardmore when I got to know Molly Keane, that delightfully aristocratic lady who lived there for many years.

After the death of her husband, she returned in 1961 to an area she knew well, to live with her two daughters, Sally and Virginia, in Ardmore. She had already given up writing as M.J. Farrell, a name sequestered from a pub, and had started to write as Molly Keane, but it took a further two decades, until 1981, for her masterpiece, *Good Behaviour*, to be published.

She was a most charming, bird-like woman, the epitome of good manners and a living connection to the big house culture of old. Molly spent the rest of her life in Ardmore. She died in 1996 and is buried beside the Church of Ireland church almost in the centre of the village.

Then I discovered another artistic connection with Ardmore, one that drew me even further into its embrace: two outstanding painters of the 20th century, Joan Jameson and Norah McGuinness. Joan, like Molly, came from an aristocratic background; she was the eldest daughter of Sir Richard and Lady Musgrave of Tourin near Cappoquin.

Educated at the Sorbonne, she eventually returned to Ireland, where a frequent guest at the family home in Ardmore was Norah McGuinness, the coal merchant's daughter from Derry. The two became great friends and Norah often stayed with the Jamesons in Ardmore.

That artistic tradition in the village is continued to this day by Mary Lincoln at the Ardmore pottery and craft shop, high up on the road that leads to the cliff walk, overlooking the pier and boat cove. She started doing her pottery 30 years ago and her shop is a remarkable emporium of her own work, that of other potters and general craftware. It's the kind of place where you have to fight hard to suppress the urge to buy armfuls of stuff before you leave.

Mary's mother-in-law, Siobhan Lincoln, wrote a marvellous book, published in 2000, with many anecdotes and recollections about old Ardmore. It's a very detailed description of life in Ardmore in the old days,

The round tower at Ardmore, Co Waterford, a familiar landmark on the cliff walk above the village and bay

not just everyday life in the village, but that of the landed gentry.

She tells how the first privately owned motor car, owned by Fred Keane, had come to Ardmore only in the second decade of the 20th century. Running water was installed in 1937; exactly a decade later, a branch of Muintir na Tíre started in the village. The rural electrification scheme was extended to Ardmore and the lights went on for the first time on May 24th, 1954.

In her book, Siobhan recalls many fascinating snippets, such as how Ardmore people going to nearby Youghal would, until the late 1960s, go to Monatrea and take the ferry across the Blackwater estuary at 2d for a passenger, 2d for a bicycle. You can read lengthy extracts from her book, *Ardmore: Memory and Story*, on the website of the Waterford County Museum at Dungarvan.

For many years, from the 1920s onwards, the Cliff House Hotel in Ardmore was the social hub of the village. Molly Keane recalled that Joan Jameson and her husband Tommy often went there to meet the Nugents, the owners, and a motley assembly that included Father Power, the local priest, and Paddy Spratt, a local auctioneer, for their school of cards. Play would go on far into the night, but the participants would all do what they had to do next day, like Father Power celebrating early Mass.

But, according to Molly Keane, when Joan Jameson died in 1953, far too young, the magic fell from the air.

On occasions, my wife and I stayed at the old Cliff House Hotel; once it was so busy we ended up in a room not much bigger than a box-room. But the restaurant and its views over Ardmore Bay more than

compensated. A brand new luxury hotel of the same name opened recently on the same site, with exactly the same views from the restaurant. It's the wonder of the area. People are said to be coming from Dungarvan, a mere 20km or so away, just to stay overnight and sample its pleasures.

Ardmore has another hotel, the Round Tower, a couple of restaurants, and a few pubs. The main beach is complemented by four or five others and, while Ardmore has lost its Blue Flag status because of the antiquated sewage arrangements in the village, that has been a blessing in disguise, because it prevented a rash of new housing developments during the lately vanished boom years.

Some historic buildings in the area have been converted. The big old coastguard station up on the heights was opened in 1867 and run as such until 1922, when it was abandoned, then burned down. In recent years, it has been lovingly restored into a family home.

Treasures of the area include the cliff walk, the ruins of the early medieval cathedral and the perfectly preserved round tower. St Declan, who made Ardmore the first Christian settlement in Ireland in 416 AD, just before St Patrick arrived, is remembered at such spots as his well and hermitage on the cliff walk. And that completes the picture: few man-made excitements, no raucous entertainment.

At this stage, yet another Keane comes into the picture. Fergal Keane, nephew of the late John B. Keane, and himself a distinguished writer as well as correspondent for the BBC, has spent many family summer holidays in Ardmore, which he describes as heaven on earth.

As descriptions go, that's pretty near the ungarnished truth.

An Irishman's Diary

Hugh Oram

WHEN I'M out for a night-time walk around the neighbourhood where I live, in Ballsbridge, Dublin, and I come to the junction of Clyde Road and Elgin Road, I often hear heavenly music. It emanates from St Bartholomew's Church, as the organist gets in a spot of practice. Then the distinctive chimes of the church clock ring out the quarter-hour or hour.

St Bartholomew's was consecrated in 1867 for the parish formed three years previously from two neighbouring parishes in Donnybrook. It's hard to imagine now, but when the church was built, Clyde Road was open fields.

The church was designed by an English architect, Thomas Henry Wyatt, later described by John Betjeman as one of the dullest of the Victorian architects, a verdict that seems a little unfair when you look at St Bartholemew's. The original plans called for a spire to top the octagonal tower, but this never happened – whether the reason was financial or structural, no one knows today.

All the decorative work around the sanctuary was designed by Sir Thomas Deane, who took his inspiration from Monreale cathedral in Sicily. This medieval cathedral has vast mosaics, created with a strong Byzantine influence. The angelic frescoes in the Clyde Road church are complemented by the stained glass windows, the mosaics on the floor and the hammerbeam roof. Fortunately, the structure and interior of the church, full of vibrant colour, remain in good condition.

Next door to the church, the vast vicarage and parish hall were opened in 1872; they are now owned by the Knights of Malta, although St Bartholomew's still has the use of the hall. Mainie Jellett, one of Ireland's most noted artists, was a regular communicant at the church and held one of her first exhibitions in this parish hall.

Hardly surprisingly, the design of the interior reflects St Bartholomew's determinedly High Church beginnings and it has continued so right up to the present. It may be Church of Ireland, but the vicar is known as "Father". As for its large and dedicated congregation, more socially diverse than the vicar had expected, it comes from as

St Bartholomew's Church: a bastion of choral music in Dublin's Ballsbridge

far away as Co Wicklow.

The church has a new, youthful team at the helm. The new vicar, appointed early this summer, is Andrew McCroskery, who previously ministered in Youghal, Co Cork. He is 34, while the new organist and director of music, Fraser Wilson, who was appointed at about the same time, is 24. Previous clerics at the church included George Otto Simms, who went on to become Primate of All Ireland.

Ever since the church opened, music has been integral to its tradition and one of Fraser Wilson's predecessors, William Henry Vipond Barry, was organist and choirmaster from 1884 until 1938, an astonishing record. The manual organ is regarded as one of the finest of any church in Dublin and its most recent renovation was completed eight years ago.

The warm acoustic of St Bartholomew's was discovered many years ago; the first radio broadcast of an organ recital at the church was made in 1935. These days, the church is used frequently for recordings and rehearsals. Christ Church Cathedral Choir's latest commercial CD was recorded here earlier this year and is due to be released shortly. A singer specialising in weddings recorded her demo CD here recently and the National Chamber Choir has been using the church for rehearsals.

But it's for its own choirs that St Bartholomew's is best known. It has the only remaining all-boys choir in a Church of Ireland parish church in the Republic. Recently, nine new boys were recruited. The girl's choir is more recent, founded about five years ago. The two children's choirs between them have 44 children. The church also has about 15 men in its men's choir. It has plans to set

up a chamber choir in the near future. Happily, say Fraser and Andrew, there's a strong appetite in Dublin for choral performance.

In addition, the church has the services of the Elgin Chorale, composed largely of members of the congregation, but also including regular members of the men's choir and people from outside the parish, who sing services during choir holidays.

One choral member at St Bartholomew's has a particularly distinguished record: Bobby Barden has been a member of the the choir, boy and man, for the past 66 years. Years ago, Dr Houston Colleson, a musical collaborator of Percy French, sang in the church choir in his student days. Another former choirboy is Malcolm Proud, one of Ireland's foremost harpsichordists. Tim Thurston, presenter of Lyric FM's *Gloria* programme on Sunday mornings, is a regular current member of the choir.

As Fr McCroskery explains, St Bartholemew's wants to expand both its liturgical and musical traditions. The church takes part in the Voice for Life scheme, a training programme for church singing, which is run by the Royal School of Church Music in Salisbury. It so happens, very usefully, that the man who runs this scheme here in Ireland, Peter Parshall, also happens to be the assistant director of music at St Bartholomew's.

As Fraser Wilson comments, Christmas is party time. During November, the church will have a concert every week, while the candlelit Advent procession, with singing by the boys and men, will be on November 30th.

The service of carols and readings, featuring Alan Stanford, now in its 20th year, will be on December 14th. On December 16th the AIB Choral Society will perform, the service of lessons and carols is on December 16th. Midnight Mass on Christmas Eve will feature the world premiere of a piece by composer Peter Macintosh, while the traditional Christmas Day Eucharist is at 11am.

The church is still basking in the rave reviews of the Irish première of the very earliest Spanish opera (1665) *Celos aun del aire matan*, performed there in July.

It's a church deservedly admired for its interior design and for the musical refreshment it offers, even for night-time walkers.

September 29, 2008

An Irishman's Diary

Hugh Oram

IT'S THE same in every town and city in Ireland, indeed throughout the so-called developed world: old shops and streetscapes have given way to the new, functional yet characterless. Donnybrook in south Dublin is a perfect example of this irreversible tide of transformation.

For many years, Furlong's newsagents on Morehampton Road, close to its junction with Marlborough Road, was an informal social club for the great and the good of Donnybrook. A small, narrow shop stocked with a vast array of newspapers and magazines, it was presided over for many years by Gerry Callanan, a fount of local information, always a mischievous twinkle in his eye. His family, too, including his wife, Máire, presided over the convivial proceedings.

One of the many people whom I used to bump into there was Derek Mooney, then beginning his ascent of the heights of RTÉ, its mast at Montrose clearly visible from the street outside. Often, in Furlongs, from chatting to one of its regulars, one heard the latest scandal surrounding Donnybrook's often nationally known personalities, and it all added to the frisson of excitement. At one stage, the Callanans also had the post office a little further along Morehampton Road.

After Gerry Callanan retired and gave more of his time to the Fitzwilliam Lawn Tennis Club just down the road, the shop lay derelict for a number of years. Just recently, however, the old shop and the florists next door have been converted into a branch of Boots the chemists. The new shop is shiny, modern and efficient, very smart, yet utterly devoid of any character. Des Brady's pharmacy close by, there for years, has undergone a sea change to survive the new competition.

Near this spot was once the Panorama Travel shop; in those days, you popped into a travel agent and booked your latest trip, as we did on various occasions. Now of course, it's all done online, with none of the personal interchange across the counter. These days, there isn't a retail travel shop in Donnybrook; the Donnybrook Travel shop just off the Main street has been transformed into a print shop.

The Roy Fox food shop in Donnybrook: one of the few survivors of an older era in this century

Another big change in Donnybrook has been the disappearance of the family grocer. Nylands was an old-fashioned grocery store, almost next door to Furlongs. Only recently, Anne Casey, one of the Nyland family, died. At the other end of Donnybrook, Stynes grocery shop was another old "institution" that tried in vain to adapt to new trends. Today, the place is a Balti restaurant. Across Donnybrook Road, the Spar supermarket, for so long the domain of the Woods family, is now a 24-hour affair. A little up the road from Stynes was Cunninghams, an old fashioned radio shop, a lingering relic of the original wireless era.

Yet another old-fashioned shop that disappeared into the ether was O'Connors hardware shop on Morehampton Road, filled with every kind of gadget and widget for the house and garden; you could rummage around happily for hours. Almost next door was a bakery shop, Quinlans, renowned for the succulence of its cakes.

Garages and petrol stations have been obliterated, too. The Morehampton petrol station, near Furlongs, has long since closed down, as has the filling station next door to Madigans pub, itself on the list for redevelopment. Breens garage had a wonderfully dozy dog that kept a lazy guard on the pavement outside; today, what was once a garage, filled with antiquated machinery, is an über chic modern office.

Pubs, too, have reinvented themselves. Kielys pub, which got its first licence in 1739, once had an upstairs art gallery, giving rise to the quip that this was one of the few places in Dublin were art was above drink.

These days, there's a restaurant in place of the art gallery, while Kielys has transformed itself with its all-day food and big screen TVs for sport and it has wi-fi. Down the road, Longs pub also modernised itself.

Happily, McCloskeys pub has remained as it was, with a lovely, warm atmosphere, even if it is now doing melts on the menu.

A few shops have kept going through the years. Roy Fox, the greengrocers, is still going strong, despite the recent demise of Des Donnelly. Molloys, the game and fish shop, is still there and in an amazing makeover, Donnybrook Fair, there for countless years, has done a complete transformation. For long, it was owned by Winifred Murray and it was a rather staid but incredibly useful mini-supermarket. These days of course run by Joe Doyle, it's the height of sophistication, aimed at the moneyed classes, with all kinds of exotic foods that you never knew you needed.

Another shop that's been going for years is Lyk-Nu cleaners in the mall. A remark made by the Liverpool poet Roger McGough has always stuck in my mind: one day, whizzing past on his way to RTÉ, he spotted Lyk-Nu flashing past and thought "Ah, Donnybrook' s Chinese restaurant".

Donnybrook a century ago bears no resemblance to the Donnybrook of today. From the time when I first got to know Donnybrook well, in the mid-1970s, change has been relentless, yet somehow, through all the constant sweep of closures, openings and refurbishments, Donnybrook has managed to retain some of its impermeable village atmosphere, even though it badly needs somewhere like the old Furlongs, where people could simply wander in and while away the time in a good old gossip.

October 23, 2008

An Irishman's Diary

Hugh Oram

The Diceman, Thom McGinty, taking part in a street parade

ARE the present-day Dublin street characters as interesting as those of previous generations? There's a real conundrum. Admittedly, one of my favourites was one of the most recent – the Chilean man who squatted by the side of Brown Thomas in Wicklow Street, playing the pan pipes. He was making a genuine contribution to the well-being of everyone in the vicinity, but I haven't seen him for a while. Years ago, Wicklow Street had another resident musician, the woman who played the harp.

Some of the street characters of earlier generations had an expansiveness to their zaniness that made them memorable. It was part of a tradition whose origins date back centuries, no doubt to the very beginnings of the city.

Recently I read a publication of the Old Dublin Society, dated December, 1939, in which one of the articles was devoted to the old Dublin street characters. Many of those mentioned dated back to the 18th century and their names would mean nothing now. But one stuck in my mind: Mary-Anne Night-and-Day. She got her nickname because in the earlier part of the 20th century she walked endlessly in an area bounded by Grafton Street, St Stephen's Green and Harcourt Street. Mary-Anne wasn't a street performer, but because she walked the city streets so constantly, day and night, she became embedded in the public consciousness.

Other "characters" from the 20th century included the Hickey Brothers, who also walked the city streets incessantly. As they walked, they gesticulated flamboyantly as in their heads they rearranged all the buildings round Dublin's centre, creating an utopian city in their own minds. During the recent boom years, developers took over their function in a more concrete way.

Many readers will remember the woman with the rosary beads who used to dance animatedly on the central plaza in O'Connell Street, in front of the GPO, warning heathen Ireland of the error of its ways. The last time that I saw her, she was enjoying afternoon tea in what was then the Berkeley Court hotel.

Bang-Bang was probably the best-known of all the street characters in the latter part of the 20th century, active from the 1950s onwards. His real name was probably Thomas Dudley (no one is quite sure) and he was addicted to cowboy films. As he roamed the city, he used to do mock shoot-outs on the buses, pretending that his key was a gun. Dubliners often took part in his games by shouting his name at him or, better still, falling down "dead". On occasion, he even got into theatres and walked across the stage during performances, much to the amusement of audiences. When it came to performance art, Bang-Bang was a true pioneer.

But sadly, like Mary-Anne Night-and-Day before him, and many other street characters, poor Bang-Bang probably suffered from mental illness. He died in 1976.

Another old-time favourite Abraham was Feldman, the son of a Ukrainian who had fled to Dublin in the late 19th century. Abraham, born here in 1901, grew up on Dublin's northside and discovered his life's vocation behind a camera, using a made-up name, Arthur Fields.

Dressed in a long raincoat, regardless of the weather, and sometimes with a scarf for effect, he always wore a battered pork-pie hat at a jaunty angle. His camera was slung around his neck. For the best part of 50 years, until the late 1980s, he was a fixture on O'Connell Bridge and generations of families coming up to Dublin for matches in Croke Park would get their photographs taken by him.

Arthur was a devoted family man, whose three sons and a daughter were brought up on the proceeds of their father's photographic work on O'Connell Bridge. He died in April, 1994 at the age of 94.

In these days of mobile-phone pictures, there's no place for that old-fashioned, almost instant photography. Similarly, the old-style news boys selling newspapers on the street have also become part of history.

In more recent times, perhaps the most memorable figure was the Diceman, who assumed all kinds of roles, and also, perhaps, marked the point at which old-style characters became superseded by street performers. Born and brought up in Glasgow, Thom McGinty was someone who contributed enormously to the gaiety of his adopted city during the late 1980s and early 1990s. He became so famous that in 1989 he appeared in a production of Oscar Wilde's play *Salome* at the Gate Theatre. Then there was Pete with his woollen cap who sold copies of *In Dublin* magazine, in its early years, outside Bewleys in Grafton Street.

In recent years Grafton Street has featured a whole crop of street performers who have often moved on to better things – like Glen Hasard, who left school at 13 and began his career by busking there. Two of my current favourites are the man and the woman who paint themselves from head to toe in gold or silver and become living statues.

They and many others help to keep the tradition of the Dublin street character alive in a technical and impersonal age.

January 6, 2009

An Irishman's Diary

Hugh Oram

NELL KANE was once so well known in Dublin music-making that, just to test her popularity, her father sent her a Christmas card addressed simply: "Miss Nell Kane, Dublin". It arrived safely and promptly. When Nell opened it, the card simply read: "Ha, ha".

For decades, she played a key role in music teaching and playing in Dublin, and had her own orchestra. She gave up private music teaching only five years ago. Nell recently celebrated her 91st birthday and has the clearest and most accurate memories of her time in music.

She was born in Wicklow town and her family moved to Dublin when she was three. By the age of six, she was starting the piano and at nine she began playing the violin. Her mother, Margaret, was very musically inclined and gave her plenty of encouragement. Her father, Joe, also loved music; by day, he worked in CIÉ, which is why the family home for years was in Kilmainham, close to the railway works in Inchicore. She and her ensemble, which later evolved into her orchestra, won the Lord Mayor's prize in the Father Mathew Feis three years in a row before they decided they should give someone else a chance to win.

After Nell completed her music training and got her teaching diploma in music at the then School of Music in Chatham Row, she began working there part-time, going on to teach there for 47 years.

She has the fondest memories of the school, which had started as the Municipal School of Music in 1890. It has been in Chatham Row since 1904 and is now the Conservatory of Music and Drama in Dublin Institute of Technology. "Michael McNamara, the then principal, was a great favourite," Nell says, "'Mr Mac' to me and everyone else".

Always a free spirit, in between her teaching sessions at the school of music she taught in many schools, such as Sion Hill in Blackrock, Muckross Park in Donnybrook and the Cross and Passion College in Kilcullen, Co Kildare. She also did much music work for the Department of Education.

At one stage, she was asked by the Christian Brothers in Crumlin to start music lessons there. She told the brother in charge that it would cost him money for her fees and all the musical instruments he'd need to buy, but he replied that the school was already so much in debt for its new building, that a little more wouldn't matter.

About 60 years ago, her ensemble evolved into the Nell Kane Orchestra, which at its height had about 30 players. The idea was to mix very experienced players with relative novices. Nell says that they never got a penny for their performances; all the money they raised was for charity.

Rehearsals were held every Saturday in the studios of the Desmond Donegan Ballet School in Parnell Square. The orchestra played at many venues, such as the Royal Hibernian Hotel in Dawson Street and the Aberdeen Hall in the Gresham Hotel, and at many hospitals. It also broadcast frequently on Radio Éireann, in the days when the studios were still at the top of the GPO. The music was very varied – from light music such as *Tales from the Vienna Woods* and *the Gypsy Baron* to works by Beethoven and Elgar, her own favourite classical composers.

The orchestra brought another benefit too: a few romances started among the players.

Nell toured extensively in the US, with the St James's Choir and Orchestra led by Fr John O'Brien. She reckons that the musical life in Dublin in the 1950s and 1960s was even better than it is now, though people now have better venues to attend, such the National Concert Hall, whereas in her heyday it was the Phoenix Hall and then the St Francis Xavier Hall off the top of Gardiner Street.

Nell's star pupils include John Sheahan of the Dubliners, whose playing of his well-known composition *The Marino Waltz* must owe something to Nell, because it was she who taught him violin. Another pupil was John Kinsella, now a leading composer. Many of her former pupils went on to become teachers, so the teaching tradition continues to be regenerated.

As if all that wasn't enough, Nell was active in charity work, first with the Red Cross, then with the St Vincent de Paul Society. She remembers going to visit people in top-floor flats in the old tenements in York Street and being given a lighted newspaper to see her way back down the stairs, so that she could avoid the rats and mice. In another house she visited, the man of the house had TB and the family were so poor that they had only old boxes to sit on in the livingroom.

After she gave up teaching music, Nell found another passion – painting. She is still very active in religious affairs in Wicklow town, as president of the local Dominican laity and with a group that visits Medjugorje. For the past 30 years she has lived in the original family home in Wicklow town, which was fortunately kept on. She rarely goes to Dublin these days and says that everything you could possibly need is available in and around Wicklow town. She has a wide circle of relations and friends so there is never a dull moment.

"Once you have good health and good friends, that's all you need," she says. "I completely forget my age. You just get old, but I never think old."

Nonagenarian Nell Kane played a key role in Dublin music-making for many decades: Photograph: Cyril Byrne

April 7, 2009

An Irishman's Diary

Hugh Oram

The Rotunda hospital, which dates back to the 1750s, is one of the few old city centre hospitals still in its original location

IN THE OLD DAYS, Dublin city centre had an amazing variety of hospitals, most of which have now either disappeared or been redeveloped in the suburbs. The first Dublin hospital was set up in 1180, in what is now Thomas Street and since then, some 100 hospitals were established in the city.

By present day standards, the specialities of those old hospitals were often extraordinary.

One of the strangest was the Westmoreland Lock Hospital, one of three Lock hospitals in Ireland (they were also popular in England and in various parts of what was then British empire). The one in Dublin was founded in the 1750s, and in 1792, it was transferred from Donnybrook to Townsend Street, almost next door to the present location of *The Irish Times*. It lasted there until the early 1950s, being demolished in 1955.

The Lock hospitals were for women with sexual diseases and under the Contagious Diseases Act, women could be forcibly removed to the Lock hospitals in Dublin, the Curragh and Cork. If the patients were found to suffer from venereal disease, they were detained until such time as they were certified as cured. Often, the women were put out of their misery; the favourite form of euthanasia was "smotheration".

Another unusual old Dublin hospital was the Cow Pock Institution, set up in 1804 to provide free vaccination against smallpox. During the vaccination sessions, a tiny amount of "lymph" which contained cowpox virus, was placed in a small scratch in the arm, giving the patient immunity. As the only reliable source of vaccine was a lesion of a vaccinated patient, after patients had been treated, they had to return after one week.

During the 18th century, some of Dublin's greatest hospitals were founded as charitable institutions. Jervis Street hospital was set up in 1718 by six Dublin doctors as a charitable infirmary offering free medical services to the city's poor. From its inception, it was primarily an accident hospital.

Dr Steeven's Hospital opened in 1733, funded with the money left by a Dublin doctor of that name to his sister, Grizel. It closed in 1987 before becoming the headquarters of the Eastern Health Board. The Meath Hospital was similarly funded by charitable donations; it opened in 1753 to provide health care for the people of the Liberties. Just over a decade ago, it moved to its new location in Tallaght.

Mercer's Hospital was another charitable institution set up to cater for the sick poor. It opened in 1734 and as part of its fundraising, its board of governors invited Handel to Dublin to help raise funds. The end result, musically speaking, was the first performance, in 1742, in Fishamble Street, of the *Messiah*. Mercer's was the main beneficiary. After the hospital closed in 1983, it was put to a variety of other uses, including Mercer's Institute for Research on Ageing.

Specialised hospitals include the Rotunda maternity hospital, dating back to the 1750s and one of the few old city centre hospitals still in its original location. The Coombe Women's Hospital dates back to 1826, with an ambition to move to a new site from its present Dolphin's Barn location.

Holles Street maternity hospital, dating from 1894, has similar ambitions for a new site. But whether such projects can be realised in the current economic climate remains to be seen.

St Patrick's Hospital was opened at Bow Lane in 1757 with a bequest from Dean Swift and it has been caring for the mentally ill ever since. But the great asylum at Grangegorman, dating back to 1810 and renamed as St Brendan's psychiatric hospital in 1960, has gone. The plan is for the entire new campus of the Dublin Institute of Technology to occupy 26 hectares of the site.

The oldest hospital in or near the city centre is St James's, which can trace its lineage back to a hospital for orphans set up in 1702.

Other Dublin city centre hospitals have transferred to out-of-town locations. Simpson's, once in Parnell Street, is now in Dundrum, It was founded in 1779 by a merchant and land owner, George Simpson, who suffered from poor eyesight and gout in his old age and decided to set up a hospital to benefit "reduced gentlemen" suffering similar afflictions. The old Children's Hospital in Harcourt Street, whose origins went back to 1821, moved to Tallaght.

While many of the 18th-century hospitals were set up as charitable institutions, Catholic orders played a huge role in the following century, mirroring the strong Protestant ethos of Dublin hospitals such as the Adelaide.

The Sisters of Charity started St Vincent's Hospital in the former town house of the Earl of Meath, at St Stephen's Green, in 1834. This was the first Catholic hospital in Ireland and the first hospital to be administered and staffed by women. It remained in St Stephen's Green until 1970, when what is now St Vincent's University Hospital was opened at Elm Park on Dublin's southside.

What is now the Mater Misericordia University Hospital, still on its same site on Dublin's northside, was another religious creation, run by the Sisters of Mercy. It opened in 1861 and for many years the old Mater private nursing home was situated in a nearby Georgian terrace, before being replaced by the modern Mater Private Hospital.

When the nuns were in charge of various Dublin hospitals, discipline was strict and hygiene was such that the idea of superbugs would never have crossed anyone's mind.

While many of the old hospitals, such as Mercer's and Sir Patrick Dun's (1788), were long since converted to other uses, the latest Dublin hospital closure to be announced is that of St Bricin's military hospital at Arbour Hill. Founded in pre-independence times as the King George V military hospital and designed by the Royal Engineers in the British army, its staff and facilities are being transferred to The Curragh.

But those old city centre hospitals have left their mark on the city in unexpected ways, such as the connection between the *Messiah* and the old Mercer's Hospital. Also, when the old Jervis Street hospital staged Araby, an oriental fête, in 1894, to raise much-needed funds, little did anyone think that the name of *Araby* would live on in the title of one of Joyce's short stories in *Dubliners*.

● *The Dublin Handel Festival runs until April 19th. See* www.templebar.ie

April 14, 2009

An Irishman's Diary

Hugh Oram

A SMALL PLAQUE on the red brick wall above a bookie's shop at 37, Wexford Street in Dublin's south inner city, leads on to an extraordinary author's life and the even more astonishing creation of a classic left wing novel, *The Ragged Trousered Philanthropists*, once again enjoying a renewed burst of popularity.

It was here in this house that Robert Noonan was born in 1870, the illegitimate son of Samuel Croker, an elderly man who had retired from the Royal Irish Constabulary and who subsequently became a magistrate. The only trouble with Croker was that he had two "wives" and two families. Mary Noonan was his "liaison lady" and mother of four of his children, including Robert.

Little is known about Robert Noonan's childhood years in Dublin, but at the age of 16, he rebelled against his family and its considerable income derived mainly from absentee landlordism and left home. Despite a lack of formal education, he spoke several languages. When he was 18, he sailed to South Africa.

In Cape Town, although he hadn't been apprenticed, he started to make a good living as a painter and decorator. He married at the age of 21, but after the birth of a daughter, Kathleen, his wife embarked on several affairs and the marriage soon ended in divorce. Robert Noonan never remarried and his former wife, Elizabeth Hartel, subsequently died from typhoid fever, in 1895.

Robert Noonan was a temperamental man of many contradictions. He lived with his daughter in a wealthy suburb of Cape Town and employed a black manservant called Sixpence, of whom he was very fond. Yet he led protests against the employment of black skilled labour.

In 1898, he was active in the Transvaal in commemorating the United Irishmen and their rebellion in Ireland a century previously and then, with the second Boer war looming, he helped organise the Irish brigades there to fight on the side of the Boers against the British.

But by the time the war started, Noonan was on his way out of South Africa, bound for a new life in Sussex on the south coast of England. One of his sisters, Adelaide, and her son, Arthur, had joined Noonan in South Africa, and they accompanied Noonan and his daughter when they set sail for England.

A Wexford Street plaque commemorates Robert Tressell, whose book *The Ragged-Trousered Philanthropists*, is enjoying renewed popularity. Above, a theatrical adaptation of the book in London, 1949. Photograph: Getty Images

Despite the then recession, he soon found work as a painter and decorator and he became renowned for his signwriting skills. He tried diversification in 1905, by offering the War Office a new airship design. When this offer was turned down, he smashed the model. That same year, he had a run-in with the local police, who had used gratuitous violence against his nephew, Arthur. The fine imposed on Noonan had a seminal effect on turning his politics leftwards.

A couple of years later, he walked out of his job with a local decorating firm in Hastings because he disagreed with his employer over the time he had taken over a particular job. Noonan managed to find other painting work, but his health began to deteriorate, as TB developed.

Soon unfit to continue as a painter and decorator, he started to write in order to keep out of the workhouse. Between about 1906 and 1910, he wrote his great novel of working class life, *The Ragged Trousered Philanthropists*.

He described it as "the story of 12 months in hell, told by some of the damned". Hastings, where he was then living, was turned into the fictitious town of Mugsborough. Much of the content was autobiographical and it was long known as "the painter's bible".

The handwritten manuscript ran to 1, 600 pages. The first three publishers he approached turned it down and Noonan, who had adopted the nom de plume of Robert Tressell as a pun on the word trestle, from his painting and decorating work, was only saved from burning the novel by the foresight of his daughter Kathleen. She kept it in a metal box stored under her bed.

Come 1910 and Noonan had decided to emigrate to Canada and he planned to send for his daughter Kathleen to join him there. He got as far as Liverpool, fell seriously ill and died in a workhouse hospital, in February, 1911. He was buried in a pauper's grave, which lay undiscovered for years.

In 1913, his daughter Kathleen showed the manuscript of her father's book to a writer she knew called Jessie Pope. In turn, Pope's publisher took on the book and paid Kathleen £25 for the rights.

For the first edition, Jessie Pope edited the manuscript so drastically that all the socialist references were cut out. It also had the misfortune of being published close to the start of the first World War. A second edition was published in 1918, more successfully, and before long, it was also published in countries as diverse as Russia and the US. But for years, a typographical error remained in the spelling of the author's name, giving it as "Robert Tressall".

The unabridged version wasn't published until 1955, but over the years, the novel, even in its emasculated state, had been an ongoing inspiration to the working class movement in Britain, credited with helping bring about the left wing Labour Party general election victory in 1945 and the subsequent formation of the welfare state.

Kathleen did go to Canada but eventually returned to England and lived long enough to see her father and the book assume celebrity status. The original manuscript was acquired by the TUC (Trades Union Congress) in 1958 and it can now be read online on the TUC website. In 1967, the BBC made a television dramatisation of the novel, but subsequently wiped the tape.

Today, as we live through another recession, this story of the hard times suffered by the working classes is once again enjoying great popularity, its resonances as strong now as they were nearly a century ago.

In Hastings, Robert Tressell is well commemorated, while in Dublin, in 2002, he was accorded his rightful place of honour in the Dublin Writers' Museum and the first Robert Tressell festival was staged in Dublin the following year, 2003. It's an amazing novel, today regarded as one of the great fictional works of left-wing literature, yet the man from Wexford Street, Dublin, who wrote it didn't live to see it in print.

August 20, 2009

An Irishman's Diary

Hugh Oram

A scene from *Irish Destiny*, made in 1926, the year of "The Burning" in Drumcollogher. Early films were supplied on highly flammable cellulose nitrate film

THE ANNIVERSARY of the first major disaster in the Irish Free State fell recently. The Drumcollogher, Co Limerick, cinema fire happened on the evening of September 5th, 1926. It claimed 48 lives, by a strange twist of fate exactly the number of people killed in the Stardust inferno in 1981.

Just over 30 years before the cinema fire, Drumcollogher, in south Co Limerick, almost on the border with Co Cork, had been in the news for an altogether different and more positive reason. It was here that Ireland's first co-operative creamery had been set up 1889, and that fact is now commemorated in the creamery museum in the village, run by Seamus Stack, chairman of the local community council. The original creamery has been restored as part of the museum.

Drumcollogher was also known, for close on five decades, for the German-run Irish Dresden factory, which made porcelain figurines; it closed earlier this summer, a victim of the recession.

But what happened on that fateful early September evening in 1926 was tragedy on a grand scale. It should never have happened, and the cause of it was an unedifying mix of illegality and incompetence.

Two local men, Patrick Downing, who worked as a cinema projectionist, and William "Baby" Forde, came up with a scheme to make a few pounds for themselves and at the same time to entertain the people of Drumcollogher, who had seen only a few films before.

What Downing and Forde decided to do was to borrow reels of film, without permission, from the Assembly Rooms Theatre in Oliver Plunkett Street in Cork city centre. In those far off days, films weren't screened in Cork on a Sunday night, so the two men decided to purloin the current batch of films from the cinema in Cork, taking them away on the Sunday.

They planned to show them in Drumcollogher that evening, and then first thing on the Monday morning return them to the cinema in Cork, so that the cinema manager wouldn't know what had happened.

All cinema screenings had to be licensed by local authorities. In addition to cinemas, many church halls showed films and so too did travelling showmen. The showing planned for Drumcollogher wasn't licensed.

Downing and Forde took the reels of film out of their fireproof metal cases and left the cases in the cinema in Cork, to preserve the illusion that the films were still where they should have been.

They transported the reels of film up to Drumcollogher in a Gladstone bag.

The cellulose nitrate film material that was used in the early days of cinema, indeed up to the early 1950s, was highly flammable, so a sequence of events was set in train that ended in disaster.

The films were shown to the audience that crammed into the upstairs loft above a hardware shop in Drumcollogher. The audience got up into the makeshift cinema by means of wooden steps up the outside of the building.

The loft had only one door.

During the film, a couple of candles were left burning to create a little illumination on the table where the takings were counted. The candles had been placed there haphazardly, simply secured with molten wax. The first candle burned out and then the second candle tipped over on to one of the reels of film that was lying around and set it on fire.

There were some suggestions later on that some young lads in the "cinema" had tried to extinguish the candle to help them escape with the takings.

Within seconds, the building was alight. Two gardaí were in the audience, to keep an eye on the local "boyos"; they managed to escape, but the fiancée of one of them was killed.

Other people escaped through a window in the room; during the War of Independence the room had been used for clandestine IRA meetings and the bars on the window had been cut to allow for a speedy exit if the RIC raided the place.

One former IRA man and the sacristan in the local church, John Gleason, was in the audience and knew this. He helped many people jump through the window. This escape route worked well until a plump woman got stuck and blocked the window.

Soon afterwards, the floor of the "cinema" collapsed into the shop beneath, which had highly flammable items in stock, like wood and petrol.

Within half an hour, the whole building was completely engulfed. The nearest fire brigade unit was in Limerick city, over 50km away. Local wells were empty after a very dry summer.

A total of 46 people died in the fire and two died later in hospital. All but one of the dead were buried in a mass grave surmounted by a Celtic cross, beside the local church.

Later, Downing, Forde and Patrick Brennan, who owned the shop and the loft, were tried in the Central Criminal Court on manslaughter charges, but were acquitted.

Forde emigrated to Australia and he died there after apparently putting strychnine that he was using to hunt rabbits into bread that he was baking.

In those days, cinema and theatre fires were more common than they are in these more regulated times. Three years after the Drumcollogher fire, a fire in a cinema in Paisley, central Scotland, killed 71 and back in 1887, a fire at the original Paris opera house had killed 200.

In the Drumcollogher disaster, half of those who died were below 25 years of age, another eerie echo of the Stardust tragedy.

The tragedy in Drumcollogher generated an enormous amount of international news coverage. It took *Time* magazine in New York until its September 20th edition to carry its report. It described how "a crowd of eager Irish peasants had climbed the single rickety ladder and sat down in rapt expectance of Drumcollogher's first cinema show". The tone of the report caused much local annoyance, as people considered it disparaging.

Locally, the dreadful fire became known as "The Burning".

September 21, 2009

An Irishman's Diary

Hugh Oram

Michael Hartnett, who died 10 years ago today, began his life with a mistake. Photograph: Frank Miller

MICHAEL HARTNETT from west Limerick, one of the finest Irish poets of his generation, died 10 years ago today. Like so many poets before him, he succumbed to the fatal charms of that literary currency, the pint, and he died on October 13th, 1999, aged 58, from alcoholic liver syndrome.

Hartnett began his life with a mistake; his parents' name was Harnett, but when his birth certificate was being written, he was called "Hartnett". He stuck with this name, as it was closer to the Irish version of his surname, Ó hAirtnéide.

He was born in the local hospital in Croom, not far from Adare, but was brought up in Newcastle West, where the family eventually secured a new local authority house. Michael Hartnett's father was a house painter, and there was much discord caused by his drinking and there was not always a lot to eat.

Michael Hartnett had his first- and second-level schooling in Newcastle West, but he spent much time with his maternal grandmother, Bridget Halpin, who lived in the townland of Camas, in the countryside, but close to Newcastle West.

Although she had been born in north Kerry, she lived much of her life in west Limerick and was one of the last native speakers of Irish in that part of the country. She had a great array of Irish words in her vocabulary, many related to the animals of the countryside and life on the farm, although she and the family didn't use Irish in everyday conversation. But her knowledge of Irish had an immense influence on the young lad, who became as fluent in Irish as he was in English. She was the first person to recognise Michael Hartnett's poetic vocation.

The day after Hartnett finished secondary school, he emigrated to London, where he worked as a tea boy on a building site. He also worked there as a dish washer in a restaurant, developing a relationship with a cashier. Being beautiful and a Gaelic poet from Connemara, she was the perfect combination for the young aspiring poet. Hartnett also spent some time in Madrid. When he returned to Ireland, it was to start a new life in Dublin.

There he saw himself in the same mode as Patrick Kavanagh, a country poet among Dublin's sophisticated literati. Hartnett's first job in the city was on the night shift at the international telephone exchange in Exchequer Street, Dublin. At one stage, he was curator of what is now the Joyce museum in Sandycove.

But he fell in with the literary set with remarkable ease and his ability was soon recognised by John Jordan, another poet, who taught English literature at UCD. Jordan encouraged Hartnett to study at UCD, but the young poet gave it up after a year: he and academia did not mix.

For a while, he co-edited the literary magazine, *Arena*, with James Liddy; later in his career, Hartnett was for a while poetry editor of this newspaper. For a couple of years, he presented a poetry programme for RTÉ.

His first book, *Anatomy of a Cliché*, was published in 1968, to critical acclaim. Hartnett's poetic career was well under way, resulting in the publication of many works in both English and Irish.

He became that literary cliché, the difficult but charismatic artist. In 1975, he declared that in future, he was going to write only in Irish, a move greeted mainly by indifference. At the time, he said that English was a language well suited to selling pigs. During this period, he was also teaching at Thomond College, Limerick, a rare settled job in a nomadic existence.

His sense of humour and mischievousness never abandoned him. In the ballad he wrote about Maiden Street, in Newcastle West, he declared that the one thing that wouldn't be found there were maidens.

In London, he had met Rosemary Grantley, whom he married in 1966. They had two children, Lara and Niall. The marriage broke up less than 20 years later, after the Hartnetts had moved back close to his native place, when they settled in Templeglantine in West Limerick. Many people believed that Rosemary Grantley was Jewish, but Michael Hartnett had made up this to bemuse people. For the last 15 years of his life, Hartnett's partner was Angela Liston, who supported him as his alcoholism grew worse.

Apart from his fondness for drink, Hartnett also had a great liking for women, as seen in his book, *Poems to Younger Women* (1989). Michael Hartnett had a predilection for romantic yarns. If they weren't true, he was amused by the way they were taken up, including by the media.

After the break-up of his marriage in the mid-1980s, partly caused by his drinking, Hartnett moved back to Dublin, living in Inchicore. The last place he lived there, in Emmet Road, two doors from the Richmond House pub, has a plaque in his honour, put up five years ago by the Kilmainham and Inchicore Heritage group, which assiduously preserves the memory of Hartnett's time in the district.

Ironically, two other great artistic talents who had close connections with Inchicore also died young, Francis Ledwidge, the poet killed in the first World War, and Dermot Troy, the legendary lyric tenor. One of Hartnett's most noted works was the *Inchicore Haiku*, published in 1985, which marked his return to writing in English.

Michael O'Flanagan, a local poet, closely involved with the heritage group as its secretary, recalls that Hartnett liked Inchicore, its working class ethos and the people there. He has posted a rare video clip of Hartnett; it's on YouTube and shows the poet reciting in English and Irish at the Patriot Inn in Kilmainham.

Niall Hartnett says that his father liked nature imagery, especially birds, while non-Christian spiritualism, paganism and legend, factored his imagination. His books and collections of his work number about 25, according to Niall, who reckons that his father's work is also in about 100 anthologies. Here in Ireland, he and his work are reasonably well known, helped by events such as the annual Éigse in his honour in Newcastle West, the town where he is buried.

Niall brought out a book about his father earlier this year, and while Michael Hartnett would have a long way to go to become known like Seamus Heaney, Niall hopes that some day his father will reach the same level of recognition as Patrick Kavanagh.

Poetry Ireland presents an evening of elegies for Michael Hartnett today at 6.30pm in the Unitarian Church, St Stephen's Green, Dublin, with Theo Dorgan, Mary O'Malley, Pat Boran, Michael Coady, Tony Curtis, Gerard Smyth, Hugh McFadden, Thomas McCarthy, Nuala Ní Dhomhnaill, Pauline Fayne and Moya Cannon. The evening will also feature piper Peter Browne and sean-nós singer Seosaimhín Ní Bheaglaíoch.

October 13, 2009

An Irishman's Diary

Hugh Oram

Magic of the pantomime: In Hugh Oram's first job, at 14, he met star of the show, singer David Whitfield (above), and the irreverent chorus girls. Photograph: Popperfoto/Getty Images

RATHER A long time ago, I got my first job, in a pantomime, and I've never forgotten the experience. Indeed, it helped inculcate in me a love of the performing arts, including of course, broadcasting.

I was very young at the time, 14 to be precise, and I was still at school.

We were living in Birmingham, which then existed almost entirely for its car-making industry. I'd heard that a big local theatre, the Hippodrome, was going to be staging a Christmas spectacular, in the shape of the *Robinson Crusoe* pantomime, and that extra workers would be needed to get the show organised.

With the innocence that only comes with youth, I went downtown to the theatre's stage door and found some people who were putting the production together. Despite my age, or lack of it, and complete absence of theatrical or indeed any other kind of work experience, I managed to talk myself into a job as an assistant stagehand. They mentioned the wages, cash in hand, no messy paperwork, told me to be there the following evening at 7pm for the dress rehearsal, and that was that. My entry into the raffish world of theatrical work had been so easy that I couldn't quite believe what had happened.

Two nights later, the curtain went up on the first performance for the paying public. I always remember the tremendous air of anticipation as the band in the orchestra pit struck up the first few notes, the curtain flew up and the show got under way. With the powerful footlights, I could see little of the audience, but it was a full house and their enthusiasm was quickly evident. As the show progressed, act followed act.

It was a very complex show to stage, with many variety acts. These included Wilson, Keppel and Betty, a music hall trio of great renown who did an ancient Egyptian style dance; later, I discovered that Joe Keppel was a Corkman. Other acts included the Singing Mariners and Kirby's Swimming Ballet, performed in a large onstage pool.

The star of the show, pop singer David Whitfield, made his appearance, to a deluge of applause and friendly cat calls. The audience got into the spirit of the performance and enjoyed it tremendously.

In the wings, one of my jobs was to help work the dry ice machine that produced clouds of "smoke" to drift across the stage. For the first time in my life, I made close acquaintance

with the girls in the chorus. To me, they were incredibly exotic, with costumes to match, but what appealed to me most was their sheer zest for life and their enthusiasm for their work as the Hippodrome Dancers.

Their language was colourful and I added many words to my vocabulary that I'd never heard of before. In those far off days, it was unknown for anyone to utter even the mildest profanity in public, let alone on radio or television. Sex, too, was on another planet, scarcely mentioned in polite society, and it soon became clear from what they were talking about, that their personal lives were exciting and fun-filled, to say the least.

The chorus girls were so outgoing, vivacious and irreverent, it was a delight to be in their company. Then right on cue, they trooped on stage to perform their high-kicking routines with immaculate precision. Something else I remember vividly was all the scenery, the way it was stacked and how each relevant piece had to be moved swiftly into place within seconds for each scene change. The smell of that scenery also stuck in my mind, a combination of size and paint.

The stage was brightly lit, but in comparison, the heights above the wings were in pitch darkness. With the stage lights shining in on the part of the wings where the stage hands stood, the air was full of dancing dust particles. At the end of the show that first night, the curtain came down and shot up again, several times, as the audience applauded the cast. Then it was out into the still, silent night; the sense of exhilaration after a successful first night has stayed with me ever since.

Some years later, I read of the sudden death, at the age of 54, of David Whitfield. He had been touring in Australia, when he collapsed suddenly and died. Later came the news that despite his tremendous successes in the pop charts, he had died virtually penniless. His many women friends had helped him spend the vast sums he had

been earning.

As for that job in the pantomime, it must have been in the genes. When my father was a young man, dangerously addicted to high speed sports cars, he mixed in the theatrical set in Birmingham and one of the women with whom he did a serious line was one Noelle Gordon, who later became the first soap star, "Meg Richardson" in the *Crossroads* TV series (famed for its wobbly sets), all about life in a motel. I'm often amused that I nearly had a soap star for my mum! Another theatrical event in Birmingham, at a slightly later date, also had a huge impact. One night at the Alexandra Theatre, just up the street from the Hippodrome, I went to a one man show by a noted Irish actor, Micheál MacLiammóir. At that time, of course, everyone thought he was Cork through and through, not a product of London's Cockney East End with a ferocious appetite for languages, including Irish.

He was doing his performance in homage to Oscar Wilde and the torrent of words was intoxicating. That theatrical night was one of the deciding factors in my own life, when I came to the conclusion that I was living in the wrong country and decided to come back to Ireland for good.

It's all years ago now, but the memories of that pantomime job are as fresh as ever. Every time I go into a radio studio and the microphone goes " live", that very same sense of first night excitement is there.

Many years later, I came to know Laurence Foster, former head of RTÉ radio drama, and now very much involved in the Page to Stage project with the Dublin City library service, and was delighted to discover that he had came from that very same geographical and theatrical milieu with which I had been so familiar. And I still remember fondly those impossibly glamorous chorus girls and their salty turns of phrase that appealed so much to that young teenager.

December 14, 2009

An Irishman's Diary

Hugh Oram

A PIONEERING electric train, the creation of Dr James J Drumm, was Ireland's first green revolution on the railways. The battery-powered train worked well, but the shortages caused by the second World War and the usual political machinations here at home, saw an end to the experiment 61 years ago, after nearly 20 years in service.

Drumm, a brilliant student of chemistry, came from Dundrum, Co Down, and his first education was at the local national school, where his mother was a teacher. He received his secondary education at St Macartan's College, Monaghan, before third-level studies at UCD, where he was awarded an Honours BSc in chemistry, followed by an MSc degree.

He spent three years working with a chemical company in England, before returning to Ireland, where his first invention, in Dublin, was a fine quality soap. Then he worked to keep peas green after they were canned.

In 1925, he attended a lecture on batteries that sparked his interest in the subject and he began developing an alkaline battery cell that could be rapidly charged and discharged.

His work in developing this traction battery coincided with the construction of the hydro-electric dam at Ardnacrusha, which was completed in 1929. It started producing far more electricity than the country needed at the time, so using some of it as motive power on the railways was a tempting option.

Nearly a century previously, the Rev Dr Nicholas Callan, that great electrical pioneer in Maynooth, had proposed a battery-operated train between Dublin and Kingstown, now Dún Laoghaire. But what worked well in the laboratory didn't transform into commercial reality. Drumm was able to make that quantum leap.

His invention was first made public in 1927 and attracted widespread interest, not just here, but across Europe and in the US. The government of the day, through the then minister of industry and commerce, Paddy McGilligan, was enthusiastic and promptly allocated development funds. A Great Southern Railways permanent way inspection car was fitted out with 60 nickel-zinc rechargeable battery cells, each the size of a one gallon (4.5 litres) drum, wired in sequence.

The initial tests were held during August, 1929, between Kingsbridge and Hazlehatch, Co Kildare. The train could get up to to 50mph (80 kph) in just 50 seconds. Extensive testing followed, including at UCD. The longest test run was from Kingsbridge to Portarlington

Green shoots: James J Drumm created the first battery-powered train, which ran for almost 20 years. Above, a third class coach on a Drumm electric train running between Dublin and Bray, Co Wicklow in 1932.
Photograph: Fox Photos/Getty Images

and back, all on a single charge.

One of the people most closely connected with those tests was the late Gerard de Sachy, who lived in Ranelagh, Dublin. His family were close friends of my family, (he and my late father-in-law, Hugh Quinn, were great friends), yet in his latter years, I never once heard him talk about his work in developing the Drumm train.

By early December, 1931, the first Drumm train, with 13.5 tonnes of batteries fitted underneath it, was ready, capable of carrying 140 passengers. This newspaper reported " the Drumm train proved itself no longer a pre-vision of the future, but rather a concrete achievement" . By 1939, four Drumm trains were in regular daily use. The longest Drumm trains had up to eight coaches.

The trains were built at the railway works in Inchicore, a remarkable feat, considering that the previous experience of the workforce there had been entirely with steam locos. The batteries were charged at Amiens Street (now Connolly station) and Bray, and a train could easily do 200 miles (just over 320km) and more a day.

It didn't all run smoothly. On one occasion, when Eamon de Valera's government had just come to power, a trip was organised from Dublin to Gorey, with Dev aboard. All went well until the return journey, when a director of Drumm's company, a Prof Nolan, decided he wanted to get off the train at Blackrock. The battery became so run down that the train barely made the rest of the journey to Westland Row, although none of the VIPs on board was any the wiser.

For most of the 1930s and into the emergency years of the war, the Drumm train plied, very efficiently, between the old Harcourt Street station and Bray, sometimes continuing to Greystones. Fuel for steam locos was in short supply, so the Drumm trains were a godsend, at least to commuters in south Dublin.

Drumm's own company had to close down in 1940, as it was

no longer possible to try to promote the system abroad. The batteries had been designed to last 10 years and getting components for them proved increasingly difficult.

By the summer of 1944, when electricity was in short supply, the Drumm train had been withdrawn from regular use. In the Dáil that summer, Seán Lemass was non-committal as to whether the trains would ever be used again. After all, it hadn't been developed under a Fianna Fáil government.

The last Drumm train ran on July 12th, 1949; most of the coaches were converted to ordinary railway working and no relics were preserved of the pioneering train. At around the same time, the last of the old electric trams in Dublin city were withdrawn from service, two early blows to the idea of green public transport.

One development at the same time helped undermine the Drumm train. In the early 1930s, the Great Northern Railway company had started producing diesel locos at its Dundalk engineering works. Eventually, diesel became the sole motive power of the railway system in Ireland, a cheap replacement for steam, but dependent on imported oil, not a very green solution.

A couple of years before Drumm died in 1974, at the age of 77, Gregg Ryan, who is heritage officer with Irish Rail, met the great pioneer at Drumm's house in Rathgar. Drumm may have been elderly, but he had perfect recall of his battery-operated train and also remembered vividly how the war-time shortages combined with political intrigues had helped finish off his unique train.

Electricity didn't re-emerge as the motive power for railways in Ireland until the Dart was launched in 1984. Then Luas light rail followed 20 years later. In both cases, there's an overhead power supply. Following the ending of the Drumm train, the idea of battery power wasn't again considered, despite its impressive efficiency and green credentials.

February 1, 2010

An Irishman's Diary

Hugh Oram

Changing times: You may have a problem finding parking space in Adare these days, but not in times past.
Image: from *Bygone Limerick*

IT ALL BEGAN with an almost throwaway remark by George Stacpoole, the antiques specialist from Adare, Co Limerick. He's the head of the Irish Antique Dealers Association and I've known him for years. One day, he said to me that he had lots of old photographs of Adare, suggesting they might make a book.

Simple as that, the beginnings of a long quest that is finally completed, with the publication due in April of my next book, *Bygone Limerick*, with many photographs taken 100 years ago. I've known and written about Limerick, city and county, for years, but researching this book introduced me to wonderful people I'd never met previously and I heard many intriguing stories.

I soon discovered a veritable network of people, each a passionate expert on the history of their own locality: John Cussen from Newcastle West; John Harrold from Bruree; Noel Collins from Kilmallock; Tony Browne from Limerick city; Tom Keogh of the city museum, with his personal collections of thousands of old picture postcards; Frank O'Connor, an expert on Limerick's postal history; Michael F O'Sullivan, the creamery historian from Hospital; Fr Mark Tierney, that prodigious historian from Glenstal, and Vincent Browne, a thoroughly unlikely altar boy in his native Broadford, Co Limerick.

Introductions to other people were equally rewarding. From Lady Vivienne Lillingston of Kilmallock, I found that her husband, Allan, rode a one-eyed horse called Winning Fair, to victory in the Cheltenham Champion Hurdle in 1963.

Other curious historical facts came to light from the time of the War of Independence and Civil War. I was told about Tomás Malone, whose nom de guerre was Seán Ford, head of the old IRA in east Limerick. He was able to travel around the county with impunity, never discovered, because he was good friends with a judge, O'Callaghan Westropp, who had an Armstrong-Siddeley car with a capacious boot. He was never asked to open it for inspection.

Peter Tait, commemorated by the Tait Memorial Clock in Limerick city centre, had extraordinary business achievements in Limerick. He arrived in the city in the early 19th century from his native

Shetland Islands as a penniless orphan and he began his career in the city as a pedlar. He went on to invent the notion of mass production clothes, with the same principles that Henry Ford applied to car production. This notion made Tait a fortune.

The last business venture in his life was a cigarette factory in northern Greece, which failed. His life ended, almost penniless, in a desolate hotel room in what was then southern Russia, now part of Georgia.

On the contemporary side, Denis Leonard, the driving force behind the Limerick Civic Trust, was enormously encouraging as soon as I approached him. The trust has done much restoration in Limerick in recent years. Sadly, he died at a comparatively young age, at the end of last year.

I also discovered all about Seán Ó Riada's father, who was the garda sergeant in Adare for 28 years. At weekends, when he went to sit on a wall at the top of the town at 2.30am, all the local publicans knew it was time to shut up shop. During the week, he used a special knock on the doors of local pubs late at night; 20 minutes later, he would go in and find the place miraculously empty. Adare never had any "found-ons" in his time!

Another great personality I unearthed was John Enright, who made fishing rods in Castleconnell, just outside Limerick city. In the late 19th century, the runs of salmon on the Shannon at Castleconnell were vast and the Enright rods were so well regarded around the world that Tsar Nicholas II of Russia once declared that he would use none other. The opening of the Ardnacrusha hydro-electric dam and power station on the Shannon in 1929 finished the glory days of fishing

at Castleconnell.

Just over a decade later, the ferry across the Shannon here ended when a bridge was built; I found that one of the ferrymen became blind in later life, but was able to navigate the Shannon with unerring accuracy.

Someone else I heard much about was the late Tommy Bowen, who by day worked in a hardware shop in Kilmallock. He was a walking encyclopedia of genealogical and historical information about the medieval town and did much to keep the town museum going.

The places, too, that came up in my research were amazing: the old bacon factories in Limerick, the Cleeves dairy factories and the short-lived soviets in Limerick, Bruree and elsewhere. One day, a friend of mine in Dublin, Denis Bergin, asked me whether I'd heard of Limerick's hanging gardens. I hadn't, but soon found out that a Limerick banker, William Roche, in the early 19th century, had constructed vast roof-top hanging gardens in the centre of the city that were the talk of the populace. I also discovered that Roche had managed to survive the great banking crash of 1820, an event which surely proves that much history merely runs in an endless loop.

Of all the century-old photographs used in the book, those that most captured my imagination were those of Adare and all its thatched cottages.

The streets are absolutely deserted, not a car in sight, just the odd pony and trap. For anyone who has done what I've done recently, driven through Adare to try to find a parking space, it was a salutary lesson.

Bygone Limerick is published by Mercier Press, Cork, next month.

March 23, 2010

An Irishman's Diary

Hugh Oram

VINCENT GILL was the founder and long-time editor of the *Longford News*, the closure of which was announced last week. He had a truly original approach to journalism; if he was short of copy, he simply made it up. On one notorious occasion, when he was a full page short, he simply reversed a printing block so that it printed solid black on an entire page in the paper and put a caption beneath it: "Blackout at Drumlish".

These days, you practically need a PhD to get into entry level journalism, but in Vincent's day, you just did it, usually with no training at all. In his case, when he was a schoolboy, he started the *Canal Herald*, and charged people a penny a look. Later, he became one of the most unlikely people to ever enter the Garda Síochána, a career that came to an abrupt end following an incident in the bar at Limerick Junction railway station. He and a fellow garda were escorting a prisoner to Limerick Jail and they managed to lose him. Rather than be sacked, Vincent resigned from the force and started the *Longford News*.

That was in 1936, and for years he produced the paper by himself, with very little if any assistance, in his cottage by the canal in Longford, writing the copy, selling the ads, printing each week's edition, then selling the copies.

In his heyday, he was quite a good writer and in the late 1940s, sold several articles to the *New Yorker* magazine, but curiously, never cashed the cheques. After that, he concentrated on his own paper, often writing with what was described locally as a "poison pen". He often linked his news copy with his commercial needs, frequently describing how he had seen courting couples on the banks of the canal or men taking the wives of other men home from dances and threatening to name them in the following week's paper, unless they took out a subscription. Every time, it resulted in about half-a-dozen new subscriptions.

One unfortunate shopkeeper in Longford suffered badly because of a piece Vincent wrote. This man had declined to advertise in the paper, so Vincent wrote that such-and-such a shopkeeper was going to give all his customers a Christmas box, contrary to the advice of the local Chamber of Commerce. The shopkeeper had to write to all his customers saying that this wasn't in fact

If ever a *Mad Men* style television series was to be made about journalists, Vincent Gill (above), founder and long-time editor of the *Longford News* would be right up there, near the top of the list

true; he went out of business shortly afterwards.

When people wanted to put a planning notice in the paper, they simply dropped whatever coins they could afford into a bowl in the front room of his cottage. Whenever a big bill came in, as from the ESB, he did the rounds of his advertisers looking for handouts. Vincent had an equally original approach to the Revenue Commissioners; he told them that he had nothing but that they were welcome to share the paper with him.

He was very anti-establishment and loved to take pot-shots at bigwigs in the town and nationally. On one occasion, he wrote an account of a large wedding in the Travelling community and said it had been attended by the President and every member of the diplomatic corps. When he was reporting on any big society wedding in Longford, he reversed this procedure and listed all the members of the Travelling community as having been present. Yet another time, he reported on a past pupils' reunion dinner at St Mel's College, naming everyone he knew from Longford who had ever been detained in Mountjoy, describing them as having attended the function.

In the early 1960s, a BBC television crew from the *Tonight* programme arrived in Longford, attracted by a wedding report which had described how the bride wore knuckledusters and the groom was the best man. Following this, a journalist from a Canadian newspaper came to Longford to profile Vincent Gill, but had to admit defeat: "I was always one pub behind".

The north midlands seemed to specialise in producing newspaper eccentrics, among them another newspaper owner

and editor, Jasper Tully of the *Roscommon Herald*, who died just after Vincent Gill had started his own paper in Longford. After Tully's wife died, he readdressed letters to her "Not known at this address: try Hell". He also had a peculiar attitude to labour relations. Once, a trade union official was sent from Dublin to negotiate with Tully, who lay in wait behind the door to his printing works, armed with a metal ems rule. As the poor man came in, Tully knocked him out and promptly had him bundled on to the next train back to Dublin.

Vincent used to travel the county in his van, packed with a dozen of his pet cats and dogs, stopping off at every pub to sell copies of his paper.

Yet despite his often vicious style of writing, which many times resulted in him being thrown into the canal, he favoured the underdog and often gave elderly people cash and parcels of groceries, as well as buying First Communion outfits for children from needy families.

When he decided to retire, in 1974, he wanted to make sure that his deadly rival, the *Longford Leader*, didn't get hold of his beloved paper.

On the strength of the fact that one of his grandfathers had been called Reynolds, he sold the paper to Albert Reynolds for £12,000. When Reynolds took over, he and his wife Kathleen also took to a van, making sure that the paper was distributed on time around the county. The Reynoldses started off their ownership of the paper by driving their delivery van round the county, beginning at 5am on publication day.

Five years later, Reynolds sold the paper to Jack Davis, then owner and editor of the *Meath Chronicle*, who in turn sold it on to Derek Cobbe, who had worked with the *Longford Leader*, something which cemented the enmity between the two papers. By the time the *Longford News* closed, it was in the hands of the Northern Ireland-based Alpha Newspapers group, run by a former Unionist MP, John Taylor, now Baron Kilclooney.

Vincent Gill was a true original; if ever a *Mad Men* style television series was to be made about journalists, he would be right up there, near the top of the list. At the end of his life, he was living in a clapped-out caravan in Ardagh and on the day of his funeral in 1976, the heavens opened, drenching the mourners. It could be seen as a two-fingered gesture from the Almighty, of which no doubt Vincent himself would have thoroughly approved.

September 7, 2010

An Irishman's Diary

Hugh Oram

IT MAY HAVE been the first act of defiance towards the brand new Irish Free State but these days, the extraordinary occupation of the Rotunda in Dublin, in January, 1922, led by the writer Liam O'Flaherty, isn't much more than an absorbing footnote to the history of radical politics in 20th-century Ireland.

O'Flaherty, whose family lived on Inishmore in the Aran Islands, had been born there in 1896. In 1912/13, when he was at Blackrock College, he organised his first protest movement, among his fellow pupils, in favour of the nationalist cause. Then, still at a young age, he made the unlikely decision to become a priest, enrolling as a postulant with the Holy Ghost Fathers.

But his priestly ambitions were soon overturned and he joined the British army to fight in Flanders; there, in 1917, he was injured, mentally, rather than physically. For the next year, he was treated in hospital for melancholia, before being discharged from the Irish Guards.

He then began his wanderings, sometimes working on ships, around the Mediterranean and as far away as South America, as well as in Canada and the US. His political views took an abrupt left turn and in Canada, he joined the Wobblies, the international workers union, while in New York, he signed up with the Communist Party.

Eventually, he returned to Ireland, to Dublin, where he quickly became embroiled in radical politics. He had helped found the Communist Party of Ireland, not long before the Rotunda occupation. Dublin was teeming with former soldiers, like himself, who were out of a job and soon he saw his opportunity.

On Monday, January 16th, 1922, the provisional government of the new State was announced.

During the Wednesday of that week, a group of about 200 unemployed people, led by O'Flaherty, who declared himself to be the chairman of the Council of the Unemployed, occupied the concert room of the Rotunda. They formed a garrison, divided into companies.

The Rotunda had been built in 1764 as an assembly hall and social rooms; the adjacent maternity hospital was named after it. For O' Flaherty, the place was highly significant: Sinn Féin had been founded here in 1905 and the Irish Volunteers followed suit in 1913, as detailed in Aengus Ó Snodaigh' s book on the history of the Rotunda.

O'Flaherty said that the occupation of the Rotunda, led by himself, was a protest against the apathy of the authorities towards the unemployed. He told *The Irish Times* that if they were taken to court, they would not recognise that court,

'Liam O'Flaherty said that the occupation of the Rotunda in 1922, led by himself, was a protest against the apathy of the authorities towards the unemployed. He told *The Irish Times* that if they were taken to court, they would not recognise that court, "because the government that does not redress our grievances is not worth recognising".'

"because the government that does not redress our grievances is not worth recognising" . Among the occupiers were unemployed dock workers from Dublin port, one of whom was Sean McAteer, who 15 years later was executed in the USSR as a spy.

At the time, workers were taking over factories and creameries in several parts of the country, including Cork and Limerick, and declaring them to be "soviets". O'Flaherty determined to do this with the Rotunda occupation, but when the Red Flag was hung out from a window, it drew considerable hostility from the growing crowd in the street outside. The occupation also met with considerable disapproval from O'Flaherty' s new- found colleagues in the Communist Party, who didn't favour what they saw as an attempted putsch.

But the manifesto that O'Flaherty wrote for the occasion was his first literary work and its fiery language was compared with that used during the American war of independence and the first French revolution.

The group of people inside the concert room grew in number, sometimes occupying their time with impromptu concerts, while they also paraded in Parnell Square, once known as Rutland Square. A local bakery, Boland's, then in Capel Street, donated 500 loaves of bread, which helped feed the insurgents.

Policing was in a state of transition; the old Dublin Metropolitan Police was still in existence and some of its members went to the Rotunda, along with members of the Republican Police, former IRA members who supported the new pro-Treaty government. Thanks to the police, the angry crowd of some 500 people milling around outside didn't storm the building. An elderly woman in the crowd was heard describing O'Flaherty as "the man that tried to sell Dublin to the Bolsheviks".

Shots had been fired over the heads of the crowd, from inside the Rotunda. On the Thursday night, one of the occupiers, who had gone out into the square to try to collect money, was attacked and this raised the tension still further.

By the Saturday, when O'Flaherty had the option of either surrendering or having the building stormed, he decided to call off the occupation and it ended peacefully. The declaration of a soviet republic in the heart of Dublin had come to nothing. All the protesters walked out of the Rotunda and the occupation ended with a whimper. O'Flaherty himself managed to slip away unnoticed and with two companions, made his way to Cork, where he spent the next six months.

One probable side-effect of the shock caused by the Rotunda occupation, which received much coverage in the newspapers at the time, was that O'Flaherty lost both his parents at home on the Aran Islands. Shortly afterwards, his mother, Maggie, collapsed in front of her husband, and within 10 minutes, died from a massive heart attack. His father, Mícheál, soon followed, suffering from a stroke; later, he was described as "dying on his feet" .

As for O'Flaherty, he returned to Dublin in June, 1922, as the Civil War gained momentum, but the following month, he managed to escape the city and made his way to Liverpool. Once he had settled in England, he turned away from involvement in political activity and began writing in earnest, drawing on his own dramatic experiences.

His first short story was published there in 1923 and later that year, his first published novel, *Thy Neighbour's Wife*, was issued in London, a mere 18 months after the abortive Rotunda occupation.

For the rest of his life, O'Flaherty garnered the reputation of being one of Ireland's leading novelists and short story writers of the 20th century, although his last novel was published in 1950. But his radical political views remained constant.

He died in Dublin in 1984, aged 88, and the bureaucratic description of his profession on his death certificate said that he was a writer (retired) .

His nephew, Breandán Ó hEithir, was also a distinguished writer and a long time contributor of a weekly column to this newspaper. Another relative, a cousin, was John Ford, the film director, who made a memorable Hollywood version of O'Flaherty' s 1925 novel, *The Informer*.

Liam O'Flaherty's reputation as a political activist in the Rotunda may have faded at the expense of his literary reputation, but one constant remains: the problem of mass unemployment is as grave a national issue now as it was nearly 90 years ago.

March 19, 2011

An Irishman's Diary

Hugh Oram

WE DON'T make a habit of visiting celebrity graves, especially literary ones, but there's no doubt they add much cause for thought to any expedition at home or abroad.

The first "celebrity" grave that I saw was that of WB Yeats, in the churchyard at Drumcliff, in the shadow of Ben Bulben in Co Sligo. He had been buried there in 1948 after being repatriated from the south of France, where he had died nine years previously. I was struck by the "horseman" quotation on the gravestone, which has since become something of a literary cliché. I was a teenager at the time, rather a long time ago, and then, and as now, addicted to the poetry of Yeats.

'Graveside trips inculcate a strong tide of history, yet are strangely life affirming.' Above, WB Yeats's grave in Co Sligo

But the next literary grave that I saw was infinitely more romantic, that of Keats, in the Protestant cemetery in Rome. I was 17, it was my first time in the city, and my visit to what is officially called the "non-Catholic cemetery for foreigners at Testaccio" was extraordinarily moving.

Keats's grave bears the inscription "Here lies one whose name was writ on water". He had died in Rome in 1821, aged just 25, as he sought a cure for TB.

The following year, the ashes of another great poet, Shelley, were interred here. The cemetery, with its cypress trees, masses of other greenery and flowers and its colony of cats, is very serene and peaceful. (The cats, incidentally, have their own website, www.igattidellapiramide.it). Its tranquillity had inspired Shelley to write that it might make one in love with death to be buried in so sweet a place.

Much later, I found a visit to the grave of James Joyce in Zurich even more evocative. Joyce, who knew the city well, returned there after he and his family had to flee Paris in 1940, as that part of France fell to the Nazi occupation. Joyce was only in Zurich a short time when he became seriously ill and was operated on for a perforated duodenum. He died at about 2.15am on January 13th, 1941, and was buried in a non-religious ceremony in the Friedhof Fluntern in Zurich. Later, he was joined there by his wife Nora and son Giorgio.

One cold, damp winter's morning, we took a tram from the centre of Zurich up to the heights of the Zürichberg suburb, close to the zoo, to go grave hunting. There was the life-size statue of Joyce, created in 1966 by the American sculptor, Milton Hebald,

depicting Joyce sitting cross-legged, reading a book. We were amused to see, in the palm of his hand, an Irish coin that had evidently been there for years; had this been Dublin, it would have lasted no length of time.

Next to our favourite European city, Paris, where during one trip, we travelled out to the Père Lachaise cemetery in the rather grimy 20th arrondissement. The place is vast, with a galaxy of stars buried there, Balzac, Proust, Piaf, Jim Morrison, to name but four from a cast of thousands. Yet in this vast city of the dead, it's impossible to miss the tomb of Oscar Wilde. Wilde had died, aged 46, on November 30th, 1900, in the seedy Hôtel d'Alsace in the sixth arrondissement.

Today, the hotel has been suitably gentrified, as L'Hôtel, and people can pay good money to stay in the suite where Wilde was once a guest, the place where he said that either he or the wallpaper had to go. The wallpaper survived.

His modernistic tomb was created by Jacob Epstein and has been defiled by graffiti over the years. The sphinx on the side of the tomb was vandalised at one stage and the penis was hacked off, only to be replaced in 2000 by a sterling silver prosthetic. What a pity Wilde wasn't around to deliver one of his epigrams! After the hurly-burly and the social animation of Père Lachaise, where many local families go to picnic, we found the Cimetière Montparnasse in the 14th, the burial place of Beckett and his wife, Suzanne, austere and clinical, close to where they had lived, very much the resting place of the haute bourgeouisie. Beckett had decreed that his gravestone could be any colour, so long as it was grey. The shiny stone top bears the name of Beckett and his wife, the woman who had saved his life when he was stabbed by a Paris pimp in 1938; Beckett and his wife both died in 1989.

Over the years, we've seen other celebrity graves, such as

that of Richard Burton, the actor, in Céligny in Switzerland, where he was buried in 1984 in a red suit, to signify his Welshness, accompanied by a copy of the collected poems of Dylan Thomas. We were staying in Lausanne at the time, got off the Lausanne to Geneva train at the small station of Céligny, beside Lake Geneva or Lac Léman; and climbed the hill to the village's tree-shrouded *vieux cimetière*.

On another occasion, this time in Germany, we saw the grave of Richard Wagner and his wife, Cosima, a daughter of Liszt, at the Wahnfried, the Wagners' villa in Bayreuth, Bavaria. Inside,we listened to early recordings of Kirsten Flagstad, the great Norwegian dramatic soprano. Outside, the sun was streaming down and so too was a hail of jinny-joes. It was a memorable moment, in contrast to the bleak formality of the Wagner grave outside in the back garden.

All these graveside trips inculcate a strong tide of history, yet are strangely life affirming. Once, quite a number of years ago, when I was recording a radio interview with Douglas Gageby, a former editor of this newspaper, he rather startled me when he said at one point, in his matter-of-fact way, that at that time he and his wife Dorothy had long since planned to be buried in Clifden, Co Galway, a place that had particular resonances for them. Now that I'm that much much older, I view such utterances with much more understanding.

We're not finished yet; we still have another grave in mind; that of Patrick O'Brian, that great master of the maritime novel, who pretended he was Irish. He died in a hotel on St Stephen's Green in Dublin in 2000 but is buried in the extraordinary seaside town of Collioure in south-west France. We know Collioure well, but the last time we were there, O'Brian was alive and well, living and working in Collioure; already, I can feel the urge for another trip taking shape.

An Irishman's Diary

Hugh Oram

THE OTHER night, in one of the lanes in our neighbourhood in Dublin, the sounds of a very lively party drifted across the still air. Animated chatter and the sound of clinking glasses were evidence of a large group of people thoroughly enjoying themselves.

Ah, perhaps it's the students, I thought, but on further discovery, found that it was a 1930s-style party being given by one of our neighbours to celebrate her 90th birthday. The lady in question is Aileen Chapman, someone who has a voracious appetite for life and loves nothing better than a good party or a trip away. She has travelled so much in recent years that our nickname for her is "Mrs Dubai". She's also still driving her car.

In 1981, she was a passenger on an Aer Lingus flight from Dublin to London. It was the only time an Aer Lingus aircraft was hijacked and the man responsible, a former Trappist monk, wanted the third secret of Fatima revealed. Our friend and neighbour took the whole episode nonchalantly. She thought it was all bit of a hoot, but was delighted when the aircraft eventually landed at Le Touquet airport in northern France and the passengers and crew were rescued and able to have a good party to celebrate their release. Mrs Dubai was in her element.

Another neighbour of ours, who is the same age, is a whizz at computing and if I want a serious discussion on a topic like cloud computing, he's the person to whom I turn.

All this set me thinking: are the 90s the new 60s? Examples abound of people well into their 90s who fortunately still enjoy good health and are reasonably well-off, who make the most of what's on offer.

Last year, I spoke to Dr TK (Ken) Whitaker, a truly remarkable man who devised the economic plan that set Ireland on the road to economic regeneration in the early 1960s.

I was working on a book about old Drogheda, and one afternoon I had the most delightful and lengthy conversation with Dr Whitaker about the Drogheda he grew up in during the 1920s.

He reminded me just recently that he is now in his 95th year and that such longevity must be in the family genes, as his mother lived until she was 100.

Liam Cosgrave: sense of humour a key to his longevity

When Dr Whitaker was young, the family home in Drogheda was the appropriately named Paradise Cottage. He has remarkably wide-ranging memories of Drogheda all those decades ago and that afternoon conversation was almost like recreating the town exactly as it was, 80 and more years ago. His memories of the town are crystal clear, down to the smallest detail, of people and places and the fourpenny cinema matinees.

As an aside, he mentioned that he has always loved fishing and still enjoys going to his beloved west of Ireland to pursue his favourite sport, despite the unseasonably cold weather there recently.

Recently, I was talking to a former taoiseach, Liam Cosgrave, now 91. He was in charge of the government between 1973 and 1977, a grim time of dire economic conditions and widespread unrest and atrocities when the Troubles in the North were at their height. His public image then was of a gruff and rather stern man doing his solemn duty for his country. Occasionally, a humorous comment would slip out, as during the Fine Gael ardfheis in May 1977, when he suggested that one or two of our blow-ins could usefully blow out.

The truth is that Liam Cosgrave has a totally different private persona; he has a wonderful sense of humour and loves a good story or amusing tale. He also has an amazing memory for people and places, spanning many generations and much geography. But he was a little doubting of my thesis, saying, "I don't know about that," even if he is a perfect candidate for inclusion.

Another well-known public figure who beyond doubt qualifies and who's full of zip is Maureen O'Hara, 91 in August. She lives in Glengarriff in west Cork and very recently has been active in promoting her classic film festival this summer, as well as her legacy centre in Glengarriff, which will include an international film academy. A Hollywood icon to her fingertips, this native of Beechwood Avenue, Ranelagh, Dublin, where she was born Maureen FitzSimons in 1920, is still movie glamour personified.

Louis le Brocquy, widely regarded as the most outstanding Irish painter of the past century, is also from Dublin, where he returned to live with his wife, Anne Madden, after they had spent many years in Provence. He was born on November 10th, 1916, the same year as Ken Whitaker.

One side-effect of the emergence of the 90-year-olds as the new trendies have been various efforts to find Ireland's oldest working person.

Last year, for instance, a gentleman called Maurice Gaffney revealed on RTÉ Radio that he was still working as a barrister, aged 93.

Stories of great longevity have long been in existence. I'm always reminded of JP Hayden, who founded the *Westmeath Examiner* in Mullingar in 1882 and who edited it for the next 72 years, probably the longest editorship in Irish journalism. He was a rare example of great longevity among people in the media.

Then just the other day, I was looking at a marvellous new booklet on *Donegal's Farming Heritage*, produced by the heritage office of Donegal County Council.

There, on page 18 was a 1927 photograph of Miss Jane Clark of Raphoe, busy wielding a scythe. She was 95 at the time and looked a very active lady.

If anyone feels like celebrating these remarkable achievements, one place to go is the Friends of the Elderly in Bolton Street, Dublin, any Wednesday afternoon. Then you will see and hear the Bolton Street Band, described as the world's oldest boy band.

One of its members is Sean McGuinness, 92, who has had a very successful 78-year-long career as a musician, having begun at the tender age of 14. Not so long ago, he played to an admiring fan, Dame Vera Lynn, ahead of him by two years, and now aged 94.

I find it so encouraging and inspirational to see so many people very active well into their 90s. And as with Liam Cosgrave, perhaps the key ingredient is a good sense of humour, a wonderful prescription-free tonic.

July 25, 2011

An Irishman's Diary

Hugh Oram

In the 1940s and 1950s, this part of Dublin had a vibrant artistic community and many artists and writers were regulars in the shop, the likes of Brendan Behan (right) and Paddy Kavanagh

THE WEE STORES in Pembroke Lane, Dublin, were once an integral part of life in this part of Dublin 4, and are still remembered with great affection.

The shop was typical of countless small grocery shops up and down the country that survived until supermarkets began to develop. The name of the shop was a tribute to its status as probably the smallest shop in Dublin and it may also have been derived from the background of the Harrisons, Mary Catherine and John, who ran the shop for many years. Mary Catherine was Co Monaghan born and reared, while her husband had gone to school in Castlewellan, Co Down.

Originally, the Wee Stores had been a coachhouse, built about 1850 at the back of a house on Pembroke Road, but the era of horse-drawn travel eventually faded. The first car mechanics and chauffeurs had started living in these lanes about 1910. This particular building was converted into a shop around 1920. During the 1930s, it was run by a Miss Hanley, then in 1941, the Harrisons took over.

John Harrison had already plenty of experience in running shops in North King Street and on the quays near the Four Courts; eventually, he concentrated entirely on the Wee Stores. It stocked everything in the line of groceries; biscuits were then sold from tins and one whole wall was devoted to tins of biscuits, from which customers bought bags of biscuits by the quarter or the half pound. Fresh tomatoes came from the greenhouse of a man who lived nearby in Waterloo Road, while a dairy further down Pembroke Lane supplied fresh butter and cream. Ice cream was another popular line in the Wee Stores, as were sweets, minerals, potatoes, coal and briquettes. Sugar came in hundredweight sacks from which 1lb bags had to be filled.

One of the Harrisons' children, Anthony, remembers that his father used to drive a van which he used to collect goods from wholesalers all over the city. Some items like bread were delivered. In the early days of the Wee Stores, horse-drawn vans from the bakeries, like Johnston, Mooney & O'Brien, then in Ballsbridge, and the old Kennedys in Parnell Street, used to delivery bread daily. One customer of the shop, who lived round the corner in Wellington Road, used to come armed with a metal bucket and a shovel every morning to scoop up the natural fertiliser for his garden.

Later, in what was an early incarnation of the green movement, the bakeries switched to using battery-driven vans for their deliveries.

The Emergency period of the second World War was a fruitful time for the shop and Anthony Harrison remembers on one occasion his father getting delivery of a big box of cigarettes from the US, which despite requiring coupons, were all gone within a week. Pipe-cleaners sold well, much in demand by women for when they were doing their hair. Other times of the year created other demands, like the big red candlesticks the shop used to sell coming up to Christmas.

The shop was open all hours, from seven in the morning until eleven or later at night, seven days a week, even opening for a few hours on Christmas morning. St Stephen's Day was a rare occasion; the shop usually stayed closed. Sunday mornings were very busy, with queues forming down the lane after Masses at the nearby St Mary's in Haddington Road.

Pembroke and the other lanes in the area were much more rural and they were filled with birdsong then, before the lanes were so extensively developed. Pembroke Lane once had a piggery, as did Heytesbury Lane, but both are long gone, as are the orchards that once blossomed in the lanes.

In the 1940s and 1950s, this part of Dublin had a vibrant artistic community and many artists and writers were regulars in the shop, the likes of Brendan Behan and Paddy Kavanagh, although the two arch enemies didn't come in at the same time. Sometimes, when Kavanagh was going through a hard phase, John Harrison would give food as a present to the poet. Those were the days when a shop like the Wee Stores would happily sell a customer a single cigarette, because money was so scarce.

Many visual artists were also regular patrons, the likes of the late Cecil King and the late Richard Kingston, as well as Pauline Bewick and Michael Kane – both happily still with us. Musicians, too, often came in, like Barney McKenna of The Dubliners. The Wee Stores was almost as much of an artistic mecca as Parson's Bookshop, just up the road on Baggot Street Bridge.

The much-loved George Otto Simms, later a Church of Ireland Archbishop of Armagh and Primate of All Ireland, used to come to the shop when he was curate at St Bartholomew's in Clyde Road. The Wee Stores even got the odd aristo, like a Lady Nelson whom Anthony Harrison recalls dropping in.

Anthony remembers that the people who ran the grocery shops in Upper Baggot Street all got on together, in Findlaters, the Monument Creameries, Leverett and Frye and Liptons. When supermarkets started to arrive in the 1960s, the patterns and pace of shopping began to change, drastically. Another impediment for small shops was the introduction of turnover tax in 1962, which helped make them less competitive.

As for the Wee Stores, it kept going until the early 1990s. Anthony's mother had died in 1991, four years after the passing of his father. In recent years, the premises has been home to such shops as a branch of Sheridan's Cheesemongers and most recently, until earlier this year, a French-run boutique that specialised in jewellery and other crafts. Now Anthony is hoping that a coffee shop will open in the premises in the coming weeks.

The Wee Stores may be long gone, as conclusively as the trams that once trundled along Waterloo Road, and the thriving artists' colony that once lived, worked and drank, often with abandon, in this area, but they are fondly remembered as a symbol of a vanished and a quieter, simpler way of life.

September 2, 2011

57

An Irishman's Diary

Hugh Oram

'Eva O'Flaherty's main claim to fame was setting up the St Colman's knitting industry in Dooagh. It became a life-long enterprise for her, providing at its height, employment for about 30 women.' Photograph: Cyril Byrne

TAKE THE STORY of an enthralling island in the west, mix in the extraordinary social enterprise of a local woman from a wealthy family, and you have the recipe for a vivid tale being written by a Co Galway based author, Mary J Murphy. The book, *Achill's Eva O'Flaherty: Forgotten Island Heroine*, is due to be published next summer and she has hopes that it could be made into a film,with with Meryl Streep perfect as the heroine.

Murphy studied at NUI Galway, where President Michael D Higgins, was her sociology lecturer, then at DCU, before working as a feature writer and broadcaster in Dublin, London, Nashville and Iceland. Her first book, *Viking Summer*, celebrated the making of the 1968 film on Alfred the Great at Caherlistrane near Tuam in north Co Galway, where she and her family live.

Not long ago, Mary's husband, Gerard, introduced her to a local man, Brendan Gannon, who knew Eva well and indeed, had made her funeral arrangements in 1963. Eva's family home, long before she got involved in Achill, was in Caherlistrane. The mansion on its own estate is now an upmarket guest house.

Mary, her husband and their three children, Morgan, Mason and Minette, often spend time at the family's second home, on Achill Island, a place described by Mary Murphy as " gloriously wild and windy" , somewhere she regards with boundless affection, a rich source of inspiration. The connection between Caherlistrane and what Eva O'Flaherty did on Achill started to fall into place after the meeting with Brendan Gannon, and the creation of the book began.

O'Flaherty was born into a well-heeled and well-connected Catholic landed gentry family; both her mother's and father's side of the family was steeped in nationalism and Eva could trace her pedigree back to Grace O'Malley, the pirate queen. Eva trained in millinery and by 1900, was in Paris, modelling headgear for people to wear when driving the motor car. Surprisingly, she didn't stay in Paris but moved to London, where the world of millinery was gloriously exciting in the years before the first World War. A renowned society beauty, she held court in the Café Royal in London, a city that was then a hotbed of Irish literary and political revival.

But she had made trips to Irish-speaking locations in the west of Ireland. A doomed romance may have led her to settle in her own Hy-Brasil,

Achill Island. Eva also had a burning desire to help relieve the desperate poverty on the island; for most men and women on the island, just about the only way they could earn money was to go potato-picking in Scotland during the summer.

Eva helped found Scoil Acla in 1910, revived over the past quarter century and now considered Ireland's oldest summer school. But her main claim to fame was setting up the St Colman's knitting industry in Dooagh a couple of years later. It became a life-long enterprise for Eva, providing at its height, employment for about 30 women. They knitted all kinds of what were then high fashion garments, such as cardigans, smart suits and twin-sets, which were sold in such outlets as Arnotts, Brown Thomas, Sloweys and Switzers in Dublin, indeed exported all over the world, and regularly exhibited at the RDS Spring Show.

Knitting had a long tradition on Achill, going back to around the mid-18th century, when local women knitted stockings for French mariners who put into the island.

Achill historian John "twin" McNamara recalls that when his mother worked at St Colman's in the 1930s, Eva O'Flaherty had a favourite saying when someone turned up late for work: "Seven hours sleep for a man, eight for a woman and nine for a fool".

Eva O'Flaherty kept the knitting industry going until she died at nearly 90 years of age. By then, fashions had changed and demand for its products was falling. Eva never married and had no children, so there was no one to pass the torch to and the industry closed in 1970.

Of the various industries set up on Achill over the years, the knitting industry was by far the longest lasting and most durable in terms of creating employment.

Besides the knitting, Eva had her own modest house at Dooagh; her lamp-lit salon there drew an amazing variety of artistic figures, mostly painters; personalities from the church;

legal figures and political names. Those who were on first name terms with Eva and came to see her included Paul Henry and his wife Grace, Graham Greene, Heinrich Böll, Ernie O'Malley and Eamon de Valera. On one occasion, in July, 1950, ballet dancer friends from Sadler's Wells in London came all the way to Achill to see her while at the same time, Jack MacGowran was there, from the Abbey Theatre.

Achill, in the earlier part of the 20th century, drew an amazing mix of high name figures, drawn by the natural attractions of the island itself and the personality of Eva O'Flaherty.

By all accounts, she was an extraordinary woman, contributing much to an enchanting island. Mary Murphy says of her: " She was a can-do woman of initiative, driven by the impulse of charity, exuding extreme kindness, grace, warmth and generosity, convivial, independent, cultured and with a refined literary sensibility" .

Yet as is inevitable with such stirring stories, they fall into abeyance. Nearly 50 years after her death, Eva has become Achill's forgotten island heroine. So Mary Murphy determined to rescue the story from oblivion. A letter to this newspaper early last year yielded some delicious vignettes.

One was from a now elderly lady who had attended Mount Anville in the 1930s, just as Eva O'Flaherty had done in the 1880s. When Eva met this lady, then a schoolgirl, she asked her whether the girls still had to speak French to the nuns, curtsey and wear a shift while having a bath. Mary Murphy's book is wending its way towards completion and is due to be launched at Scoil Acla next summer; the Eva O'Flaherty story will have come full circle, back into the limelight, an engrossing tale of high society on Achill and community self-help. Mary Murphy is contactable at: morma@eircom.net

January 4, 2012

An Irishman's Diary

Hugh Oram

FROM years ago, I remember a catchy cartoon advertisement that was often seen in Dublin cinemas, about Johnston, Mooney & O'Brien, the bakery firm, then in Ballsbridge. The characters were spindly but the jingle was one of those musical melodies that once it's lodged in your brain, it simply refuses to remove itself.

For a century, Johnston, Mooney & O'Brien had a vast bakery enterprise in the heart of Ballsbridge, complete with a shop, close to the bridge, that sold tempting bread and cakes for picnics in nearby Herbert Park. It had been built on the site of the early 19th-century Duffy's calico mills (from a previous great industrial activity in Ballsbridge).

The bakery firm had its origins in the early 19th century and was made up of three separate bakeries, which came together in 1889. The Johnstons were a family from Kircudbrightshire in south-west Scotland, who emigrated to Dublin in the 1820s and promptly set up a bakery in the city. Mooneys and O'Briens, on the other hand, were much more "real Dub" bakeries. Today, the same names are also renowned as those of a trio of recently famous Irish cricketers.

It was a huge concern and the Ballsbridge bakery, at the height of its prosperity, employed 500 people. Its horse-drawn carts were a familiar sight around the city for years; many gardens in and around Ballsbridge benefited from the natural manure. That was until in a very early manifestation of green power, the bakery introduced battery-driven bread vans. They had another claim to fame, too; they were the first bakery in Ireland to produce wrapped sliced pans.

I often wonder about the expression "the greatest thing since sliced pan". What did people use for comparative purposes before Johnston Mooney & O'Brien brought out the first wrapped bread?

The bakery in Ballsbridge closed down in 1989 and moved to a new location in Finglas. Much controversy erupted over its Ballsbridge site and its subsequent redevelopment. The Herbert Park Hotel now stands where that enticing little bakery shop once functioned. Next to the hotel were the offices of Cablelink, which moved, over a decade ago, to East Point and transmogrified itself into UPC. On another part of the old bakery site, there are newspaper offices, a new phenomenon in Ballsbridge, those of the *Irish*

'On one memorable occasion, the renowned German writer Heinrich Böll, was nearly knocked down in Dublin by a Swastika laundry van. For one awful moment, he thought that the Abwehr had set up a branch in Dublin.'
Photograph: Gordon Standing

Daily Mail and the *Irish Mail on Sunday*.

Johnston Mooney & O'Brien is of course still trading successfully today, far removed from its Ballsbridge origins. It's in what was once the Downes Butterkrust bakery in Jamestown Road, Finglas.

Another old establishment in Ballsbridge generated loads of controversy in its latter days, the Hospitals' Sweepstake. Started in 1930, it was soon scooping in so much money than within eight years, it was able to move into vast new headquarters in Ballsbridge, designed in a very modern style and billed at the time as the largest office space in the world, built on the site of Ramsay's Royal Nurseries.

Upwards of 5,000 people, mostly women, toiled there, sorting Sweep tickets in readiness for the majestic draws, when the tickets were plucked from the drums by white-uniformed hospital nurses.

The first crack in the edifice came in 1973 when a reporter called Joe McAnthony revealed what really went on inside the Hospitals' Sweepstakes. It turned out that less than 10 per cent of the cash generated had been going to hospitals, while the three founders and their families were enormously enriched. Joe McGrath, one of those founders, had close links with the old Irish Glass Bottle company in Ringsend and Waterford Glass.

McAnthony's report in the *Sunday Independent*, one of the first instances of investigative journalism in Ireland, caused such uproar that he was forced to work for the rest of his career

in Canada. Two recent books on the subject, one by Marie Coleman, the other by Damien Corless, revealed the unsavoury behind-the-scenes story of the Sweep.

The Sweepstakes carried on until the National Lottery was established in 1987. The Sweepstakes may have been swept away, but controversy continued for a long while after, over payments to the many elderly women who had worked there for years. When the premises were demolished, all that was preserved was the hardwood flooring. These days, the name of the Sweepstake lives on in the subsequent developments on the site.

In present day Ballsbridge, right next to the Horse Show House pub, is a red-brick building once called, with great originality, the Red House. Once, there were recording studios here, where the Sweepstake programmes on Radio Éireann were recorded, with *When You Wish Upon A Star* as its signature tune. They and the studios are still well remembered by the likes of Val Joyce, once a familiar radio voice, now retired.

Yet another firm that traded for years in Ballsbridge also went the way of the Ballsbridge bakery and the Sweep, the Swastika laundry in Shelbourne Road. It had been founded in 1912, when the Nazi symbol was an innocent motif with Sanskrit links, long before it was sequestered in Germany. But its delivery vans, decorated with the the swastika, trundled around Dublin for years. On one memorable occasion, the renowned German writer Heinrich Böll, was nearly knocked down in Dublin by a Swastika laundry van. For one awful moment, he thought that the Abwehr had set up a branch in Dublin.

The Swastika premises, long since taken over by the Spring Grove laundry company, were demolished nearly a decade ago and the Oval development put up on the site. The old laundry chimney is still there, wrapped inside the Oval, but without the old swastikas that once adorned its sides.

Ballsbridge has changed immensely, especially in the past 10 to 15 years, but somehow, a little of those three astonishing undertakings can still be sensed in the air around Ball's Bridge, its original title, named after a man called Ball who ran a mill here in the 17th century.

For many years, what is now Merrion Road, outside the RDS, was called Ball's Bridge Road. It was all a far cry from the present connotations of Ballsbridge, the luxury embassy belt.

March 6, 2012

An Irishman's Diary

Hugh Oram

'The Saltees form Ireland's largest bird sanctuary and have an astonishing reputation among bird watchers from all over the world for the incredible number of seabirds that come to the islands.' Above, a gannet chick is protected by its parent on the Saltees, Wexford. Photograph: Cyril Byrne

LOOKING out to sea from the harbour at Kilmore Quay, Co Wexford, two islands stand like tempting forbidden territory, about 5km off the coast. The Saltee Islands, Great and Little, may be small in size but they encompass much history and a great variety of natural life.

Provided that the weather is calm, the boat journey across from Kilmore Quay is an easy passage. Declan Bates or others at Kilmore Quay harbour are happy to take people for a boat trip around the islands, or else to land, much easier on the big island. Declan says that it's possible to land on either of the islands, which rather amazingly, were once joined to the mainland.

The first people to have settled on the Saltees did so during the New Stone Age, about 3500 to 2000 BC. In modern times, the first family recorded on the islands were the Boxfels, in the 16th century. They were farmers, but one of the Boxfel brothers soon discovered that smuggling was far more profitable. The caves around the coast of the bigger island, with such names as Hell's Cave, were ideal for smugglers and it's said that if anyone probes deep enough into these caves, they will find material left by the smugglers 200 or more years ago.

The Saltees became an ideal base for a very motley crew of smugglers, pirates and brigands, while there were also a vast number of shipwrecks, about 1,000 in all, in this area of the south-east.

During the 1798 rebellion, the islands became a hiding place for some of the south Wexford rebels. Two Protestant leaders in 1798, Beauchamp Harvey Bagenal and John Henry Colclough, hid in caves on the islands, but were captured and then hanged on the town bridge in Wexford.

Early in the 19th century, the Parle family bought the islands and started cultivating wheat, barley and potatoes. The Parles formed the 52 arable hectares of the big island, with a third in tillage, the rest in pasture. One of the family, John, had a great reputation as a strong man; he could lift up two sheep, one under each arm, and put them into a cot (small boat) to take them to the mainland. By 1860, about 20 people were living on the Great Saltee.

The Parles lasted until 1904, when they sold the leases on the islands to Martin Pierce, of the family that owned the famed foundry in Wexford. But his interest was short-lived. In 1907, he took one of his employees on a rabbit shooting expedition on the Saltees, but when they were leaving the islands, a storm blew up and their boat filled with water and sank. They were rescued, but Martin Pierce died a few days later.

For the next 20 years or so, other members of the Pierce family used the islands for sport but didn't live there. In 1930, the Great Saltee was sold to a sporting syndicate from Dublin for £5. Then, in the late 1930s, a man called Claude Francis took over the big island and farmed there. He abandoned the island after the death of his wife and in December, 1943, a Co Wexford man, Michael Neale, a farmer's son, bought the main island.

When he was 10 years of age, he had declared to his mother that one day, he was going to own the Saltees. He also declared himself Prince Michael of the Saltees, although his "coronation" was delayed until 1953, the year of the coronation of Queen Elizabeth II. Prince Michael built a throne on the big island, as well as an obelisk with his own likeness, and put up a flagstaff. He left a peculiar decree, that if none of his family could take over the islands after his death, they were to be governed by the Absent Twelve, after the Twelve Apostles, who could come from any country in the world, as long as they were fishermen.

Prince Michael planted 34,000 trees and shrubs on the great island and the palm trees that he planted can still be seen. He also learned to fly, so as to visit his island easily. One of his airlifts was very controversial; in 1949, he flew in a plane load of cats, 46 in all, to deal with the vermin on the island, but the cats died out after about eight years. As for the prince himself, he died in 1998 and is buried in the family vault at Bannow Bay on the nearby Wexford coast. He was succeeded in his ownership and title by his eldest son, who became Prince Michael the Second.

Little Saltee, half the size of the main island, remained inhabited up until the end of the second World War. Then in 1977, Henry Grattan Bellew and his partner, Shirley, made the restoration of Little Saltee Island their active retirement project when they came back to Ireland from southern Africa.

Today, much of the main island is covered in thickets and brambles, but in one respect, the two islands retain their main point of interest. They form Ireland's largest bird sanctuary and have an astonishing reputation among bird watchers from all over the world for the incredible number of seabirds that come to the islands – thousands upon thousands of gannets, guillemots and puffins, as well as many other species. Other wildlife, too, can be seen, such as seals and dolphins. In 1950, Major Robert Ruttledge, with the help of John Weaving, turned the original island farmhouse into a bird observatory, which lasted until 1963. Major Ruttledge himself died 10 years ago, at the age of 102.

For anyone who loves nature and an unspoiled environment, the two islands are ideal for a fascinating summer trip. They have been written about, mainly by Wexford writer Richard Roche, while Henry Grattan Bellew also put pen to paper with his account of his stay on Little Saltee, called *A Pinch of Saltee*. But the ideal way of exploring this magic and unspoiled islands is by taking a boat there from Kilmore Quay.

June 26, 2012

An Irishman's Diary

Hugh Oram

'At about the same time, Rathlin Island off the north coast, also got bottled gas. One of the men working on the installation had spent three months there before head office realised that he hadn't returned. The harbour and jetty area on Rathlin Island.
Photograph: Bryan O'Brien

NOT ALONE is the past a different country, but one that's totally unrecognisable in present day Ireland. The way in which we live and work has changed so dramatically over the past 60 years or so that the old days just seem incredibly archaic. How did we ever manage? I was struck by all these fundamental social changes when I was researching and writing a recently published book about the 75-year history of Calor Gas in Ireland.

When McMullans, the Belfast oil company behind the Maxol brand, brought Calor Gas to Ireland in 1936, it started its publicity with features in various newspapers, including *The Irish Times*, extolling the virtues of this new fuel, a byproduct of the oil industry.

The first big rollout was at the 1937 Spring Show at the RDS; the Spring Show itself, to the regret of many people, became a casualty of progress. In those far off days, for anyone fortunate to be well off, the ultimate in holiday luxury was having a caravan somewhere like Brittas Bay or along the Wexford coast.

Portable gas cookers were promoted as the ultimate holiday accessory.

Few people went abroad for holidays and for those lucky enough to have a job, a day at the seaside, somewhere like Bray, was the most they could hope for.

When Calor Gas restarted after the second World War, the working conditions for the company's employees were primitive. One man I met was Jack Noonan, from Rooskey, Co Roscommon, who started as a sales rep on the road with the company in November, 1946. He recalled that the depots around the country were no more than galvanised tin sheds, with no lighting, no heat and no telephones. The van he used had no heating, a big drawback in the terrible winter of 1947. Neither was it possible in those days to get even a cup of coffee anywhere on the road, he recalled.

On the odd occasion he needed to phone head office in Dublin, he had to go to the nearest post office to make the call, which had to be put through manually. Direct dialling for any but local calls was unheard of. When head office wanted to communicate with its reps around the country, it put triplicate memos in the post. Just compare that with all the mobile online and digital paraphernalia of today.

The atmosphere at work, too, was very paternalistic. In the 1950s, after McMullans had given up the Calor Gas franchise and started Kosangas, with a Danish company, in competition with Calor (eventually, Calor took over Kosangas), this old-fashioned relationship between bosses and workers continued. Coming up to Christmas, all the women working for Kosangas had a half a day off so they could do their shopping. All employees had to attend a yearly dinner dance at the Gresham Hotel in Dublin, while another mandatory treat was the annual visit to the orchard near Limavady, Co Derry, owned by one of the McMullan family.

In those days, it was almost unknown for women to drive cars and for many, getting married meant leaving work. It wasn't until 1973, when the civil service marriage bar ended, that this time-stained ritual ended.

Everyone used to go home for lunch, which the stay-at-home woman of the house cooked. From 1955 for 20 years, one of the most popular radio programmes was the *Kennedys of Castleross*, the first Irish soap; many factories altered their lunch times so that their workers could get home to tune in over lunch. But even then, times were changing fast. When RTÉ ended the show, it got just one letter of complaint.

When Jack Lynch was taoiseach, around 40 years ago, he always made a point of going home to lunch nearly every day, to Garville Avenue in Rathgar. For years, there used to be a Housewife of the Year competition to promote bottled gas; even though it only ended in the mid-1990s, it seems incredibly out of date now.

Even by 1963, when a Kerryman, Larry Hickey, started with the company, many housewives in that county were still using ranges, or else a crane over an open fire, a custom that had persisted for centuries. Many homes in rural Ireland still had to get electricity, so candles or oil lamps remained essential.

Life was even more deficient in modern appliances on the offshore islands. When the 30 inhabitants of Inisbiggle, just off Achill in Co Mayo, got bottled gas in 1970, the cookers and other appliances had to be brought from Achill by currach, then transported around the smaller island by donkey cart. In one hilarious episode, a donkey laden with cookers refused to move, until it was given a thwack with a stick. It then shot off, at high speed, disappearing over the hill until it upturned itself, the cart and its load into a bog.

At about the same time, Rathlin Island off the north coast, also got bottled gas. One of the men working on the installation had spent three months there before head office realised that he hadn't returned. But during his time there, he became so knowledgeable about the island and its history that he wrote a book on the subject. These days, when it's usually so easy to get in touch with someone, it's hard to imagine any head office not realising that someone had disappeared off the radar for three months!

In those days, the same key would open the locks of any particular model, such as the Ford Zephyr, a popular car among wealthier motorists in the 1960s and into the 1970s.

One night, the sales manager with the bottled gas company, and his wife were enjoying themselves at the Castle golf club in Rathfarnham, south Dublin. In the early hours, they got into what they thought was their Ford Zephyr. They had only gone a short distance before they were stopped at a Garda checkpoint in Dundrum. Unknown to them, the then Garda Commissioner, Paddy McLaughlin, had also been in the golf club that night and had parked his identical Ford Zephyr, his own personal car, outside the club. It was this car that the couple from the bottled gas company had unwittingly driven off in. But it was all sorted out and no one ended up in Mountjoy!

Those were simple times, devoid of all the gadgetry we have today, and in recollection, they have a certain quaint, easygoing charm. But the chasm between the realities of then and the realities of today is so big that it can only be bridged by a little humorous recall of events.

An Irishman's Diary

Hugh Oram

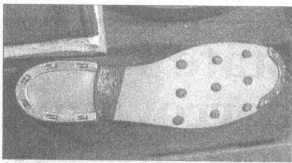

A shoe from the Barracks Life Room at the National Museum of Ireland, Dublin. "The Irish shoe manufacturing industry, once so vibrant, has been practically wiped out . . . We're now a nation of shoe importers." Photograph: Frank Miller

WHEN JOHN McCarthy, of McCarthy's shoe shop in Ranelagh, Dublin, was a youngster, his father, Con, had a great way of bringing the family on day trips all over the country. The McCarthys have had their shoe shop in the same spot in Ranelagh since 1949 and Con McCarthy used to visit many of the big shoe factories around the country.

These days, such trips would be impossible, because the Irish shoe manufacturing industry, once so vibrant, has been practically wiped out.

Back in 1984, the Guaranteed Irish organisation listed 530 clothing and footwear manufacturers; by last year, a shoemaking company called Whelan's, in Cootehill, Co Cavan, was the only one on that list still manufacturing. The others had either closed down or have transferred their production outside Ireland. It's hardly surprising that the people who used to work in shoe-making form such a devoted band of enthusiasts dedicated to a bygone trade – and they love to reminisce.

As late as the 1930s, practically every town throughout Ireland had its boot- and shoemakers hand-making their wares; just in Co Waterford alone, Tramore had three, while Dungarvan had five. But the 1930s represented the apogee of shoemaking, as British companies set up factories here to get around the tariff barriers on imports.

In Dundalk, part of the Army barracks was taken over by Rawson's, an English firm that set up its factory in the town. It survived until 1967. An even bigger factory with English origins was Hallidays, which was linked with Clarks shoes. Even into the early 1970s, it was employing 1,250 people. Other firms that were synonymous with Dundalk and shoemaking included Blackthorn. No wonder Dundalk prided itself on being the shoemaking "capital" of Ireland.

Not far away, in Carrickmacross, Co Monaghan, the Stedfast shoe company traded so well that in 1958, it set up its own brass band. The factory closed in 1988, but the band plays on. Even Kells, Co Meath, got its own shoe factory, Kenlia Shoes.

Drogheda, too, benefited in similar fashion. Woodington's arrived on the Marsh Road there from Bristol in 1932.

Up to the end of the second World War, it made working men's boots and farm boots, but the arrival of the Wellington boot displaced those lines, so Woodington's went into ladies' fashion shoes.

It had agreements with various English brands and its Sno Cats bootees sold well here in Ireland as well as in Canada and the US. It also made

Symphony fashion shoes. The other big shoe company in Drogheda was Donaghy's, set up in 1936 at West Gate.

The most unlikely places got thriving shoe companies, such as Edenderry, Co Offaly.

It too had a great name for ladies' fashion shoes, but in the end, found itself taken over by a property company, stopped making shoes and became an investment vehicle called European Leisure, which owned various entertainment and night club venues in England.

Some of the big shoe companies were much longer established, like Winstanley's in Dublin's Liberties, which continued a tradition in the area of shoemaking that was centuries old. Winstanley's started in 1875 and lasted for the best part of a century. Some of its workers went on to set up Skipper shoes, which themselves faded out.

In Limerick, O'Callaghan's had a huge shoemaking factory that dated back to 1830. In more recent times, the Limerick shoe and slipper works were set up in Mulgrave Street, Limerick, in 1933.

In Cork, the Lee Boot Company was a big employer and became even bigger by absorbing Hanover Shoes.

In Carlow, the Governey family started a shoe company in 1903 and used the outline of Carlow Castle as its trademark. It lasted until the early 1970s. In Killarney, Tuf Shoes, whose origins date back to 1881, once made all the boots needed by the Army, the Department of Posts and Telegraphs and the ESB. When the company celebrated its centenary, helped by the then minister of state at the department of justice, Dick Spring, the company was still making 8,000 pairs of shoes a week.

A couple of brands went on to garner international reputations, but phased out their shoemaking in Ireland. Padmore & Barnes was famous for its shoemaking in Kilkenny and became renowned for its Mocassin Wallabees. For a 30-year period, it was owned by Clarks, the noted English shoemakers.

Dubarry was once an

industrial mainstay of Ballinasloe, Co Galway, where it was founded in 1937 as a co-op by the local chamber of commerce.

Still renowned for its shoes and fashions, Dubarry transferred its shoe production to Portugal in 2004 and says it makes very little here now.

In the old days, leather shoes could take up to a month to break in, but these days, people want shoes that are ready to go. We're now a nation of shoe importers.

It was the same story in Northern Ireland. Down Shoes had a huge factory on the outskirts of Banbridge, Co Down, that managed to last, making Lotus shoes, until 2002. All over Ireland, shoemaking was once such a big industry that the British United Shoe Machinery company had extensive sales operations here. Once, the Irish Shoe and Leather Workers' Union was a strong entity in the trade union movement.

Just a couple of companies have managed to keep going. Whelan's footwear was founded in 1931 by Gerard Whelan when he was just 21. During the 1960s, its shoes were very popular with showband performers, the likes of Joe Dolan, Brendan Bowyer and Big Tom. Today, among its various lines, it is noted for its Irish dancing shoes.

In Naas, Co Kildare, Tutty's handmade shoes, started in 1946, are still going strong and the company is also renowned for its orthopaedic shoes. It has a workforce of 10, a far cry from the time when Ireland had close to 20 shoe factories, as well as ancillary factories, such as the Nugget shoe polish factory in Bluebell, Dublin.

The Anglo-Irish trade agreement in the mid-1960s, and then Ireland's joining of the EEC in 1973, meant that the industry was very susceptible to imports – and succumb it did.

Shoemaking became part of Ireland's disappeared manufacturing tradition, like car assembly, but these days, the powerful memories of those who once worked in shoemaking keep its spirit, if not its physical manifestation, alive.

September 8, 2012

62

Hugh Oram

An Irishman's Diary

Nice for Christmas; there's no better place, as we've found on a couple of occasions. The weather in Nice, the capital of the Cote d'Azur, is generally very mild during December, sunny, too.

Arriving at or departing from Nice airport in clear weather is spectacular; the airport is built into the sea at the western end of Nice and the views from your plane are astonishing. The other big plus about Nice is the Promenade des Anglais, that great seaside boulevard, opened in its present form by the Duke of Connaught in 1931 and a great walking treat.

These days, Nice is so packed in summer with tourists that December is a far better time to explore. Mind you, we weren't particularly turned on by Nice, despite all its museums, parks and gardens, or by the two other big conurbations along the coast here, Cannes and the principality of Monaco.

They are all too glitzy glam, reeking of super-rich perfume. But we found Nice an ideal place from which to explore the whole Cote d'Azur. From the main railway station in Nice, it's easy to reach the towns along the coast.

The most distant we travelled to was St Tropez, all of 108km away. St Tropez, with its quayside restaurants and legions of big yachts tied up, is quiet and appealing in December, the opposite of what it's like in August.

Going in the other direction from Nice, eastwards, towards Italy, which once ruled this corner of France, we discovered Menton. The town has preserved much of its 19th-century charm, despite the destructive earthquake of 1887. Menton remains delightful, with its old town rising from the harbour to the 17th-century church of St Michel Archange.

From the end of the 19th century, Menton, whose symbol, a lemon, denotes its mild microclimate, was very popular with English and Russian aristocrats. These days, the new Russian oligarchs find home from home here but the town gives a better insight into the old days of the French Riviera than anywhere else. Menton has also attracted many creative spirits, none more so than William Butler Yeats, who died on January 28th, 1939, in the ironically named Hotel Idéal-Séjour in Roquebrune- Cap-Martin.

He was buried in the town, which is really a western extension of Menton, and wasn't repatriated to Sligo until 1948. Over the years, it has been suggested from time to time that the man who is buried at Drumcliffe isn't Yeats at all, but a French dentist.

Out of all the trips we did from Nice, none was so striking as that on the Train de Pigne, from Nice to Digne-les-Bains, an old Provençal lavender town, high up in the mountains of Haute Provence. The train is named after the pine cones that were once used to fire up the old steam locos on the line. The first section of the railway was opened in 1891 and it took 20 years to complete. These days, the 151km journey takes three-and-a-half hours through mountain scenery and along gorges, climbing to a high point of 1, 000 metres above sea level.

I'm glad that when we did the trip, it was from the old station for the line in Nice, just a few blocks from the main SNCF station. The old Gare du Sud was dark and dingy but full of character. In recent years, it has been replaced by a nearby modern station that's the exact

These days, Nice is so packed in summer with tourists that December is a far better time to explore

opposite. We were also lucky in taking the trip on the old-style train – seriously deficient in amenities – before it too was upgraded. Yet as the train bumped slowly upwards along an uneven track, we enjoyed the baguettes and grande bouteille of rough red wine we had bought at the station.

At the other end of the line, Digne-les-Bains was high enough up to induce what felt like a touch of altitude sickness after a vinous Sunday lunch at the Hotel Grand Paris.

On this particular trip, we were destined to move on to Paris itself.

From Digne-les- Bains, we took an exceedingly meandering bus trip to Valence, on the main TGV line from Marseilles to Paris. We were whisked by TGV to Paris in just over two hours, but when we arrived at the Gare de Lyon late on New Year's Eve, we had to wait an hour in a vast queue for a taxi. *Plus ça change, plus c'est la même chose!*

December 18, 2012

Hugh Oram

An Irishman's Diary

Oh for the days of the working lunch that went on until 5pm and the raft of great characters, major and minor, who once worked in Ireland's advertising industry. That was in the pre-digital days when all the ad agencies were locally owned, before the multinationals moved in.

The standard had been set in this newspaper, around 65 years ago, in the days when GJC Tynan O'Mahony was the general manager. He had a wooden leg; the story goes that in the early 1920s, he got trapped in a lift in London and performed a DIY amputation with his penknife. Never lost for a *bon mot*, years later, he announced one night that he was going to go to a fancy dress ball dressed as a toffee apple, an excellent example of lateral thinking. He was also said to have burst into a meeting of Freemasons in Molesworth Street, Dublin, bringing fraternal greetings from his Holiness the Pope.

Unsurprisingly, O'Mahony set the pace for a legion of characters in the Irish advertising industry. He prepared the stage for his son, Dave Allen, the TV comedian.

One of the best of the characters in advertising here wasn't Irish, but American, Mack Kile, the man who ran the Irish International agency until he left Ireland in 1975. It was he who created the perennial conundrum about how you get the figs into Jacob's fig roll biscuits.

Many other stories were told about Kile, including the apocryphal one about how he arrived at a presentation for Dunlop tyres curled up inside a gigantic tyre.

Some of the characters attracted apt nicknames. The late Peter Owens had learned much from his time working in Madison Avenue, New York, when the Madmen there were in full swing. After he set up his own agency here in Dublin, he used to glide around town in a very posh car. Not for nothing was he known as "the little grey gnome from the West (Mayo)". He was noted for the sharpest elbows in adland.

On the other hand, the late Bill Walshe of the Innovation Group, was known as the greatest and most amusing spoofer in advertising.

Any deficiencies in the jokes department were always made up for further down the line, as some of the copywriters and artists in the agencies were always up for a little jape or two. One of the well-known agencies in Dublin in the old days was Janus, then based at Parnell Square. One day, Denis Garvey, its boss, gazed out of his window with not a little bemusement, to see a brassiere dangling from a line. It turned out to have been a little prank devised by certain members of the creative department.

The old McConnells, founded by Charlie McConnell, was then the number one agency in town and, handily, the Red Bank restaurant was nearby, in D'Olier Street. Deals were often done and creative themes dreamed up over interminably long lunches, heavy on drink and wreathed in smoke, a typical scenario for ad agencies in those innocent days.

This predilection for drink extended to the annual advertising awards festival, founded in Kinsale, Co Cork, in 1962. In its early years, it was notorious for the sheer quantity of drink consumed. In one famous incident, in Acton's Hotel, late one night during one festival, a suitably inebriated senior advertising sales figure from RTÉ astonished everyone by appearing among the multi-

> **The standard had been set in this newspaper, around 65 years ago, in the days when GJC Tynan O'Mahony was the general manager**

tude dressed in nothing but a paper hat.

This tradition of outrageous behaviour carried on until quite recently.

Once, the late Don O'Connell, the former seaman who walked with a decidedly imperfect gait and who ran the old Doherty Advertising agency, was entertaining a potential client in his office. He took the man's very expensive overcoat, then promptly flung it out of the window; it was caught by someone stationed on the pavement below. O'Connell's reasoning behind this bizarre act was that even if he didn't get the advertising account, the man who had come to see him would never forget Doherty Advertising.

The original madmen of Madison Avenue have been well captured in the television series of the same name. But the truth is that once, we had a cast of great characters in the Irish advertising industry who were among the best of the breed.

March 22, 2013

64

Hugh Oram

An Irishman's Diary

One of the most inventive geniuses ever, to emerge in this country was one Richard Pockrich, who lived in the 18th century, and who came from a wealthy family in Co Monaghan. He was lucky, because his father left him enough money for him to spend his entire adult life indulging his voracious appetite for invention. The vast family estate was at Derrylusk, Co Monaghan; the Pockrich family had settled in the country from Surrey during the 17th century.

Pockrich had an incredibly inventive mind, although many of his ideas seemed mad at the time. These days, in hindsight, some seem remarkably prescient. His first move came when he was just 20 and decided to settle in Dublin. He set up a brewery and distillery at Islandbridge, which promptly failed, leaving him with substantial debts. After he lost all his money and the bailiffs came in pursuit, he played them a prelude on a set of wine glasses. These glasses were filled with the correct amount of water, so that tunes could be played. The rather implausible story goes that the bailiffs were so mesmerised by Pockrich's playing that they forgave him his debts!

In any event, when he was 25, he inherited his father's fortune, estimated to have been worth anything from £1,000 to £4,000 a year. The musical glasses weren't a new idea, as making music by tapping glasses had been practised in Persia in the 11th century, so whether Pockrich invented or re-invented the idea is a moot point. In any event, this method of making music became very popular in the 18th century and Pockrich profited from his performances. This was the only one of his ideas that worked well in his lifetime. He had another musical idea, of forming an orchestra from 20 drums, but unsurprisingly, this one didn't work.

He wanted the drums to be placed in a circle, with one person standing in the middle who would play them all. His other ideas were extraordinarily wide-ranging. At one stage, he spent much money cultivating geese on vast areas of mountainous land in Co Wicklow and reckoned that he could rear enough geese to supply the entire market for geese in Ireland, England and France. The venture failed. He wanted to build an observatory on one of the Wicklow hills and to use the midland bogs for cultivating vines (but neither of these projects came to fruition). In addition, he wanted to link the Liffey and the Shannon, a very sensible idea that didn't come about until long after his demise.

He also wanted to build naval ships from metal that would be unsinkable, equipping each with 500 small boats made from tin that would float away in case of shipwreck or collision. In the event, metal didn't start replacing wood for ships' hulls until the 1870s and the idea of lifeboats didn't materialise until long after his time.

Richard Pockrich had ideas for aviation too. He wanted everyone to have a pair of wings that they could use for flying around, believing that people would then give up walking. This particular idea is not impossible these days, but is still far from a practical proposition. Medical ideas infused his brain, too. He wanted sick or old people to get blood transfusions by tube from healthy young people, and he also devised a plan for using brown paper and vinegar to revitalise wrinkled skin. Social problems concerned him and he devised a scheme that would help Dublin's many beggars find paid work, but like so much of what he devised, nothing came of it. He wanted to become an MP so that he could put his social policies into practice, but his two attempts to get elected, once in Monaghan and once in Dublin,

This method of making music became very popular in the 18th century and Pockrich profited from his performances

failed.

He was so busy inventing that he didn't get married until he was 50. Pockrich's wife believed he was wealthy, whereas most of his fortune had been dissipated. He considered his wife to be wealthy, also an entirely erroneous view. She eventually ran away with an actor called Theophilus Cibber; the two of them sailed off to Scotland, but en route, the ship sank and everyone on board was lost. As for the inventive Mr Pockrich, in 1758, when he was 63, he was in England on a tour with his musical glasses. He was staying in lodgings at a coffee house in central London and it's thought that while he was doing experiments in his room, he set fire to the place. Several houses were destroyed, as well as Pockrich himself.

Was he merely a fantasist, as many of his contemporaries thought, or a genius who was too far ahead of his time? These days, the latter view tends to prevail, but what's clear is that he was one of Co Monaghan's most creative sons.

May 2, 2013

Hugh Oram

An Irishman's Diary

One book I have at home that provides constant inspiration is a copy of Cook's *Continental Timetable*. The date of publication is especially poignant, August, 1939. The month after it came out, the second World War started and many of the railway journeys listed were no longer possible and indeed, never resumed.

The book has an incredible feeling of transience about it, quite apart from all the detail about long-forgotten possibilities in rail, steamer and air journeys around Europe and further afield. For Dublin, the book lists the old Thomas Cook office at 118 Grafton Street, telephone 21036. It was close to the main entrance to Trinity and for years it was a mecca for long-distance travellers. Years ago, I went there on many occasions to get travellers' cheques. They have long since become almost obsolescent.

While the book lists all the diplomatic representation in London in that fateful year, 1939, it has no listings for Ireland. It includes all the renowned golf courses across Europe and beyond, from Algeria to Turkey, but again, there's no mention of any in Ireland. At least in terms of diplomatic representation and a plethora of fine golf courses, we've long since put those omissions right. But the book does point out that a telephone service is available between Great Britain and Ireland and all Continental countries, except Albania. That was long before the days of direct dialling to anywhere in the world! The book made no mention of how long it might take to get through, via an operator, to some far-flung destination in Europe, a connection that now takes seconds.

Some of those 1939 railway journeys are still possible, like Berlin to Moscow and on to Vladivostok; the book described how you could continue this particular trip by travelling a further 508km from Vladivostok to Harbin in China. From Harbin to Tokyo took another four days, continuing by sea and making a journey time close to a fortnight.

Once we had a glimpse of what those old-fashioned long distance expresses were like, when we travelled on the Moscow to the Hook of Holland express, the carriages kept warm in the middle of winter by great stoves, installed at intervals in the train. If you fancied taking the *Star of Egypt* express from Cairo to Luxor, going to Jerusalem by train, or in Europe, taking the long distance steam-hauled train all the way from Berlin to Cannes, it was all here.

One of the most appealing trains was the Cote d'Azur express, departing Paris at 10.15, arriving Menton, 23.10. The sheer glamour and romanticism of those trips, as listed in the Thomas Cook book, is potent stuff. I well remember the first long-distance train journey I did on the Continent, an overnight express from Paris to Rome. Seeing the sun rise as the train sped through the Italian Riviera, close to the sea, was an unforgettable experience. I had never before seen sunlight of such intensity and brilliance.

More prosaic journeys are also here, like the LMS trains from Euston to Holyhead, finally delivering passengers to Westland Row in Dublin, and the Great Western Railway service from Paddington to Fishguard and on to Rosslare. The Fishguard to Rosslare Harbour ferry service had begun in 1906. Bus journeys,too, were included, really esoteric stuff, like links to obscure places in Norway. Air

Some of those 1939 railway journeys are still possible, like Berlin to Moscow and on to Vladivostok

services, too, were listed, like London to Deauville in 60 minutes and Amsterdam to Java and Australia by KLM three times a week. All sorts of steamer services are there, including the German and Hungarian river steamers and the Pharaonic Mail Line from Beirut to Alexandria, Tripoli and Marseilles. Interestingly, the book lists all the electric railways in Switzerland, a significant innovation for the time, although it doesn't have the Drumm battery train between Dublin and Bray.

Some of the advice still holds good. In 1939, Thomas Cook strongly advised passengers to insure their baggage at very low premiums. As it turned out, this 1939 book was the last that Thomas Cook produced in the format it had launched in 1873. For the duration of the war, publication was suspended and with the war, so many of those great long distance express train journeys simply vanished into history, never to be resurrected.

Hugh Oram

An Irishman's Diary

What an incredible life history, the story of Irishwoman Kate Meyrick, brought up in a respectable middle class environment, who went on to become "queen of the night-clubs" in 1920s London. Kate Evelyn Nason had been born in 1875 at No 24 Cambridge Terrace in what was then Kingstown, now Dún Laoghaire; her father was a well-off doctor, who died a year later. Her mother remarried, this time to a clergyman from Lancashire; but she too died within seven years. The young Kate returned from England to Dublin as an orphan and lived with her grandmother who had the young girl educated by governesses. Subsequently, from the time she was 15, she attended Alexandra College,

then in Earlsfort Terrace, Dublin, where the Conrad Hotel and the adjoining office complex are now located. But even then, she was showing signs of independence, claiming to have been the first woman in Dublin to ride a bicycle.

When she was 19, she married a medical man in Dublin, Ferdinand Merrick, who was a physician and specialist in nerve diseases. They soon opted for the posher sounding surname "Meyrick" and moved to England. So far, so good, with Kate a dutiful doctor's wife. But soon after the end of the first World War, when she was 44, her marriage collapsed. She went to London, where she soon became involved in the hectic and louche *demi-monde* that was

emerging as a reaction to the recent war. She became the manager of Dalton's Club in Leicester Square, as well as a part-owner. With three sons at Harrow and three daughters at Roedean, she had substantial funds to find for her children's education.

The club had a notorious name as a pick-up place and many disillusioned young men, who had recently returned from the battlefields, made their way there. For a pound or two, the young women who worked in Kate's club offered sympathy and sex. Kate also gloriously ignored the official closing time of 10pm and soon she found herself in court on vice charges. In her defence, she said that the women she employed were bringing comfort to the terribly disfigured young men who had come back from the war. It was to no avail; she was fined for keeping a disorderly house and the club closed.

Not deterred, she opened her own place, the 43, on Gerrard Street in Soho, which soon became a fashionable jazz night club. It attracted as members such artists as Augustus John and writers JB

Priestley and Joseph Conrad. For a time, the club was run respectably, but then Kate once more started ignoring the licensing laws. One of the regulars at her club was American actor Tallulah Bankhead, the Lady Gaga of her day; she smoked over 100 cigarettes a day, drank gin and bourbon like water, kept a suitcase full of drugs, had numerous affairs with men and

The club had a notorious name as a pick-up place and many disillusioned young men, who had recently returned from the battlefields, made their way there

women and used sailor-like language. Other patrons of the club included peers, army officers and rich young businessmen. Again, the law caught up with Kate, who went to prison for six months for selling alcohol without a licence.

Her clients, including the King of Romania and the Crown Prince of Sweden, protested against the sentence, but to no avail.

Kate owned several other nightclubs and also had an interest in a club called the Folies Bergeres in Newman Street, just off Oxford Street. She had become a celebrity in her own right and her fame and her own joy were cemented when one daughter married a baron and another an earl.

But her downfall came when her dealings with a police sergeant called George Goddard came to light. He was earning £6 a week, but lived in a large freehold house in London, had two flashy cars and a couple of safe boxes bulging with money. It turned out Kate had been paying him £100 a week not to raid her clubs. In one of the most notorious cases of police

corruption during that era, Kate was sentenced to 15 months hard labour for bribery and corruption. This came at the time of the Wall Street crash in 1929; the ensuing great depression effectively ended London's libertine nightlife that had flourished during the 1920s.

All the time that Kate spent in Holloway prison had a disastrous effect on her health and she died in 1933 at the comparatively young age of 57, from bronchopneumonia. She died a poor woman, having breezed through £500,000 during her career, paying for lawyers' fees, money for blackmailers, payments to swindlers and other incidentals. Just before she died, she wrote her memoirs, called *Secrets of the 43*, but when the book came out, it was promptly banned. Kate had revealed too many dark secrets of London's elite.

She was buried at Kensal Green cemetery in London. For a well-educated and brought up former pupil of Alexandra, Kate Meyrick had come a long way and fallen even further, a remarkable story indeed.

November 27, 2013

Hugh Oram

An Irishman's Diary

Bohemian Paris in the 1920s was a wonderful place for journalists, who could enjoy the city's non-conformity; the city was awash with vinous and many other libertarian delights. Not only were mainstream newspapers flourishing, but the city at one stage had four English language newspapers and a plethora of literary publishers. The comparison with Dublin was astonishing.

The collapse of the French franc against the US dollar precipitated an influx of Americans to Paris, including many literary figures. Paris became home to the likes of F Scott Fitzgerald, Ernest Hemingway and Ezra Pound. They could live for next to nothing in Paris and while away many hours in the literary cafes of Montparnasse, then the cultural centre of Paris. The seismic shift to the boulevard St Germain came much later.

One noted writer who contributed occasional newspaper pieces was James Joyce, who was paid between $8 and $10 for each piece he wrote for the Paris edition of the *Chicago Tribune*. This paper was by far the most interesting of the three American newspapers in Paris, although after 17 anarchic years, it merged in 1934 with its better-off rival, the Paris version of the *New York Herald*. This was the progenitor of the present day *International New York Times*, still produced in Paris. The third paper, the *Paris Times*, had a far briefer existence. The fourth English language paper in Paris was the *Continental Daily Mail*, founded in 1905.

The Chicago paper had a staff of about 30 and how it managed to survive for so long on such perilous foundations remained a mystery. Cafe life was a constant distraction and its business editor always said that he made the office each day just in time for lunch. On one occasion, F Scott Fitzgerald, who had just arrived at its offices with Zelda his wife, announced that he had just been to a brothel and that he had enjoyed the experience so much that everyone on the staff should try it; most already had.

A young French woman called Louisette managed to have relations with most of the staff of the Chicago paper in Paris and after she died in her 20s, it was said that she had lived herself to death. Staffers working on its newsdesk had a great ability to fashion two columns of text out of a 20-word cable. Inventiveness was everything; the paper also did a Nice edition during the height of the winter season on the Côte d'Azur, and on one occasion, the editor in Nice was

The mainstream Parisian newspapers were also going through a golden age in the 1920s, with the best part of a dozen dailies, the same number then as New York

so short of copy that he simply had the entire edition set in 10 point type.

One man on the Paris newsdesk once took this creative spirit to new heights. The then Prince of Wales was on a visit to a Paris orphanage and Spencer Bull rewrote the handout about the prince's trip. Bull was well under the influence, when he customarily could make no distinction between fact and fantasy. In his rewrite, he had the prince ask a young lad what his name was. "None of your goddamned business, sir," the youth replied, at which the prince seized a riding crop from his equerry and beat the young lad's brains out. Unbelievably, the copy made the front page of the paper next morning, with the banner headline: "Prince of Wales Bashes Boy's Brains Out With Bludgeon". This sense of anarchy was widespread.

When Charles Lindbergh, the American aviator, arrived in Paris in 1927, a young Jean-Paul Sartre pulled off a celebrated hoax when he announced that the flyer was going to get an honorary degree from the École Normale. Some newspapers reported it verbatim.

The mainstream Parisian newspapers were also going through a golden age in the 1920s, with the best part of a dozen dailies, the same number then as New York. The splendidly titled *L'Intransigeant* was very popular, *Paris-Soir* even more so, selling two and a half million copies a day. Yet many of those papers failed to survive the start of the second World War – some didn't even last through the 1930s – and just about the only Parisian paper to still exist from those heady times to the present is *Le Figaro*, then owned by François Coty the perfume magnate.

Like all good times, 1920s Paris couldn't continue and the 1930s were much more sombre for print there. Ironically, another great Irish writer, Samuel Beckett, managed to arrive just as the party was finally ending, at the tail end of the 1930s.

Hugh Oram

An Irishman's Diary

It was the first Wikileaks-style revelation of its kind, creating a worldwide media sensation; it all happened in a Derry newspaper in January, 1946. Five months before, the US had dropped atomic bombs on Hiroshima and Nagasaki in Japan. Then came the front page story in a local paper in Derry, the *Londonderry Sentinel*, that the Soviets were making such advances in nuclear technology that not only were they overtaking the Americans but they were developing much more sophisticated systems than the US, having produced an atomic bomb that was no bigger than a grapefruit.

Sidney Buchanan was the long-standing editor of the *Sentinel* and the source of the scoop of his journalistic career was right on his doorstep, one of his regular contributors. The effect of his front page story was startling.

At the paper's offices, then on Pump Street, in Derry city centre, not far from St Columb's Church of Ireland cathedral, the calls started flooding in from newspapers and news agencies around the world. Newspapers as far away as Australia majored on it. Everyone wanted to know: was the story true? Had the Soviets stolen a march on US atomic weapons? Even the then US president, Harry S Truman, was forced to enter the fray, almost immediately, and he denied its veracity, a sure sign to the man with whom the story had originated that it was in fact perfectly true.

The man responsible for this sensational scoop (no-one ever found out how and where he sourced his incredibly accurate information) was a doctor from west Africa who had been practising in Derry since 1938, Dr Raphael Ernest Grail Armattoe.

During the second World War, Dr Armattoe worked at the civil defence first-aid post in Brooke Park in Derry, then after the war, he opened his own practice in the city. At the time, an African GP or hospital doctor anywhere in Ireland was a rarity, but Dr Armattoe was warmly commended by his many patients, who found him marvellously sympathetic and efficient. Born into a prominent family in west Africa, he had originally gone to Germany to study medicine, but as that country turned Nazi, he moved to France, and then on to Edinburgh, where he qualified. Then he came to Derry, with his wife, Leonie Schwartz, a tall, willowy woman from Switzerland.

In Derry, Dr Armattoe also proved very popular as a speaker on a variety of topics to various societies and organisations. He had an intense intellectual curiosity about an amazing amount of subjects.

One of his many interests were the ancient herbal cures of Co Donegal while another and much wider involvement was decolonisation in Africa. He even found time to write plenty of poetry; some foreshadowed his early death.

The publicity resulting from the newspaper story ensured many more speaking engagements, this time on science in the Soviet Union. He talked about this topic in the Mansion House in Dublin (where he was very friendly with Erwin Schrödinger, the Austrian physicist at the Dublin Institute for Advanced Studies), and as far away as Sweden and the US. Such was Dr Armattoe's reputation that in 1949, members of the Dáil, the Northern Ireland parliament at Stormont and three Westminster MPs from the North, wanted to nominate him on two counts for a Nobel prize, for his scientific research and his dedication to peaceful understanding between nations and races. However, they omitted to forward documentary evidence to back their assertions, so Dr Armattoe didn't even make the shortlist.

Soon afterwards, he became much more interested in the fate of his homeland and left Derry, moving the family home back to west Africa. In 1953, he addressed a United Nations committee in New York on the question of the reunification of the Togoland mandates in west Africa, one British, the other French. Dr Armattoe had been born in Togoland just before the first World War when it was still a German colony. He didn't want the Togoland mandates amalgamated with the Gold Coast, which became Ghana, but that was precisely what happened. On his way back home to West Africa, he stopped off in Dublin to visit his eldest daughter, Irusia, who was in boarding school, and went on to Germany to meet old friends there. He died in hospital in Hamburg on December 21st, 1953, aged just 40. His wife remained convinced he had been poisoned, but by whom was never discovered, although his political enemies in west Africa were suspected.

To this day, however, Dr Armattoe is well remembered in Derry and in 2011, a blue plaque was unveiled by the Ulster History Circle at what was once his home and practice on Northland Road. It was dedicated to the physician, anthropologist and writer from west Africa. His was an extraordinary life story and his revelation about Soviet nuclear advances, made in the *Londonderry Sentinel*, remains one of the best Irish newspaper "scoops" of all time.

The man responsible for this sensational scoop was a doctor from west Africa

February 25, 2014

Hugh Oram

An Irishman's Diary

Ballsbridge, Dublin's embassy belt, once had its very own slum, Turner's Cottages, close to the top of Shelbourne Road and almost opposite the present day Oval development.

Richard Turner, a noted 19th century ironfounder, opened his Hammersmith Works on Pembroke Road in 1834. They made the roof of what is now Pearse station in Westland Row, the great botanical greenhouses at Glasnevin, Belfast and Kew, most of the garden railings in Ballsbridge and did business as far away as Russia.

Today, Hume House is there, while next door, the Number One, Ballsbridge, scheme of luxury apartments and offices is being built on the old veterinary college site.

Turner built a collection of cottages at the back of his site to house his workers and they remained in place for many years after the iron works moved in 1876 to North King Street, on the other side of the city. The cottages weren't demolished until just over 40 years ago, at which stage, there were still close on 20 left. Outsiders, but not the people living there, called it "The Gut".

The cottages each had two large downstairs rooms; most had no kitchens, although in later years some had tiny kitchenettes. People cooked on either a large open fire or on a range. Coal was fetched from a nearby coal yard in prams and stored beneath the stairs. Upstairs, there were two bedrooms, with wrought iron fireplaces and a small box-room, but no lavatory or bathroom. In earlier days, a different family lived in each room, so that one house had four families.

People living there had to queue to use the outside lavatory in the yard and wash themselves in front of the fire in the living room.

Families living in the cottages shared a tap in the yard for water and for washing clothes, which were hung to dry on lines, worked with pulleys that stretched from one side of the small enclave to the other.

Many of the families living here had five or six children, who often went barefoot, so the little street with the cottages was always full of children playing and having fun. When the rag and bone man arrived at Turner's Cottages, children rushed in home to collect any old clothes or bottles, knowing they would be rewarded with a toffee or a plastic ring.

The menfolk worked at menial jobs, including at the Volkswagen assembly factory in the old tram depot on Shelbourne Road, the old bottle factory in Ringsend, at the original Johnston, Mooney & O'Brien bakery in Ballsbridge or in the coal yards that

Some of the women worked in the old Swastika Laundry, just across from the cottages on the other side of Shelbourne Road

then traded in the area.

Some of the women worked in the old Swastika Laundry, just across from the cottages on the other side of Shelbourne Road. A surprising number of families took in boarders to make ends meet.

Despite the lack of facilities, this was a strong working class community, right in the heart of Ballsbridge. Not so long ago, I met a lady called Breda Keogh, who had been brought up in the cottages and was married from there when she was 23. Initially, she and her husband lived in a flat in Sandymount for three years before buying a house on the northside. She recalled that it took her years to get used to living in that part of the city; even in recent times, it still sometimes felt a little strange to her after the neighbourliness of Turner's Cottages.

When the cottages were pulled down, her parents were rehoused in a maisonette in Macken Street, which they hated. Breda's mother died not long after the move and her father died a couple of years later. The residents of Turner's Cottages were scattered all over the city, some to Crumlin and Drimnagh, others to Beech Hill in Donnybrook, so that today, the only time former residents get to meet up is at funerals.

A similar slum once existed in a narrow laneway nearby, beside what is now Mary Mac's pub on Merrion Road. A whole cluster of families lived here in absolute squalor, with water from an outside tap and a communal lavatory. Further along Merrion Road, beside where the RDS sale ground once stood, another group of cottages had similarly deplorable conditions. Today, the headquarters of AIB stands on the site.

It's 90 years since the Germans established the first diplomatic legation in Ballsbridge. These days the area is awash with over 30 suave diplomatic missions; ambassadorial residences, too. Turner's Cottages have long since been airbrushed out of history.

April 25, 2014

Hugh Oram

An Irishman's Diary

Helen Waddell died almost 50 years ago and her status as an Irish literary superstar in the 1930s is almost forgotten, except in certain academic circles, yet she had an extraordinary mind and career to match.

Her origins were truly exotic. She was born in Tokyo in 1889; her father was a Presbyterian missionary. Tokyo in those far-off days was largely undeveloped, long before it became a metropolis. Many traditional aspects of Japanese life had an indelible effect on her.

She spent the first 11 years of her life in Tokyo before the family returned to Belfast, where her mother died shortly afterwards. Her father remarried, but he too soon died and Waddell found herself in the care of her stepmother.

At school in Belfast and at the then small and nascent Queen's University, her literary and social abilities were quickly noticed.

But life during Helen's 20s was largely fallow as she looked after her stepmother at their modest home in north Belfast, a far cry from the exotica of Tokyo.

Her stepmother Martha was a domestic tyrant, besides becoming a secret whiskey addict. It wasn't until Martha died in 1920 that Helen was able to escape this stultifying home atmosphere.

By the time she went up to Oxford at the age of 31, her hair was already streaked white. But her immense skills in medieval studies were soon apparent, heightened by the two years she spent in Paris in the mid-1920s.

Her lectures at Oxford and elsewhere drew audiences that today would almost compare with rock-star status.

After Paris, she settled in London, which she loved, although she made frequent trips home to see her family in Co Down, except during the second World War.

She worked for a noted London publisher, Constable, which also published her works. She also had a long affair with the elderly Otto Kyllmann, the chairman at Constable. She had many suitors, but never married.

Her first big literary success was *The Wandering Scholars*, in 1927, a study of the medieval goliards, devoted to conviviali-ty, licence and the writing of ribald and satirical songs in Latin. In 1933, her only novel, *Peter Abelard*, the medieval love story of Abelard and Heloise, was published and it was an incredible success, with 15 printings in its first year. It also made her a lot of money and she defied her many friends, one of whom warned her that a writer should never buy a house. Helen did just that, at Primrose Hill Road, close to Hampstead in north London.

With the publication of *Peter Abelard*, Helen Waddell, who already knew most of the then

Waddell's immense skills in medieval studies were soon apparent

current literary "greats", was propelled into mega-stardom, just like any top selling chick-lit author today, except Helen's work was grounded in intense academic research. Her closest friend on the literary circuit was AE, George Russell, a fellow Northerner, from Lurgan.

The then prime minister, Stanley Baldwin, became a firm friend, introducing her to another fan, Queen Mary, wife of the king.

Yet this hectic upper-class social whirl, as well as increasing domestic concerns, helped dull her literary output. Although her literary output was substantial, many of the books she planned remained unwritten.

Living in London during the second World War was a recipe for chaos, and when a bomb fell on her house later in the war, the damage it caused took several years to put right.

But in 1942 she took part in a protest against the death sentence imposed on six young IRA men in Belfast who had shot dead RUC policeman Patrick Murphy, Catholic and father of nine children.

She wrote a letter to the London *Times* pleading clemency. In the end, the leader of the six was the only one hanged.

By the end of the war, her career was beginning to fade, along with her fine literary skills and her extraordinary understanding of religion, including Catholicism. By the time she was 60, she was starting to develop dementia. She died in 1965, at the age of 76, by which time it had totally engulfed her.

Although she died in London, she was buried close to Banbridge, Co Down, in the graveyard of the church with which her family had many connections and near the home of her sister, Meg, to whom she had been particularly close.

Waddell's life had been one of immense literary erudition and great writing skills, but today, her best-selling works about the medieval world are no longer fashionable.

June 17, 2014

Hugh Oram

An Irishman's Diary

A century ago, Dundrum, in south Dublin, had a mere 500 inhabitants. Today, it has the largest shopping centre in Ireland.

Some of its old facilities have been remade, especially the former railway line from Harcourt Street station to Bray, which closed down nearly 56 years ago. Open for just over 10 years now, the Luas Green line tracks most of its route, as far as Brides Glen, and the old station at Dundrum has been turned into a busy commuter stop.

The old, small railway bridge at Dundrum has been transformed into the vast crossing of the new bridge, named after William Dargan, the railway pioneer.

Dundrum also once had an Odeon cinema, subsequently changed into the Apollo, closed down 47 years ago. Apart from films, it often presented live shows by local artistes; these days, the venue for live performances is the Mill Theatre in the Dundrum Town Centre.

When the brand new Odeon opened its doors in 1942, it had underground parking for 500 bicycles, then the favoured mode of transport for most people. The enthusiasm for bicycles has come full cycle, helped by Daly's long-established bicycle shop by the Luas bridge in Dundrum. The local cinema-going tradition is continued by movies@dundrum, in the Dundrum Town Centre.

The whole area was once characterised by big houses, set in spacious grounds, but most of them were replaced by housing developments from the 1960s onwards. Today, one of the few big old houses still surviving is Airfield at Dundrum. The wealthy Overend sisters, Letitia and Naomi, lived there for years and kept a working farm, renowned for its Jersey milk in green-topped bottles.

Today, their house has been meticulously restored and one of the delights there for visitors are old copies of *The Irish Times* going back over 60 years. The farm has the only local dairy left out of 30.

Letitia Overend had a 1927 Rolls-Royce and she had a habit of gaily parking it any which way in the Main Street when she went shopping. In those days, traffic wardens were unimagined. Now, her Rolls-Royce, together with the sisters' other two cars, are immaculately preserved in the garage at Airfield.

She went shopping in the likes of Findlater's and Leverett & Frye, but those old grocery shops, with counter service and much chat, have long since disappeared. Today, Main Street in Dundrum, which can be politely described as an architectural melange, has one remaining traditional

Letitia Overend had a 1927 Rolls-Royce and she had a habit of gaily parking it any which way in the Main Street when she went shopping

shop. It's Campbell's Corner, run by the genial Paul Campbell; the family has been doing shoe repairs there since 1900. His son, also Paul, has his shoe business, in Enniscorthy, Co Wexford. Mulvey's Pharmacy, too, has long antecedents in the village.

Old factories vanished years ago. The Manor Mill Laundry closed down in 1942 and its premises were taken over by Pye, which for over 40 years was the biggest employer in Dundrum. One renowned employee was Albert Reynolds, who got a job there as a cabinet polisher, something he replicated in later life when he became taoiseach. But in those days, trade union membership was mandatory to work in Pye. Albert Reynolds's tenure was brief, since it turned out he didn't after all belong to a union.

After Pye came the renowned Dundrum Bowl, also short lived. Following lengthy tribunal inquiries, the land was eventually used for the Dundrum Town Centre. Its construction started in 2001; next March will see the 10th anniversary of its opening.

Dundrum has also had some memorable residents, including the late Seán Mac Réamoinn, of RTÉ and Cumann Merriman.

Once, in his later years, he declared that he was like the census: "broken down by age, sex and religion".

A noted and highly controversial writer, Francis Stuart, lived for years at Windy Arbour, just down the road from Dundrum, and after he died, in Co Clare, in February 2000, *The Irish Times* published an extraordinary front-page photograph of him taken on his deathbed.

The present Dundrum may bear little resemblance to the once small country village to which well-off people from Dublin repaired for the fresh mountainy air and goat's milk.

But you can still travel to and from Dublin city centre and Dundrum by Luas, rather than by steam train, in just under 15 minutes.

August 20, 2014

Hugh Oram

An Irishman's Diary

Dr John Fleetwood is well remembered for his many radio and television appearances; he also happened to be a very popular and well-liked GP in Blackrock, Co Dublin. He had a great gift for combining two careers, one in medicine, the other in the media.

He was born in Edinburgh in 1917, into a well-established Scottish medical family. From Edinburgh, he and his family moved to Plymouth. When he was in his early teens, the family moved to Ireland and he went to Presentation College Bray, progressing to Blackrock College.

Then at 21, when he was studying medicine at UCD, Radio Éireann put on an elaborate programme for rag week and John Fleetwood was in his element. For presenting a 30-minute show, he was paid the grand sum of four guineas.

Cricket

He also wanted to become a cricket commentator on the Dublin station, but one was already in place. Another opportunity presented itself, a competition for contributors to the *Question Time* programme. The trainee doctor was successful, at the age of 21, and a radio career began, lasting for 60 years.

Graduating from UCD in 1941, he became a medical officer in the Local Defence Force, during the Emergency, as well as holding other positions, such as assistant master in the Coombe hospital.

From 1944 to 1947, he worked in Dr O'Grady's practice in Donnybrook, before starting his own practice in Proby Square, Blackrock. One of his four children, John jnr, eventually joined him in the practice, then took it over when his father retired. Today, he is part of the Carysfort Clinic, still in Proby Square.

In his younger days, when Dr Fleetwood snr was doing house calls, if he was in the Sandycove area, he had a habit of taking a little time off for a "dip in the nip" at the Forty Foot.

If he was accompanied by a male medical student, he'd ask them if they wanted to join him – all rather unorthodox for a GP!

In later life, Dr Fleetwood became well-known for his many *Sunday Miscellany* pieces on RTÉ Radio 1. His mischievous sense of humour was never far distant.

Recently, when I was reading one of his scripts in the Fleetwood collection of papers in the Royal College of Physicians of Ireland, it was hard to suppress my laughter. The good doctor and his family were holidaying in a remote

■ John Fleetwood became a medical officer in the Local Defence Force, during the Emergency

At 21, when he was studying medicine at UCD, Radio Éireann put on an elaborate programme for rag week and John Fleetwood was in his element

rural house in Normandy when the drainage system seized up. The owner sent for a local tradesman, who happened to be called Jean-Paul Sartre, a source of much amusement for Dr Fleetwood. But said tradesman managed to blow up the whole system, and as Dr Fleetwood so graphically described, *merde* was flung everywhere in the house, even the ceiling.

He often appeared on the *Late Late Show* on television and Gay Byrne recalls that he was very popular with viewers. Dr Fleetwood often demonstrated the Heimlich manoeuvre, to clear the airways of someone who is choking.

Gay Byrne and his wife Kathleen say that even now people come up to them and say that the advice of Dr Fleetwood had saved a loved one's life.

Dr Fleetwood also wrote extensively, including a number of books, on such subjects as the history of medicine in Ireland and the Irish body snatchers. He also liked to travel a lot and he and his wife Ann O'Connor – they were together for 55 years –

made a pioneering trip to the Soviet Union in 1961. Everywhere he travelled, he shot 8mm colour film.

When RTÉ was doing a television series a decade ago on home movies, Dr Fleetwood's collection made one of the programmes.

Versatility

His versatility and innovation, both in medicine and the media, knew no bounds and having met him on several occasions in the RTÉ Radio Centre, I can testify to his avuncular approach to life.

His wife predeceased him by five years and he died in 2007, leaving four children and 12 grandchildren.

At the time, one of his granddaughters was studying medicine, making her the fifth generation of medics in the Fleetwood family. One of his passions had been care for the elderly, at a time when the subject was barely considered. He was a cofounder of the Irish Gerontological Society in 1950 and he became an international voice for healthy and active ageing. When he died, he was in his 91st year.

December 30, 2014

Hugh Oram

An Irishman's Diary

Another aspect of Dublin's heritage is about to disappear but will anyone really bother when the perjorative D4 is turned into DO4, which doesn't have quite the same ring to it. Dublin's postal districts will be transformed into new sets of letters and numerals with the imminent new postcodes, which will also give individual addresses their own alphanumeric "identity". The old postal district numbers will form the basis of the first part of these new postcodes. But nowadays, when hardly anyone writes personal letters any more, will many people take notice of the nationwide switchover?

The postal districts in Dublin date back to 1917, when they were also introduced in cross-channel cities. Postal districts had started in London in 1857, but it took 60 years for them to reach Dublin.

But before postal districts took shape here, the daily postal service was little short of miraculous, with up to six collections and an equal number of deliveries daily. In the days when the postcard was the equivalent of today's email, people in Dublin could write to other addresses in the city and the note would be delivered the same day, very handy for dinner parties and soirées among the better-off.

The idea of postcodes has also been slow to take off; they began in England in 1959 and they've been used in Northern Ireland for the past 40 years. There, the BT part of the postcode was extended from Belfast to include every northern address.

This part of Ireland has remained the last bastion of the old postal districts of Europe, a distinction that's soon going to disappear, as the postcode project, something like 10 years in gestation, comes to fruition. The only quick thing that happened was when the pillar boxes were painted green, almost overnight, in 1922. The then new British postal districts were retained.

Postal districts were centred first on the heart of Dublin and as the city expanded, so too did the postal districts. In most cases, districts north of the river Liffey got odd numbers while those on the southside got even numbers, another case of southside one-upmanship!

One of the two exceptions to this rule are the Phoenix Park and Áras an Uachtaráin, which are in Dublin 8. There's a practical explanation for this anomaly. After the post office and sorting office in James's Street were built in 1892, it began delivering the mail for the vice-regal lodge in the Phoenix park, since it was much more convenient than the old Phibsboro sorting office. So the park and the Áras got roped into Dublin 8, just as Chapelizod village, north of the Liffey, is in Dublin 20. This means that just two of Dublin's 24 postal districts span the Liffey.

Mind you, the public in Dublin didn't start using postal district numbers until 1961, as reflected in the old green street nameplates. Only the new blue ones started using district numbers. As Dublin grew in the 1970s, some districts were split, with Dublin 5 retaining its nomenclature for that part of the district nearest the sea, while its inland area became Dublin 17. Then west Dublin was divided into two new postal districts, Dublin 22 and Dublin 24. Parts of Co Dublin managed to escape altogether; places like Dún Laoghaire, Blackrock, Lucan and Swords have survived thus far without having numbered postal districts. Other parts, previously in Co Dublin, such as Firhouse, Knocklyon and Tallaght, had numbers stuck on them. Foxrock became Dublin 18.

The really big split – and the huge rows – came in 1985, 30 years ago, when Kimmage, Templeogue, Terenure and parts of Rathgar became Dublin 6W rather than plain old D6. Many residents were affronted, afraid that their houses would lose value. An Post had come up with another solution; instead of Dublin 6W, they could introduce Dublin 26. But this had created even more furore as snobbish elements considered this too close to Dublin 24, otherwise known as Tallaght. So Dublin 6W came to be accepted, reluctantly.

One other city is also about to lose its postal districts, Cork, but these are only for internal postal use; they've never been used by the public. Cork city centre is actually Cork 1, while Douglas is Cork 2 and Wilton, Cork 4.

Dublin's postal districts managed to remain a secret to the public for 44 years but Corkonians, naturally, have gone one better. This time round, I suspect that the change over will scarcely raise a murmur, even from the D4 diehards in Ballsbridge, but then, who sends a letter these days except for business purposes?

■ Westmoreland Street, Dublin 2.

PHOTOGRAPH: PETER THURSFIELD

Before postal districts took shape here, the daily postal service was little short of miraculous, with up to six collections and an equal number of deliveries daily

March 16, 2015

Hugh Oram

An Irishman's Diary

It is not every day that a contributor to *An Irishman's Diary* has a special train laid on for him and what's more, is given a pass to travel in the driver's cab.

But that's what happened to me recently, when Irish Rail allowed me to travel on an out-of-service train between Connolly and Heuston stations in Dublin to see the Phoenix Park rail tunnel. Two other tunnels on the rail system are longer but an intense mythology has grown up around the one that runs beneath the Phoenix Park.

The tunnel's construction started in 1875 and was the result of intense rivalry between two privately-owned railway companies, the Great Southern & Western and the Midland Great Western. The former operated from Kingsbridge, now Heuston, but didn't have access to the North Wall, which was controlled by the latter company.

So the Great Southern & Western built the tunnel under the Phoenix Park in just over two years. Building work uncovered an unusual find, the remains of about 35 Vikings, mostly male warriors, complete with swords, shields and spears. Despite that, the tunnel was built in far less time than it took to build the admittedly longer Dublin Port tunnel, with far less controversy.

Victorian

It runs for just over 700m under the Phoenix Park and it is a mark of Victorian construction solidity that the brick-lined tunnel is still in excellent shape. The tunnel has two parallel railway lines, so that trains going in each direction can pass each other. It's well-lit and an additional feature is the number of recesses built into the walls, every 10m on both sides of the tunnel, so that if a train approaches, a railway worker in the tunnel can step in to safety.

During the second World War, the tunnel was used to store food supplies, so it became a gigantic larder, just as over-ground, in the Phoenix Park, great stacks of turf were built.

Since then, the tunnel has continued in use, including for GAA specials taking fans to Croke Park for all-Ireland finals. Hassard Stacpoole has an encyclopedic knowledge of the historical workings of the Irish railway system; he is a son of George Stacpoole, the noted Limerick antiques' dealer. Hassard himself now works in London.

He says that scheduled passenger services ran through the tunnel until June 2001. On Sundays, there was even a late afternoon service from Galway to Dundalk and an evening one from Limerick to Drogheda.

A train enters the tunnel at Heuston Station, going under the Phoenix Park. PHOTOGRAPH: BRENDA FITZSIMONS

Two other tunnels are longer but an intense mythology has grown up around the one that runs beneath the Phoenix Park

Up to the 1980s, the tunnel was used for daily mailboat services between Dún Laoghaire and Heuston. Even earlier, around 65 years ago, the tunnel facilitated through trains from Cork via Dublin to Belfast, although it seems most unlikely that those will be revived.

Out-of-service

In recent years, the tunnel has been used mostly for out-of-service trains travelling between Connolly and Heuston and from time-to-time, by excursion trains, including those GAA "specials".

It was on an out-of-service train that I made my recent trip, in the company of Jim Evans, the driver, and John Magee, a district traction executive.

On the way there, after Connolly, the train sidled past Croke Park, through Drumcondra station, until it reached Glasnevin junction.

There, trains turn one way for Maynooth and Sligo, the other way for Heuston, through the tunnel.

When the train returned from Heuston, as it approached the tunnel mouth under Conyngham Road, I could see in the spring sunshine the Wellington Monument perched almost above the tunnel. It also runs beneath Garda headquarters.

From mid-2016, four trains an hour at peak periods are set to run from the Kildare direction through to Grand Canal Dock, catering for the growing numbers of commuters from Co Kildare. Off-peak, there will be one train an hour through the tunnel. The service won't start until signalling work has been completed, so the exact start date hasn't been announced.

The tunnel at Bray Head at 1,000m is longer than that in the Phoenix Park. Longest of all is the tunnel that burrows for just over 1,200m beneath Cork's northside and in to Kent station. That is almost twice the length of the Phoenix Park masterpiece.

There's also the Gogginstown tunnel beneath Ballinhassig, just south of Cork city. It was once part of the old West Cork Railway system but has been closed since 1961. With permission from the landowner, it's perfectly possible to walk through this deserted 828m tunnel.

Hugh Oram

An Irishman's Diary

Two misconceptions persist about Sir Edwin Landseer Lutyens, that he was the quintessential British architect of the early 20th century and that he was an architect of empire. Both conceal two statements of fact: Lutyens's mother, to whom he was very close, was Irish, and he also left a fairly substantial body of work here in Ireland. Lutyens's mother was Margaret Theresa Gallwey, called Mary all her life. She was born in Ballincollig, Cork, in 1833; her family came from Killarney. Her father Michael was an RIC officer. Mary went on to marry Charles Lutyens in Montreal in 1852. She was the sister of a brother officer of Charles. They went on to have 13 children; Edwin was the 10th, but as a result of the

rheumatic fever he suffered as a child, he was the only one of the Lutyens boys who never went to public school or university. He had some education at art school, but managed to set up his own architectural practice in 1888, when he was 19.

Lutyens, usually called Ned, never lost his youthful shyness, but had a reputation as the perfect party guest, always high spirited and witty. He had many Irish friends, including Gogarty, Lavery and Orpen. He made up his own word for the fun he enjoyed – "vivreations". He was also a keen spectator at the Tailteann Games in Dublin in 1924.

His marriage was far from successful, although it produced five children. In 1897, he married Emily, daughter of the

first Earl of Lytton, but almost from the start, the marriage was very unsatisfactory. Emily went on to show much more interest in eastern religions, slightly ironic in view of Lutyens's work in India.

His design style at first reflected the Arts & Crafts movement, then it became more classical, as his work moved from designing private residences to large-scale public edifices. Among his works here, he designed a new wing for Howth Castle in 1910/11, including a library and chapel. At the same time, he carried out a major upgrade of the 16th-century castle on Lambay Island, off the north Co Dublin coast. The island had been recently bought by Cecil Baring of the famous banking family; the bank itself collapsed in spectacular fashion 20 years ago. The island's present owner is Alex Baring, the seventh Baron Revelstoke, who has plans to turn the castle into a holiday destination.

In his earlier years, Lutyens had a great propensity for attracting wealthy clients. Another of his Irish designs was a substantial holiday home near Downings in north Co

■ Sir Edwin Lutyens: strong associations with Ireland

Lutyens, usually called Ned, never lost his youthful shyness, but had a reputation as the perfect party guest, always high spirited and witty

Donegal, Tranarossan House, for the Hon Mrs Phillimore. Yet another titled client was Sir E Hucheson Poe, for whom Lutyens designed the Italianate Heywood gardens in what is now Co Laois. For this, he used 10 salvaged capitals from the Commons chamber in the old Irish parliament at College Green. He worked with his great collaborator, Gertrude Jekyll, a noted garden designer of the time. Today, the gardens are owned and managed by the OPW, although Heywood House itself is long gone.

Lutyens also transformed a fishing lodge at Casla in Connemara into a villa, to which the owner, Joseph Bruce Ismay, chairman of the White Star Line, retreated after the *Titanic* disaster in 1912. Again, Gertrude Jekyll created the gardens. Ismay lived in the villa until his death in 1939. The great architect also did one piece of church work in Ireland, an altar and frame at St Patrick's church on Upper Donegall Street, Belfast. The triptych was created by Lavery.

These days, Lutyens is well remembered for his two designs for a municipal art

gallery in Dublin to house the Lane collection. One design was for a gallery suspended over the Liffey, while the other was for a gallery on part of the park in St Stephen's Green, opposite the Royal College of Surgeons. Both plans were rejected. Eventually, 20 years later, the the municipal gallery opened at Charlemont House on Parnell Square. Lutyens's work in designing the war memorial gardens at Islandbridge is also well recorded, commemorating those from Ireland who had died while serving during the first World War. He worked on this with TJ Byrne, chief architect of the OPW, and the gardens opened in 1940.

Outside Ireland, Lutyens is highly regarded for such monumental works as the Cenotaph in Whitehall, London, and his work in New Dehli. Construction of his spectacular design for a new Catholic cathedral in Liverpool was abandoned in 1941. Lutyens died in 1944. Part of his legacy is his work in Ireland, despite the failure of his plans for a new municipal gallery in Dublin, and it's all a tribute to his own Irish heritage.

April 7, 2015

Hugh Oram

An Irishman's Diary

Trinity College Dublin, has had a remarkable tradition of cultivating plants going back 328 years, first in the college grounds, then at Lansdowne Road in Ballsbridge, and for nearly 50 years now, at Dartry.

The college began with a physic garden in 1687, showing the then close link between plants and medicine.

The physic garden was considered essential for medical education. A new physic garden established in 1722 had some 500 species, many foreign.

Towards the end of the 18th century Trinity had a site at Harold's Cross, but this was short-lived. By 1806, Trinity had abandoned its college-based physic garden in favour of a new site in the then largely rural district of Ballsbridge. However, a new physic garden was opened on Trinity's main campus in 2011.

The RDS bought a large site in Glasnevin in 1795 for a botanic garden – now the National Botanic Gardens – and Trinity settled into a much smaller site at Ballsbridge, which it acquired on a 175-year lease.

Collection

By 1807, it had enclosed 1.2 ha with a 3m-high wall along Shelbourne Road.

In 1832, a further piece of land was added along Pembroke Road, while in 1848, an additional plot was secured in Lansdowne Road.

A screen of *Quercus Ilex* trees was planted inside the railings along Lansdowne Road and many of them are still there today. The first curator at Ballsbridge was James Townsend Mackay, who stayed in the job for some 60 years; his arrival coincided with Trinity changing from regarding plants as *materia medica* to "pure" botany. (*Materia medica* explores the therapeutic properties of any substance, particularly plants.) Mackay's 600-page *Flora Hibernica* was the first flora of Ireland.

A remarkable collection of Trinity people were connected with the Lansdowne Road botanic garden, including in the last century Prof Walter Starkie. He became Trinity's first professor of Spanish in 1926, and was also an authority on gipsy life. He lived in Botanic House in the Ballsbridge garden and died as recently as 1976.

But from the 1830s onwards, the limitations of the Ballsbridge site were obvious. In the early years of that decade Richard Turner established his Hammersmith Works next door and fumes from the ironworks constantly drifted over the botanic garden.

Ironically, it was at the Hammersmith Works that the

■ In 1968, Trinity College's botanic garden moved from Ballsbridge to Dartry in Dublin 6.

> By 1806, Trinity had abandoned its college-based physic garden in favour of a new site in the then largely rural district of Ballsbridge

great glasshouses were created for the botanic gardens at Glasnevin, Belfast and Kew in London.

Trinity began disposing of the Ballsbridge site, piece by piece, between 1942 and 1965.

Redwood

Hotels cropped up on part of the garden site. What was the Intercontinental Hotel, became Jurys and is now the Ballsbridge Hotel. Then came the old Berkeley Court Hotel, now the Clyde Court Hotel.

The Ballsbridge Hotel still has a giant Californian redwood in its grounds, another relic of the old botanic garden.

By 1968, Trinity's botanic garden had moved to Dartry and many important plants were transferred there. The site is now partially bounded by Trinity's new halls of residence.

Unlike the old Lansdowne Road site, Trinity owns the one in Dartry, a big advantage. It's a delightful place, with some 1,000 plant species as well as between 100 and 200 species of trees and shrubs, from Ireland and other parts of the world. It includes a wonderfully peaceful arboretum, as well as beehives, experimental ponds and a collection of greenhouses, all under the supervision of Steve Waldren, the curator and administrator. The current director of Trinity's botanic garden is Prof John Parnell. The Dartry botanic garden has built up a fine reputation for plant conservation work, as well as a range of plant-related research projects. The garden also hosts classes in art, gardening and wood carving as part of its outreach programme.

When I was in Dartry the other day, I met one of the residents of the botanic garden, Fluffy, a very large and delightful black cat. Steve explained that about 10 years ago, someone left a bag of four kittens at the entrance to the garden; two of the cats are still in residence, gainfully employed in rodent control. This wonderful collection of plants, shrubs and trees from many countries continues a masterly tradition of cultivation in Trinity.

Among donations in recent years was a tree fern from Australia, presented by the Royal Botanic Garden in Sydney for Trinity's quatercentenary.

June 30, 2015

Hugh Oram

An Irishman's Diary

It seems scarcely credible these days, but once Tallaght was a small and somnolent village with a strong rural flavour set in a mainly farming hinterland.

All has changed, and changed utterly, since a British town planning expert, Myles Wright, began work in 1964 on his plans for the development of the greater Dublin area. Three years later, his report was published, in which he recommended the expansion of Tallaght, as well as Blanchardstown, Clondalkin and Lucan. He envisaged a population for Tallaght of 136,000.

In 1972, his report was adopted for the Co Dublin development plan and work began on creating the new suburb.

Until then, Tallaght had been a village with little more than the Main Street, a staging place on the way to Blessington. In the late 18th and early 19th centuries, a number of mills had been built along the nearby banks of the river Dodder, for making flour and paper.

Old Bawn

The townland of Tallaght covers 425 hectares. The 19th-century village centred on the Main Street, with such features as St Maelruain's 1829 Church of Ireland, a post office and little else.

Another smaller townland was that of Old Bawn, about half the size of Tallaght and even more rural.

Around 1850, the whole area had nine forges and seven pubs, one of them in Tallaght village. Old Bawn, like Tallaght itself, developed into a small village; in the mid-19th century, Old Bawn village had about 400 inhabitants.

Steam tram

Housing in the area consisted of about 140 mud cabins, over 300 cottages, more than 200 farmhouses and close on 50 more solid houses, occupied by better-off people. The first modern-age development came in 1888, when the steam tram service began, from Terenure to Blessington, before it was extended to Poulaphouca seven years later. The tram track ran through Tallaght village, beside the footpath. That footpath on the Main Street was lined by a row of small, sedate houses that opened right onto the street, and the tramway, with the occasional shop.

The arrival of the tram encouraged people in the area to do their shopping either in Terenure or Dublin city centre so the shopkeeper class never developed in the old Tallaght village. The tram managed to keep going as far as Blessington until 1932. The Poulaphouca section had closed in 1927.

■ St Maelruain's Church, Tallaght.
PHOTOGRAPH: LAWRENCE COLLECTION/NLI

Tallaght, a city in everything but name, bears no resemblance at all to the village that was buried beneath all the developments of the past 40 years

After the tram closure, most people depended on ponies and traps, bicycles, walking and the occasional bus to get around; cars were rare.

All the mills along the Dodder had closed down by the mid-19th century. At about the same time that the mills vanished, Irish died out as an everyday language in the district.

It took until 1924 for the Tallaght area to get its first major factory, Urney's the chocolate makers. But during the 1920s, the 1930s and the 1940s, if any work was available in the Tallaght area, it was mostly on farms.

While shopping in the old Tallaght village was limited, so too were the possibilities for entertainment.

Beyond Doyle's Hall, which eventually became a snooker hall, Molloy's pub and house dances, people had little opportunity for entertainment. It wasn't until the 1960s that the Embankment pub became popular for ballads.

Apart from the farm workers and their families in Tallaght, the area also had strong artistic connections. Katharine Tynan, the novelist and poet, lived in Tallaght, and WB Yeats often stayed with her.

Handel

In the spring of 1742, when Handel was in Dublin prior to the first performance of the *Messiah*, he stayed in Abbey Street, but it isn't so well known that he also went to stay in Tallaght, to recover from the excesses of food and drink he'd been enjoying in the city centre.

Tallaght was also known for Malachi Horan, who died in 1945, aged 98. He lived all his life on Killinarden Hill, in an entirely rural district, and when a local GP made notes of all his stories. The resulting book, at the end of his life, became a unique record of Tallaght's old way of life, three decades before it started to disappear for ever.

Some historical places still survive in Tallaght, such as St Mary's Priory, and vestiges of the old village can be seen along the Main Street. But these days, the modern Tallaght, a city in everything but name, bears no resemblance at all to the village that was buried beneath all the developments of the past 40 years.

August 7, 2015

Hugh Oram

An Irishman's Diary

Walking through a green area in Irishtown the other day, warm and sunny, a mere six kilometres from the city centre, I got an entirely new perspective on the southside of Dublin Bay. I could see the whole sweep of the bay, from the start of Sandymount to Dún Laoghaire, with the Dublin Mountains as a distant backdrop.

I was exploring the Irishtown Nature Park, which is on the southside of the Poolbeg peninsula. The main track through the park skirts the coastline, looking out over Sandymount Strand, with its fast-moving tides, while several more minor paths criss-cross the hilly uplands of the park, which rises quite steeply.

Along those more minor paths, trees and vegetation have grown profusely and it is easy to imagine being in the depths of the country, except for the low hum of machinery being used elsewhere on the peninsula. Just at the back of the park, you can see the incinerator being built, a highly contentious issue in Sandymount and Irishtown. You'll also see the wastewater plant close by, while two sentinels stand guard, the now disused chimneys that were once part of the old Poolbeg ESB generating station, their red and white paint fading away.

The whole genesis of the park seemed implausible. During a short-lived building boom in Dublin between 1972 and 1975, much rubble from construction sites was dumped here, while much of the Irishtown end of the strand was also used as a rubbish dump. Turning the huge mound of building rubble into a nature park seemed an unlikely idea, and when the Sandymount and Merrion Residents Association met with officials of the old Dublin Corporation in the mid-1970s, scepticism prevailed. Lorna Kelly, who has been closely involved with the association since it was reborn in 1963 from what had been the Sandymount Residents Association, says that one person in the Corporation was particularly supportive, Frank Feely, who went on to become city manager and who retired in 1996.

Jim Shannon, the then parks superintendent, also warmed to the idea. Some of the initial plans for the park included a boating lake and an area for tennis and basketball, but these never happened. Today, a number of wooden seats along the main path are the only artificial creations. One of those benches has an apposite slogan carved into it: "The trail is beautiful, be still."

When development of the park started in the 1980s, lots of trees were planted as well as seeds and the Corporation's efforts were helped by many local residents who also planted seeds. Today, says Lorna Kelly, the park has over 200 plant species. Some weren't native; tail grass, with its fluffy seed heads, came in via the nearby Dublin port. The park also has areas of grassland and scrub and all kinds of fungi.

It also has many species of sea and shore birds, butterflies, too. The park is an ideal habitat for the wren, commemorated in Sandymount by the St Stephen's Day wren boy festivities. Other birds here can include skylarks and linnets, dunnocks and stonechats and I spotted a heron just offshore. Brent geese winter in a two-hectare area of grassland close to the park.

Walking the main trail gives an entirely new way of looking at this side of Dublin Bay, much more revealing than what you can see from the walkway beside Strand Road, seen by some as being over-sanitised, a phrase that could never be used about Irishtown Nature Park. The walk through the park can be continued to the Great South Wall, as far as the Poolbeg lighthouse.

The tracks are meant for pedestrians and when I was walking the main path the other day, I passed by a young woman walking barefoot along the path despite its stones. Bikes can be a problem; local residents say that the park should be solely for pedestrians, runners and joggers.

One south-facing part of the hillside even looks like a discarded vineyard and it got me thinking. The northeast of France has over 300 huge mountains of slag from disused coal mines and viticulture has started, with grapes growing on the less than fertile soil. Perhaps one day, we could see an Irishtown appellation?

Strangely enough, there's another natural park with exactly the same name in New Brunswick in eastern Canada. It's vastly larger, with nearly 900 hectares of forests and 100 hectares of lakes; perhaps a little twinning would be in order?

In the meantime, Irishtown Nature Park remains fiercely cosseted by local people who enjoy walking its trails and a delightful green oasis waiting to be explored by those who don't know it.

The Pigeon House, Ringsend, and Irishtown Nature Park.
PHOTOGRAPH: CYRIL BYRNE

Turning the huge mound of rubble into a nature park seemed an unlikely idea but today it is home to over 200 plant species

September 8, 2015

Hugh Oram

An Irishman's Diary

For decades, the subject was taboo, but these days, fortunately, opinions toward remembering the Irish military contribution to the first World War are more open. Memorials to the fallen in Catholic churches in Dublin have become less hidden away.

Michael Pegum is an historian, whose website, irishwarmemorials.ie, has been listing the sites of war memorials around the country since 2004. He explains that seeing the graves in France of his maternal grandfather and a distant cousin, both of whom died serving in the first World War, inspired him to create his website. His book on the war memorials in the Kildare Street and University club on St Stephen's Green, *Our Fallen Members*, is due to be published in November. He says that the change in political circumstances after 1916 is only partially to blame for the absence of memorials in Catholic churches; they have had little tradition of such memorials.

But in much more recent times, memorials have included the one unveiled last year outside St Patrick's Church in Ringsend, to Joseph Pierce Murphy, the first Irishman to die in the Great War, aboard HMS *Amphion* on August 6th, 1914, aged 25. The other Ringsenders who died at sea during that war are also remembered.

The largest of all such first World War memorials, the only communal one in a Catholic church in Dublin, is that in St Mary's in Haddington Road, which lists 93 names, many of them privates, but others of more exalted ranks. At its foot, it has a neat row of red poppies.

Many served in the Royal Dublin Fusiliers. It includes some officers who were members of the Royal Army Medical Corps, and one woman, Iza Mahony, who was a voluntary nurse on hospital ships. The best-known name on the list is that of Thomas Kettle, the Nationalist MP and poet, who served in the Royal Dublin Fusiliers. When a statue of him was put up on St Stephen's Green in the 1930s, no mention was made of his war service. Also listed is Thomas Doyle, lost on the RMS *Leinster* in 1918.

Most of the people listed had local connections, but the memorial doesn't include Lieut Alan Ramsay, who was the first Dublin-born British army officer to die during the Easter Rising, in the battle for the South Dublin Union, now St James's Hospital. His father, Daniel, was the owner of the Royal Nurseries in Ballsbridge. Subsequently, the Irish Hospitals Sweepstakes head-

■ The memorial in St Mary's in Haddington Road lists the names of 93 people. Many served in the Dublin Fusiliers.

Memorials to the fallen in Catholic churches in Dublin have become less hidden away

quarters was built on the site.

Neither does the memorial commemorate soldiers who were killed in the nearby battle of Mount Street Bridge, although there's another, much smaller, memorial in St Mary's, that commemorates Charles Hachette Hyland, a 29-year-old dentist who lived at Percy Place. His father was manager of the Gaiety Theatre for many decades. But Charles, who had been unscathed while helping the wounded during the battle, was killed later that week by a stray bullet as he stood at the back door of his house.

St Andrew's in Westland Row has memorial tablets. Dermot McCarthy of that parish notes that many young men from the locality fought and died in the first World War.

Some were officers, the sons of prominent local families and educated in Catholic schools in England.

Other Catholic churches in the Dublin have first World War memorials that are dedicated to a single fallen soldier, such as St Teresa's in Clarendon Street, the Star of the Sea church in Sandymount and St Brigid's church in Cabinteely. The Church of the Visitation in Fairview records five names, while the Church of the Holy Name in Ranelagh records two members of the French family who died on war service. St Mochta's in Porterstown, Clonsilla, records Robert J McGrane, who died in German East Africa, but whose regiment is unknown.

After the Great War, many commemorative plans were sidelined. People in Flanders who had known many soldiers from the Dún Laoghaire/Rathdown area, which had about 500 military fatalities, sent a statue of Christ to commemorate them, but the Christian Brothers school and the parish church in Dún Laoghaire refused to take it and instead had it housed in a newly built oratory in the grounds of the local Dominican convent.

As Michael Pegum says, the situation with memorials from the Great War in Catholic churches around the country replicates their scarcity in Dublin. When he's looking for such memorials, he finds them in much greater abundance in Protestant churches.

September 29, 2015

Hugh Oram

An Irishman's Diary

Dublin once had one of the symbols so redolent of Paris in the old days, the Parisian pissoir, a relic of old indecency. Of course, they had a much more elegant official name, *vespasiennes*, named after the first century Roman emperor Vespasianus, who put a tax on urine collected from public toilets and used for tanning leather.

Paris introduced public urinals in 1830, but an uprising that year put an end to them, as they provided ideal material for barricade building. They weren't reintroduced until 1841, eventually becoming known as *vespasiennes*.

At the height of their popularity, in 1914, Paris had 4,000 of them, an instantly recognisable sign of the city. Even in the 1930s, it still had over 1,200. The old Dublin Corporation decided to get in on the act. Just before the 1932 Eucharistic Congress in Dublin, a big clean-up campaign began in the city and the Corpo decided to import several genuine French pissoirs from the manufacturers in France.

'Gentlemen Only'

They were put up at various locations, including Upper Ormond Quay, Eden Quay and at the junction of Fairview and the Malahide Road. Today, portable loos feature at such events as Electric Picnic, but these French pissoirs were meant to serve hard-pressed male pilgrims to the Eucharistic Congress in Dublin. Rather unnecessarily, signs were put in place reading "Gentlemen Only". No such provision was made for ladies attending the Eucharistic Congress; we never had the the traditional *dames pipi* guarding the frontiers to female public toilets in Paris.

While the pissoirs were seen as a sign of Parisian modernity in Dublin, after the Eucharistic Congress ended, it was downhill all the way. In his 2012 autobiography, *A Kick Against the Pricks*, Senator David Norris said that there was a hugely active gay sexual life in Dublin in the 1950s and 1960s, but centred on public lavatories. He remarked that strangely no-one seemed to think it was odd to have cinema-like queues during the evenings at public conveniences in the city centre, including the aforesaid *vespasiennes*.

But somehow, the Dublin vespasiennes managed to cling on, becoming useful places for advertising posters. The one on Upper Ormond Quay even had one for the old *News of the World*, with a most appropriate slogan, "All Human Life is There".

But the pissoir on Upper Ormond Quay, which was the most fanciful of these cast-iron monsters, was sold in the 1970s by Dublin Corporation to a student for a mere £10. This

■ A pissoir on Ormond Quay

Just before the 1932 Eucharistic Congress in Dublin, a big clean-up campaign began and Dublin Corporation decided to import French pissoirs

particular pissoir suffered a bourgeois fate and ended up as a gazebo in a back garden in Sandymount.

The last surviving *vespasienne* was the one out in Fairview, which staggered on until 1980, when it too was carted away. They had suffered the same fate as all the public air-raid shelters put up in Dublin during the second World War or Emergency, admittedly for an emergency of a different kind.

Public convenience

Paris suffered similar extinctions; in recent years, the only surviving *vespasienne*, leaking like hell, has been the decrepit one on the Boulevard Arago in the 14th arrondissement, close to the Santé prison. By coincidence, Samuel Beckett lived just round the corner. By the 1980s, the much more modern and hygienic *sanisettes* came to Paris, courtesy of JC Decaux, also involved in bike hire and sometimes known as "piddle and pedal".

The once respectable 70 or so public toilets in Dublin, such as the ones at Upper O'Connell Street, St Stephen's Green and College Street, also closed.

In August last year, an unusual outbreak of sentimentality erupted over a public toilet, when the city council, as part of its works on the river Dodder at Ballsbridge, suddenly demolished the public loos at the foot of Anglesea Road. They had been unused for years and there had been much talk of them being put to other uses, like a Little Museum of Ballsbridge, but in the end, the demolition artists got in first.

While the *vespasiennes* in Dublin, Paris and many other cities around the world have gone to that great toilet in the sky, at least they are remembered on film.

In the 1967 spoof Bond film *Casino Royale*, Insp Mathis of the secret police, played by that fine Glaswegian actor Duncan Macrae, introduced himself to Bond, played by Peter Sellers. The inspector is inside a *vespasienne* and says to Bond; "These are my credentials"; to which Bond replies "All in order".

Dublin's ancient vespasiennes never even got a plaque, unlike the one put up last year in the gents at Kiely's pub in Donnybrook, in honour of a certain Ross O'Carroll Kelly, who hit and missed there for years.

December 30, 2015

81

Hugh Oram

An Irishman's Diary

After nearly 56 years, the cut still rankles in Waterford and Tramore, the demise of their railway line, on which the last train ran on the last day of December 1960.

The railway was short, a little over 11 kilometres, and the journey time from Manor Street station in Waterford to Tramore was a quarter of an hour. It had opened on September 7th, 1853, after that great railway pioneer William Dargan had built the line in a mere seven months, including over Kilbarry bog near Waterford.

Originally the plan had been to build a railway from Waterford to Cork, but when that foundered, local business people in Waterford, many of them Quakers, came up with the idea of the train to Tramore. The £77,000 needed to build the line was raised locally. It was the only line never connected to the rest of the Irish railway network.

Seaside resort

For many people in Waterford and beyond in the south-east, the line provided a quick and easy way of getting to the seaside, and it was the making of Tramore as a seaside resort. In those far-off days, before bicycles were popular and before the motor car had been invented, the train was a novel mode of transport. Later, in 1929, a reporter from the *Daily Express* in London described it as "the jolliest little railway in the world".

One Waterford man who lives in Tramore, Frank O'Donoghue, a former chief executive of Waterford Chamber of Commerce, knows the story of the railway inside out, and I met him recently. In 2012, he published a superbly produced book called *The 5-Minute Bell*, on the history of the line; it proved so popular that a second edition, with even more material, was published in 2013. It is full of local reminiscences.

He detailed, minutely, the whole history of the railway and also assembled an amazing array of old images. The trains were powered by steam locomotives, unique in their own way, for 101 of the 107 years that the railway operated. All the maintenance was done locally, at Manor Street station. The line was entirely self-sufficient.

The collection of carriages was elderly and eclectic, so much so that some people called the train a "moving museum". But the trains were capacious, holding up to around 1,000 people.

The most spectacular of the few accidents happened on an August night in 1947, when the last train arrived from Waterford and sailed through the

■ The railway was short, a little over 11 kilometres, and the journey time from Manor Street station in Waterford to Tramore was a quarter of an hour

A reporter from the 'Daily Express' described the Tramore to Waterford line as 'the jolliest little railway in the world'

wall at the end of Tramore station, on to the roadway, narrowly missing the hundreds of people milling around, waiting to catch the train back to Waterford.

The train had also managed to avoid all the damage to the railways caused during the Civil War. But all the railways in the Free State were amalgamated into the Great Southern Railways in 1925, which meant that control passed to Dublin; then in 1945, the railways became part of CIÉ.

Up to 1925, under local ownership, the railway had always paid a dividend, and this loss of local control helped ensure the line's eventual demise.

Cheap fares were introduced in 1952 and they induced a short-lived boom in traffic, with 14 trains a day in each direction. All traffic records were broken and the carriages were packed. It looked like a bright future for the railway, but that optimism was a mirage.

For the last six years of its life, the line used diesel railcars, but by the end of the 1950s, the line was losing £3,000 a year. As Frank O'Donoghue says, rather ruefully, another tuppence on the fares would have cleared the deficit. When the train was replaced by buses, the bus fares were dearer. In 1959, the year before it was shut down, the line carried over 400,000 passengers.

Last year, Waterford County Council took over the old Tramore station, and it is hoped that in its new incarnation it will include a museum. Many people still have artefacts of the old line. Manor Street station in Waterford cannot be revived; it was demolished years ago.

According to Frank O'Donoghue, rebuilding the Waterford to Tramore line would be very difficult, even if Tramore now has more residents than Dungarvan. But another local heritage line, the Waterford & Suir Valley Railway, from Kilmeaden to Waterford, has already proved popular.

The five-minute bells that used to give intending passengers advance warning of train departures may have disappeared, but the memories of the marvellously idiosyncratic Waterford to Tramore train are still fresh.

January 20, 2016

Hugh Oram

An Irishman's Diary

Lambay Island may be barely five km off Rush in north Co Dublin, but it has long had an air of inaccessible mystery. When WB Yeats visited the island in the 1880s, he compared the experience to landing on a remote South Seas island for the first time.

However, in recent times, Skerries Sea Tours, run by Eoin Grimes, has been running trips to Lambay Island, where people taking the trips can disembark and do a walking tour of the island. Those sea trips are due to resume in mid-April. Otherwise, the island can be seen from aircraft coming in to land at Dublin Airport.

The island has been well recorded, for close on two millennia, since Ptolemy created his map of Ireland. It has had various names, since Roman times, while the present one is derived from Norse ("lamb island").

For centuries, it was owned by the pre-Reformation archbishops of Dublin. In 1814, it was acquired by the Talbot family, who then owned Malahide Castle. They owned Lambay for most of the 19th century.

In 1860, the tenant farmers were evicted and replaced by English and Scottish tenants. Then, the island had a population of about 140; now, it's around six.

For over a century, the island has been owned by the Baring family, who once owned the recently infamous bank, founded by them in 1762.

Cecil Baring was the first of the family to own Lambay. He had not long married his wife Maud when he noticed an advertisement in the *Field* headed simply "Island for Sale". In April 1904, he bought Lambay Island. Some sources say he paid £5,250; others say he paid £9,000.

The castle, about three centuries old, was very dilapidated, but he engaged the renowned Anglo-Irish architect Edwin Lutyens to rebuild the castle in the Arts & Crafts style, which he did from 1910 to 1911. It is enhanced by the surrounding sycamore trees and the rose gardens designed by Lutyens's professional partner, the renowned garden designer Gertrude Jekyll. Lutyens also designed the Baring family mausoleum on Lambay.

Today, apart from the castle, the island still has other buildings, including a row of old coastguard cottages and the White House, also by Lutyens, in 1930, as a holiday home for the Baring family. The island also has its own airstrip, a disused golf course, a very rare "real tennis" court and a working farm. The modern wind turbine keeps the lights burning.

■ Lambay Island: an air of inaccessible mystery

> ## When WB Yeats visited Lambay Island in the 1880s, he compared the experience to landing on a remote South Seas island for the first time

The Barings were raised to the peerage in 1885 and some were extraordinary, often eccentric, characters. Rupert, the fourth Lord Revelstoke, who died in 1994, was especially colourful. He lived on the island for six decades and passed the time there by writing doggerel. The fourth earl also cared for the castle garden, while he often spent the early hours of the morning playing chess.

My wife Bernadette once met him at a reception in Iveagh House, where she worked; he made her an offer she could refuse. His lordship offered to give her a set of gates, four metres high, from Lambay Island, for her family home, but of course, they would have been ridiculously out of place in a suburban setting.

The sixth Lord Revelstoke had many accomplishments, including being a pilot. His other interests including running the Regent Sound Studios in London, where the likes of the Beatles, the Rolling Stones and the Who laid down tracks; he was also an early developer of the internet. He died in 2012.

The current Lord Revelstoke, the seventh, known to his friends as Alex Baring, wants to attract wealthy tourists to this island destination, when it is not being used by his family.

Lambay is noted for its flora and fauna, including vast colonies of sea birds. The island also has grey seals, as well as wallabies, descended from those donated by Dublin Zoo in the 1980s.

Around 50 shipwrecks have happened in the waters around Lambay; the *Tayleur* disaster has often been compared to the *Titanic*. The *Tayleur* was on her maiden voyage from Liverpool to Australia in 1854 when she ran aground off Lambay; some people on board managed to scramble ashore, but close on 400 souls were lost. The iron hull of the ship is still lying there in about 18 metres of water, just off the south-east of the island.

For a small island, of 2½ sq km, Lambay has an amazing archaeological, historical and wildlife heritage, and in the company of Eoin Grimes, skippering his boat out of Skerries, visitors can now explore it all for themselves.

March 23, 2016

Hugh Oram

An Irishman's Diary

The Cavan & Leitrim Railway was the last all-steam, narrow-gauge railway to survive in Ireland; it had also managed to be the country's most idiosyncratic railway system.

It all began in 1887, after the 3ft-wide track had been laid from Belturbet in Co Cavan to Dromod in Co Leitrim. At Belturbet, it connected with the Great Northern Railway; at Dromod, it linked with the main Dublin to Sligo line.

The hub of the system was at Ballinamore, where the company had its workshops. There was also a link from near Ballinamore to Drumshanbo and Arigna, although the final 4½-mile connection from Arigna to the nearby coal mines was not completed until 1920. The original railway had cost £60,000 to build.

When the company started, eight locomotives were purchased and seven of them were named after the first names of daughters of directors. The eighth director refused to lend his daughter's name to the last engine, so it was called *Queen Victoria*. In its early days, the railway looked like something out of the Wild West, as the locomotives had "cow-catchers" at the front, while early passenger carriages had verandahs and platforms at each end.

The trains were often so slow that intending passengers could walk alongside and simply hop aboard. Tickets were issued wherever they got on the train. The schedules were often nominal, as train crews were liable to stop along the way and have chats with friends and neighbours. One inspector of the rails carried a gun so that he could go wild-fowling when he was not attending to his duties.

Two successive station masters at Belturbet vanished. They each helped themselves to £7 in cash, enough for a ticket to America, with £1 left over. At a crossing just outside Mohill, trains stopped on demand for the Rev J Gargan Digges, a director of the company and renowned for his beekeeping. He was the private chaplain on the Lough Rynn estate.

In the aftermath of 1916, train crews played their part. In 1917, the *Queen Victoria* locomotive was painted green, white and orange and was promptly dubbed the Sinn Féin engine.

In 1920, a man from Belfast called Capt CV Rogers was brought in to bring some semblance of punctuality and discipline to the railway workers. One night, he was awoken from his slumbers by armed men, who marched him the 12 miles to Killeshandra. The next day, he fled the area.

Whenever Black and Tan

■ The Cavan & Leitrim Railway: the country's most idiosyncratic railway system

In 1917, the 'Queen Victoria' locomotive was painted green, white and orange and was promptly dubbed the Sinn Féin engine

soldiers boarded the trains, the crews walked off. As a result, drivers and firemen often went for months without pay. In 1922, the new manager, William McFarlane, was taken to Ballinamore station and made to sign a letter reinstating the sacked workers.

The Cavan & Leitrim Railway was absorbed into the Great Southern Railways during the 1925 railway amalgamations. The railway workshops at Ballinamore were closed and overhauls shifted to Inchicore; local working practices on the railway were extinguished. The Rev Digges lost his own private halt.

Roads were improving and cars were starting to come into vogue. Fewer women used the train to go and do their weekly shopping in Mohill or Drumshanbo. The latter had a station nameplate for years, put up by the Great Southern Railways, that read "Drumshambo".

The railway finally closed down in 1959. During the 1950s, with three scheduled trains a day in each direction, station staff had so little to do that station gardens flourished.

The death knell had come in 1958, when the ESB opened a new generating station at Arigna, making the railway's transport of Arigna coal redundant. One of the old steam locomotives can now be found in a transportation museum in New Jersey, while the Ulster Folk & Transport Museum also has an old locomotive and a passenger carriage.

A new railway company was set up in 1993, with the aim of restoring the nearly six miles of track between Dromod and Mohill, but this never happened.

Until a couple of years ago, steam train trips were possible on a short stretch of track at Dromod. A substantial museum was opened at Dromod; it now includes not just railway memorabilia, but many other transport artefacts. A railway museum is also open at Belturbet, also with lots of material on the old railway.

The Cavan & Leitrim Railway was unique in many ways, much loved in the countryside through which it ran, but as with the other regional railway systems in Ireland, the economics provided unsurmountable.

June 21, 2016

Hugh Oram

An Irishman's Diary

Dublin once had two remarkable railway systems, both long vanished. One was the Atmospheric Railway between what is now Dún Laoghaire and Dalkey, while the other was the elaborate railway in the Guinness brewery at St James's Gate.

The Atmospheric Railway was opened to traffic in 1844, a decade after the Westland Row to Kingstown line had been built. The new railway ran for just under two miles, following the track of the old tramway from Dalkey quarry to the pier in Kingstown.

A pneumatic tube was laid between the rails, and the train was drawn upwards to Dalkey through the suction of a piston connecting with that tube. The train was quite fast, with the average speed around 25 mph, although the maximum speed obtained in test runs was just over 50 mph.

The service was also very regular, every half hour, between 8am and 9.30pm. The journey time was three minutes and trains could carry 200 or more passengers.

The train ran back to Kingstown by gravity, running at a sedate 18 mph, but often, on the last stretch of track, third-class passengers were required to get out and push.

It was the first railway of its kind in the world; this novel means of propulsion had been pioneered by the great English railway engineer, Brunel. But there was intense competition between him and another railway pioneer, Stephenson, who thought that trains needed locomotives to haul them. International newspaper interest in the new Dalkey railway was intense.

But the system had one fatal flaw; it needed leather flaps to keep it airtight. Extra attendants had to ensure the flaps worked properly, but rats did for the railway by gnawing at the leather to eat the grease. In winter, the flaps froze.

So 10 years after it opened, the Atmospheric Railway made way for the new main line from Kingstown to Bray, just as the rival Harcourt Street line to Bray was opening. Today, there's virtually nothing left to remind people of the old railway, except for Atmospheric Road in Dalkey, an area commonly known as "The Metals", where the Dalkey station and the engine house for the air pump were once located.

Similar railways operated on the outskirts of Paris, in south Devon and in New York City. Modern versions of the system operate at Porto Alegre in Brazil and in Jakarta in Indonesia.

The other old railway in Dublin was the eight-mile-long narrow gauge system in the

■ A 22-inch narrow-gauge railway system was constructed to carry materials around the brewery, as well as taking casks of stout to barges moored on the Liffey quays

Guinness even had a safe on wheels that took weekly wages round the brewery

Guinness brewery. In 1873, the brewery had been substantially expanded when Guinness bought land between St James's Gate and the river Liffey. A 22-inch narrow-gauge railway system was constructed to carry materials around the brewery, as well as taking casks of stout to barges moored on the Liffey quays. Guinness even had a safe on wheels that took weekly wages round the brewery.

An ingenious spiral tunnel was built to link the higher and the lower parts of the site; this tunnel was based on the design of tunnels used in the Alps. At the time, Guinness had a highly inventive Dublin-born chief engineer, Samuel Geoghegan, who had gained much experience abroad, including in Turkey and India, before joining Guinness. He did well at Guinness; he lived in Ailesbury Road. Coincidentally, his brother William was the head brewer.

The first new locomotives didn't work well, because they couldn't keep out the dirt from the tracks, but the first steam engine designed by Geoghegan, and built in 1882, proved very satisfactory. Many more were built, including 17 at the old Cork Street foundry. They lasted until diesel working started in the 1940s.

The Guinness railway lasted until 1975 and two of its engines are preserved, perfectly restored, in the transport gallery at the Guinness Storehouse. Another of the old locos is at the Stradbally woodland railway in Co Laois. Two Guinness locos, one steam, the other diesel, are in the Ulster Folk & Transport Museum. Further examples are in the Welsh narrow-gauge railway museum and in a railway museum in West Sussex.

Another intriguing feature of railway working at Guinness was the broad gauge railway that ran for about 500 yards, linking the brewery with the goods yard in what is now Heuston station. This section of track was scrapped in 1965 to improve road traffic close to Heuston station.

Fortunately, artefacts and material relating to the Guinness railway are well preserved in the Guinness Storehouse and Archives, which means that the brewery has one of the best railway museums in these islands.

August 17, 2016

Hugh Oram

An Irishman's Diary

Co Donegal once had marvellously intricate narrow-gauge railways. At 225 miles long, it was the longest narrow-gauge system in these islands, a true marvel of railway engineering. By the end of 1959, the last sections of the system had closed.

The first lines in the county opened in 1863 and 1864, including Strabane to Stranorlar.

Other lines followed, so that by the start of the 20th century, major towns in the county could be reached by rail, including Letterkenny, Burtonport and Glenties in the west of the county, and Killybegs and Ballyshannon in south Donegal. On the Inishowen peninsula, a line went as far as Carndonagh.

A small section of the network was originally broad gauge, but soon narrow gauge became the working norm across the county. The Donegal railways also ran to Derry city, which at one stage, had four railway stations. One in the docks area linked Derry with Letterkenny, Buncrana and the Inishowen peninsula, while the Victoria Road station on the east bank of the Foyle provided a connection to Killybegs.

But consolidation came quickly to the network. In 1906, the County Donegal Railway Joint Committee was set up, with help from the Great Northern Railway (Ireland) and the Midland Railway in England. In the north of the county, services were run by the Londonderry and Lough Swilly Railway company, usually called simply "The Swilly".

The railways were useful in helping Donegal people reach emigrant ships, sailing from Derry and elsewhere. They also played a vital and integral role in the everyday commerce of the county, and during the second World War, they were well-used by the people of the twin towns, Ballybofey and Stranorlar, and many others in the county, travelling in their vital quest to win turf.

They were also widely used for excursions, such as those by pilgrims to the Holy Well at Doon, near Letterkenny, as well as by Orangemen going to Rossnowlagh for the Twelfth, and the Ancient Order of Hibernians on August 15th.

The Donegal railways were also very innovative; diesel railcars were introduced around 80 years ago and proved economical and reliable. They helped the railways keep going for far longer than if they had been steam-worked. Thrift was everything, and in many cases carriages were kept in service for decades.

The railways also induced a sense of friendly competition,

■ Ballybofey station

> The lines to Buncrana and Letterkenny closed in 1953. By 1960, the last of the Donegal system had been obliterated

like the race between a diesel railcar and a motor car, driven by Maj Henry White of Lough Eske Castle, along the Barnesmore Gap.

One lethal crash happened in January 1925, when a train on the Letterkenny to Burtonport line was blown off the viaduct at Owencarrow. Four people were killed. In 1949, a railcar driver and two passengers were killed when two trains collided head-on near Donegal town.

But as happened everywhere else with the railways, motor cars and lorries provided unbeatable competition. The station at Carndonagh shut in 1935 after a mere 34 years in service. The line to Burtonport clung on, as far as Gweedore, until 1947, while the lines to Buncrana and Letterkenny closed down in 1953. By 1960, the last of the Donegal system had been obliterated. The Swilly company, which became bus-only for passengers, managed to last until two years ago.

Such was the attachment to the Donegal railways that after the line from Donegal town to Ballyshannon closed down in 1959, two of the railway workers continued to operate a freight service between the two towns for a month before the bosses in Dublin realised what was happening.

With so many railway memories still so vivid in Co Donegal, it's hardly surprising that the county has two excellent heritage sites. The old station in Donegal town has been converted into the Donegal Railway Heritage Centre, packed with artefacts of all kinds, and even an old railway carriage that can be hired out for functions.

At Fintown, you can take a trip in an old railcar along five kilometres of track, the last remaining segment of the Co Donegal railways, on the old Stranorlar to Glenties line. It opened in 1995 and now there are plans to restore the old station. Its lakeside setting is so spectacular that the late Brian Friel said that it was as scenic a stretch of railway as anything to be found in Switzerland or Minnesota.

Derry had the Foyle Valley railway museum dedicated to the Co Donegal railways, including old locos and carriages and a working track, but sadly, it has been long closed.

October 11, 2016

Hugh Oram

An Irishman's Diary

An Óige has 24 hostels in its network and some of them have considerable architectural history, not to mention history itself, attached to them.

In terms of architectural heritage, the most outstanding is undoubtedly the Trá na Rossan hostel, near Downings in north Co Donegal. The building was originally designed by the great Anglo-Irish architect Sir Edwin Landseer Lutyens, whose other Irish works included the mansion on Lambay Island and the Irish National War Memorial Gardens at Islandbridge, Dublin.

During the 1890s, the five acres of land on which the hostel stands were bought for £40 by the Hon Mr and Mrs Robert Phillimore of London. They commissioned Lutyens to design a holiday home for them, which they subsequently used for many years. After her husband died, Mrs Phillimore continued to use the house, but in 1936, decided to dispose of it. By March the following year, the house had been handed over to the An Óige trust.

The organisation was a mere six years old at that stage and until the Co Donegal acquisition, its properties had been exclusively in the Dublin and east coast area. The first hostel to open had been at Lough Dan in Co Wicklow.

The other hostel of much architectural significance is the one just outside Killarney. Aghadoe House had been built in 1828, with very wide eaves, at a cost of £12,000. The Ordnance Survey name books of the 1830s described it as being "a very fine building,

densely shrouded with trees".

During the War of Independence, local republican volunteers commandeered the house, which was burned down in 1922. It was rebuilt to the original plan, and just over 20 years later, it was noted that the house was being extensively renovated by the then owner, Robin Hilliard. It subsequently came into An Óige ownership.

One historic hostel among the 15 franchised by the organisation is the Rowan Tree hostel in the centre of Ennis, overlooking the river Fergus. It started life as an 18th-century club for aristocratic gentlemen, and as a recent acquisition, it has been extensively refurbished.

Yet another franchised hostel is Sheila's in Cork, once the first non-church school in the city, Scoil Íte, founded by Mary and Annie, sisters of Terence MacSwiney.

The Old Mill hostel in Westport, near the river, opened in 1991 and is also franchised.

The building dates back to the 18th century; the original warehouses here were used for a variety of purposes, including as a brewery, as a storehouse and as an animal shelter.

In terms of architectural heritage, the most outstanding An Óige hostel is undoubtedly Trá na Rossan, near Downings in north Co Donegal, which was originally designed by Sir Edwin Lutyens

Other hostels have interesting provenances. One of the three Co Wicklow hostels, Knockree, had been built in the 18th century as a farmhouse. It opened as a hostel in 1938 and in recent times, has been rebuilt, although the original farmhouse was incorporated in the rebuild.

The Dublin international hostel, at Mountjoy Street in Dublin, also has an historical heritage. It's in a converted 19th-century convent and the old church is now the breakfast room.

The hostel that appeals to me most is also in Co Wicklow, at Glenmalure. It was built in 1903 as a hunting lodge, constructed in the style of a traditional farmhouse. Even today, it still has no running water, no electricity, no landline phone and an intermittent mobile signal, making it the ideal place to escape today's "always on" world.

Around a century ago, this place was a holiday getaway for such noted personalities as Katherine Lynn and Maud Gonne, and it still has a wonderful escapist air.

Other hostels, too, are located in the most scenic locations, such as the one on

Cape Clear island, once a coastguard station, where visitors can enjoy the island birdlife and the profusion of marine species in its waters.

In other hostels around the country, facilities couldn't be more modern. The hostels in Dublin and at Errigal in Co Donegal have e-car charging points so that people staying there can recharge their electric cars. Errigal may have wifi, but it also has a more traditional talking point, a "green lady" ghost.

There are six more hostels in the North, run by a separate organisation, Hostelling International Northern Ireland, with which An Óige has a good working relationship.

At one point, An Óige had 55 hostels, and just over 10 years ago, at a time of financial crisis in the organisation, eight of its hostels were closed and sold off.

But these days with record tourist numbers and new attractions, such as the Wild Atlantic Way and Ireland's Ancient East, the present hostels are securely based and retain their architectural and historical resonances in abundance.

November 22, 2016

Hugh Oram

An Irishman's Diary

A recent mid-winter walk along the strand and among the dunes at the mouth of the river Boyne on the east coast was a most rewarding experience, the only sound that of waves hitting the shore, and the only sight of fellow humans was the occasional dog walker.

But not far from the Maiden Tower and the Lady's Finger, which guard the entrance to the Boyne, I spotted very strange sights, the miniature lighthouses that were built in the 19th century by the old Drogheda Harbour Commissioners to warn navigators sailing in and out of the Boyne estuary.

These lights were constructed on top of convoluted metal supports, looking for all the world like something out of an HG Wells science-fiction novel, unique in their design in Ireland. One of those three lights, the Drogheda North Light, which is easily found by walking upriver from the beach at Mornington, is being restored, in a project masterminded by the Drogheda Port Company. Financing is coming jointly from the port company and a government scheme for built heritage investment. Irish Lights has been giving technical advice, as has Keith Rankin, a marine engineer.

Restoration project

A noted Dublin-based conservation architect, Fergal McGirl, together with a company called KC Environmental, are leading the restoration project, and one aim is to preserve as many of the original features and materials as possible.

The lighthouse that is being restored was built about 1880 and it is set on an intricately intertwined set of cast-iron supports. A ladder leads up to the actual lantern, which has glazed panels. The light is set within boundary walls that also enclose the original lighthouse keeper's house.

For years, the lantern had a fixed light pattern, but when the Drogheda North Light was eventually connected to the electricity network in 1950, the signal was changed to a flashing warning. Three years later, the Drogheda North Light was changed again, to flashing red, while Drogheda West and East Lights kept white signals.

But as has happened all over the world, the Drogheda North light was made redundant by advances in marine electronic navigation systems. It is nearly 20 years since the last lighthouse keepers left Irish Lights' lighthouses as automatic systems took over; the Baily lighthouse on Howth Head was vacated by its manual operators on March 24th, 1997.

So the light at the mouth of the river Boyne that is being restored will in time form a perfect example of old lighthouse technology, long since obsolete, but fitting in well with other sea safety features in the area, such as the beacons and

Drogheda North Light
PHOTOGRAPH: COURTESY OF FERGAL McGIRL ARCHITECTS

They were built on top of convoluted metal supports, looking for all the world like something out of HG Wells

the old lifeboat house. When restoration work on the Drogheda North Light is completed, it will become part of the Boyne tourist trail. It will be open to the public for a number of days each year and for school educational trips.

Outbuildings

Another of the three old lights in Mornington, the Drogheda West Light, is privately owned, and it is planned to modify the light and the existing lighthouse keeper's house and outbuildings. This particular light is literally in the back yard of a bungalow.

The Drogheda North Light refurbishment scheme is not the only one by any means. Irish Lights developed the Great Lighthouses of Ireland initiative, which gives people the chance to stay in, or visit, 12 lighthouses. Five of its lighthouses have benefitted from extensive restoration work.

Fanad Head lighthouse in Co Donegal cost over €420,000 to restore and it reopened as a visitor centre, with self-catering accommodation, during the May bank holiday in 2016. Over €180,000 is being spent restoring another Co Donegal lighthouse, at St John's Point. The Irish Landmark Trust will offer accommodation here; it is due to open in 2017.

Three lighthouses in the North have also been refurbished. The Rathlin West Light in Co Antrim is now a seabird centre, and opened in April 2016.

St John's Point lighthouse in Co Down cost over €240,000 to renovate and opened in August 2016, with accommodation run by the Irish Landmark Trust. This particular lighthouse has a connection to Brendan Behan. His father, Stephen, had been contracted to paint a number of Irish lighthouses; Brendan was roped in to help paint the one at St John's Point. But his attempts at painting were far less impressive than his literary works.

The third restored lighthouse in the North is at Blackhead, Co Antrim, where refurbishment was recently completed; again self-catering accommodation is being run by the Irish Landmark Trust.

So while the Drogheda North Light is the latest lighthouse restoration project to get under way, it's all part of moves to preserve what is probably Europe's oldest lighthouse heritage.

Hugh Oram

An Irishman's Diary

One of the strangest therapeutic fads in Ireland was for Turkish baths; they were comparatively short-lived, although in some cases, their architectural heritage lasted far longer.

The pioneer of Turkish baths in Ireland was a Co Cork doctor, Dr Richard Barter, who had seen the benefits of water-based cures in European alternative medicine. He brought this new style of medicine to his practice in Blarney, Co Cork. Then, after reading a book on Turkish baths, he decided to build one.

He opened a vast edifice, the hydrotherapy baths at Blarney, but soon found that the Turkish-style baths were unsuitable, because the air was so moisture laden. Instead, he went back to the technology of the ancient Romans and created the dry-air systems that they used. The baths at Blarney were comparatively short-lived, but the extensive ruins can still be seen today, even though the richly decorated interior, designed to create an Oriental illusion, no longer exists.

Sackville Street

Barter went on to found Turkish baths in Dublin, in Upper Sackville Street, in 1869, the year before he died. The baths were part of a building called the Hammam Hotel, which lasted until anti-Treaty forces destroyed it in 1922. When the premises were rebuilt, they were called Hammam Buildings, and to this day it houses a tax office of the Revenue Commissioners.

Out of various other Turkish baths in Dublin, undoubtedly the best-known of them all was the one in Lincoln Place, at the back of Trinity College.

It opened in 1860, complete with a large ogee-shaped dome, a towering minaret and separate bath facilities for men and women; it even had stables for patrons who arrived on horseback.

The Turkish style was mimicked in great detail, down to the attendants dressed in scarlet dressing gown-style robes and Turkish slippers, while coffee was served from china cups.

Initially, Dr Barter was closely involved in the running of these baths, but moved on to open his own Turkish baths at the Hamman Hotel. The baths in Lincoln Place proved popular initially; in their first four years, they attracted about 90 bathers a day.

Right next door to the baths was the Café de Paris, the first French-style restaurant in Dublin. It advertised French breakfast, lunch and dinner, and even outdoor catering, a complete novelty for Dublin. This restaurant lasted for 20 years, until 1880, while the baths kept going for much longer, until 1900.

They were unable to compete with the half-dozen other cheaper Turkish baths in the

■ The Turkish baths in Bray, Co Wicklow

> **The Turkish style was mimicked in great detail, down to the attendants dressed in scarlet dressing gown-style robes and Turkish slippers**

city, including one near the College of Surgeons on St Stephen's Green.

The old baths at Lincoln Place were subsequently used by many different commercial concerns, until they were demolished in 1970. Their history has been well documented by Malcolm Shifrin and others.

In *Ulysses*, James Joyce called the Lincoln Place Turkish Baths "the mosque of the baths", but they couldn't have been one of Leopold Bloom's first ports of call on June 16th, 1904, because the baths had already been closed for four years. It's probable that Bloom went to a similar establishment nearby, on Leinster Street.

The short-lived interest in Turkish baths spread far beyond Dublin. Cork city got one, at South Mall, which closed in 1943. What was a passageway in the original baths today leads to the contemporary Jacobs on the Mall restaurant, named after the original managing director of the Turkish baths.

Belfast, Downpatrick, Dungannon, Ennis, Kilkenny, Killarney, Limerick, Sligo, Tipperary, Tramore, Waterford and Youghal also got their own versions of Turkish baths; the ubiquitous Dr Barter was closely involved.

Even that great railway pioneer William Dargan got in on the act. He and others were very involved in turning Bray, Co Wicklow, into the Irish equivalent of an quintessential English seaside town. Dargan funded the building of Bray's Turkish baths at Quinsborough Road, which cost £10,000. The baths replicated the Turkish style in every way, including its minarets. They opened in 1859 but lasted less than a decade.

By 1867, the Bray Turkish Baths had become an assembly room for concerts and other events. Eventually, the premises became a cinema in the earlier 20th century, but for many years subsequently, the building was derelict, and was finally demolished in 1980. A plain shopping precinct was built on the site.

The health-giving properties of the so-called Turkish baths, Roman style, in Ireland are little disputed today. These days, every luxury hotel worth its name has a spa, the modern hydrotherapeutic equivalent, but without the glamorous Turkish-style architecture, and with not a minaret in sight.

February 6, 2017

Hugh Oram

An Irishman's Diary

When I was working for Michelin in Paris, helping to compile its *Green Guide to Ireland*, I found a strange puritanism that was almost, by definition, totally un-French, as well as an fanatical devotion to factual accuracy.

In 1988, Michelin tourist guides had decided to launch the first such guide to Ireland. Half a dozen writers, including myself, competed to find someone to complement the Michelin staff writer.

My chosen destination was Limerick and the task was to write a Michelin-style entry about all the tourist sights of the city. I went to Limerick, did my duty, wrote my copy and thought no more about it. A couple of months later, I had a phone call from Michelin to say that I was the successful candidate.

Ireland was divided up, with the staff writer being given the northern part of the island of Ireland to cover and me, the southern part.

Assignment

My first assignment was Birr, Co Offaly. On the way there, on the October bank holiday weekend, 1988, the traffic was bumper to bumper from Leeson Street bridge to the turn-off for Birr.

The trips around the country intensified and the amount of mileage clocked up was astronomical. Exact mileages had to be returned to Michelin and they were equally precise about all other expenses; everything had to be carefully documented and receipted. Luckily, my wife Bernadette was able to travel with me on every assignment and bring her poet's vision to bear on everything. I made an arrangement with Michelin that I would be compensated only for my own expenses.

I was reminded of the apocryphal story of the Fleet Street reporter who came to Dublin years ago on assignment and when he returned to London, put in an enormously inflated expenses claim for the hire of a boat to take him to Usher's Island in Dublin on numerous occasions. The accounts staff in London were oblivious of Dublin's geography and paid without hesitation, in full. That reporter wouldn't have lasted five minutes with Michelin!

Questions

The next discovery about Michelin was its absolute devotion to accuracy. I was soon receiving convoluted questions from the fact-checkers in Paris. An underlying question was always whether somewhere was *vaut* (worth) *le détour*.

Quite often, I had to go to

■ Michelin had a strict rule, a sacking offence in fact, that no alcoholic drink was to be consumed on the premises

The trips around the country intensified and the amount of mileage clocked up was astronomical

Paris for editorial meetings at the headquarters of Michelin tourist publications, in the avenue de Breteuil. Friends remarked that I was just off to Paris on another jolly, but the reality was different. There, the meetings went on for hour after hour with a stern taskmaster, the editor, Mike Brammer, an Englishman who has spent so much of his adult life in France that he is more French than the French.

But in Paris, any thoughts of solace in the staff canteen were soon banished. Michelin had a strict rule, a sacking offence in fact, that no alcoholic drink was to be consumed on the premises. The canteen was well stocked with mineral water and soft drinks, another blow to my preconceived notions of working life in France!

It was a complete contrast to the trips we quite often made to the Champagne region to observe the progress of the latest vintage. There, in truer French tradition, any hint of abstention from alcohol was a grave and unforgiveable offence. A great friend of ours, François Bonal, a former French army colonel, who got a dream job on retirement as head of publicity for the Champagne houses, quite often welcomed us to the region with wonderful hospitality and free-flowing champagne.

Eventually, after nearly four years of arduous work, the *Michelin Green Guide* was published, in 1992. It had been such an exhaustive and exhausting experience that I had no wish to work further for Michelin.

But like every good restaurateur worth his or her salt, I soon realised how useful it was to have "Michelin" on my CV.

Coastal town

Another strange outcome, after the job was over, was that Mike Brammer and I became good friends and remain so to this day. He retired from Michelin a couple of years ago and now lives in a coastal town in north Brittany; we are planning our next meeting for later in the summer.

Michelin, in all its forms, remains an indelible part of my life, all watched over at home by a 30cm model of Bibendum, acquired in mysterious circumstances in Biarritz. But that's another story!

March 21, 2017

Hugh Oram

An Irishman's Diary

Thomas Hardy, one of the great English novelists, had little interest in Ireland, but a fortnight-long visit he paid here during May 1893 did have a long-term impact on him.

Hardy had been a friend of the father of Lord Houghton, who had been appointed lord lieutenant of Ireland less than a year previously. Lord Houghton had written some minor verse and, because of that literary interest, he and Hardy also became friends. He invited Hardy and his first wife, Emma, whom Hardy often called "Em", to stay with them in the vice-regal lodge, now Áras an Uachtaráin.

His first observation there was that their bedroom windows faced the Phoenix Park and the Wicklow Mountains. He noted that the building dated from the 18th century, 1751 in fact. Later, he referred sardonically to the "little court" at the vice-regal lodge.

He and his wife had been met upon arrival by Mrs Florence Henniker, sister of the lord lieutenant, and Hardy had been immediately smitten.

She was in her late-thirties, 15 years younger than Hardy's wife, and he found his new companion attractive and intuitive, independent and intellectually ambitious. She had already had three novels published.

That introduction began Hardy's long infatuation with Mrs Henniker, who although married to an aristocratic and military man high up the social scale, was happy to pursue a friendship with a married man, an unusual quest for late Victorian times. Hardy also became keen to have a physical affair with her, but she soon made plain to him that his passion was futile.

But their friendship continued for 30 years.

Enthused with his new-found friend, Hardy soon found another subject in which to invest considerable interest, the murders in the Phoenix Park in May 1882 of Lord Frederick Cavendish, who had only just been appointed the chief secretary for Ireland, and Thomas Burke, the permanent under-secretary, the most senior civil servant in Ireland. Not only did Hardy inspect the scene of the murders, but he also went to the chief secretary's lodge in the Phoenix Park. There, he saw the room where the bodies of the two men had been taken and relished hearing the gruesome details of the subsequent discovery of a roll of bloody clothing underneath the sofa. Hardy noted that the room had not been cleaned since the time of the murders, which he found intriguing.

Also in Dublin, Hardy ventured into the city to see the public buildings and saw some comical drunken women

■ Thomas Hardy: fortnight-long visit to Ireland in May 1893
PHOTOGRAPH: HULTON ARCHIVE/GETTY IMAGES

Not only did Hardy inspect the scene of the Phoenix Park murders, but also the room in the chief secretary's lodge where the bodies were taken

dancing in the street.

He also visited Bray, where at "the grey hotel by the shore", he met the chief secretary and the lord chancellor, as well as plenty of magistrates.

The last visit by Hardy and his wife while they were in Dublin was to the Guinness brewery, where they and Mrs Henniker went for a trip on the narrow-gauge railway that then circumnavigated the brewery. Hardy reported that all of their party had been splashed with either porter or dirty water, ruining the ladies' clothes.

That afternoon, Hardy and Emma took the 3pm train from Kingsbridge to Killarney, where they stayed in the Great Southern Hotel beside the railway station. The next day, they went to see Ross Castle and the Middle Lake, and in the afternoon, walked around Killarney town, where Hardy found that cows stood about the street like people. His further adventures outside the town took him to the Black Valley, which he found deeply impressive, as well as to the Upper Lake.

In those far-off days, Killarney and the lakes were the prime tourist destination in Ireland, popularised by Queen Victoria's earlier visits, and on that trip, Hardy and his wife behaved like typical Victorian tourists.

After their return to Dublin, the pair went straight to Kingstown, where they stayed at the Marine Hotel, now the Royal Marine, until early the following morning, they took the ship to Holyhead.

After their arrival back in London, Hardy and his wife immediately returned to the aristocratic social scene, to which he had gained entry because of his literary fame rather than his family background. His father had been a stonemason and builder.

That fortnight-long tour to Ireland made comparatively little impression on Hardy, but his new found friendship with Mrs Henniker did have substantial consequences.

In his final great tragic novel, *Jude the Obscure*, published in 1895, the heroine, Sue Bridehead, was clearly constructed on the character of Florence Henniker. Her health was uncertain, but she and Hardy maintained a close friendship until her death in 1923, five years before Hardy's own passing.

October 24, 2017

Hugh Oram

An Irishman's Diary

Brick-making has been an integral part of construction in Ireland for four centuries, creating an important part of the urban landscape, competing in earlier times against stone and in more modern times against concrete.

While the sheer number of brickworks around the country has shrunk drastically, bricks still form an integral part of urban settings and old bricks remain an important built legacy.

One of the first major buildings where bricks were used was Jigginstown Castle, near Naas, Co Kildare, whose ruins can still be seen. The castle was built between about 1637 and 1640, using both locally made and imported bricks.

Trinity College Dublin had been originally built using red Dutch bricks.

Bricks had been made in Co Wexford as early as 1550, while the earliest record of brick-making in Dublin came in 1599, when one George Burroes was making bricks on a 4½-acre site in an area that is today part of Hawkins Street.

During the 1770s, brickfields existed at Merrion in what is now south Dublin, while the late 18th-century brickworks in what is now Sandymount gave rise to the district's earlier name, Brickfield Town. The houses around Sandymount Green were originally built to house the families of men working in the local brickworks.

In the 18th and 19th centuries, locally made bricks were widely used in Dublin and other coastal towns and cities, but they were competing against imported bricks that were often cheaper. But the tremendous legacy of brickwork in Dublin can be seen in the Georgian squares and buildings such as the former Kildare Street Club and the Shelbourne Hotel.

Many of the houses built in Rathgar and Rathmines in the 1880s were constructed with Athy-made bricks, while around the same time, many military barracks around Ireland were built with bricks from the brickworks at Kingscourt, Co Cavan.

Bricks were less comprehensively used in inland areas, but the development first of the canals and then the railways helped spread the use of brick.

At its height, the industry had 150 brickworks spread throughout Ireland.

The best-known brickworks in Dublin was undoubtedly the Dolphin's Barn brickworks, based on the Crumlin Road. The clay pits extended from Kimmage to the Grand Canal at Goldenbridge, and this clay gave these bricks a distinctive yellow biscuit colour. When this brickworks was closed in 1944, the site was purchased by Dublin Corporation to build the large housing estates in Drimnagh.

William Lacey, a lecturer in

■ A brick chimney. As bricklayers' wages increased, bricks were made taller, so that by mid-Victorian times, one foot of wall required just four courses, saving on construction costs.

The earliest record of brick-making in Dublin came in 1599, when one George Burroes was making bricks on a site in an area that is now part of Hawkins Street

the School of Architecture at the Dublin Institute of Technology, and a specialist in brickwork, considers that Dolphin's Barn was the most important of the old brickworks.

While the brickworks at Dolphin's Barn and Clonsilla both produced yellow-coloured bricks, the renowned Portmarnock brickworks, just north of the city, were famed for their red-coloured bricks, made between 1850 and 1918.

South of Dublin, the brickworks at Rathnew, Co Wicklow, lasted from the earlier 19th century right up to 1922. Many builders considered that Rathnew bricks were the finest in the country.

The most important technical advance had been the expansion of Irish-made machine bricks in the later 19th century, which helped do away with the old cottage industry style of brick making.

Bricks had long been made by hand and were much smaller, often in random sizes.

As bricklayers' wages increased, bricks were made taller, so that by mid-Victorian times, one foot of wall required just four courses, saving on construction costs.

But mechanisation only offered a temporary reprieve.

By the time the Irish Free State had come into being in 1922, only five brickworks survived: at Dolphin's Barn, Dublin; Courtown, Co Wexford; Tullamore, Waterford; and Youghal.

Steadily rising costs and cheaper imports had militated against the continuation of the industry.

William Lacey says that Kingscourt, the only current clay-brick manufacturer in the Republic, still supplies an imperial range of bricks. Present-day bricks normally come in metric sizes.

Many of the older bricks used in buildings across Ireland can still be in very good condition, if properly maintained, but if bricks are needed for repairs, using imported bricks is the norm.

Since the 1980s, brick imports generally, including from the UK and the Netherlands, have accounted for up to 70 per cent, and sometimes much more, of bricks used in Ireland.

But despite all the imports, the brick making industry in Ireland is still hanging in, having travelled far from the days of hand-made bricks, which were fired in hand-stacked kilns fuelled with turf.

December 29, 2017

Hugh Oram

An Irishman's Diary

Bray once had a unique tourist attraction, an aerial chairlift that whisked passengers up to the Eagle's Nest on the heights of Bray Head, but it's the best part of 50 years since it last functioned.

The chairlift was opened in April 1952. It was the brainchild of Eamonn Quinn, father of former senator and Superquinn boss Feargal Quinn. After the second World War, Eamonn Quinn had opened the Red Island holiday camp at Skerries in north Co Dublin, which became immensely popular during the 1950s. He also purchased two sites in Bray, one a field at the bottom of Bray Head, the other, the Eagle's Nest restaurant and

ballroom halfway up Bray Head, about 150 metres above sea level. The Eagle's Nest had been opened in 1932.

Quinn was then faced with the problem of getting customers up to the Eagle's Nest; the incline was too steep to walk up. Until then, the main transport had been the Bray Head Express, a horse-drawn cart, which cost six pence per person.

Quinn was inspired by the many ski-lifts he saw in Switzerland. A total of seven steel pylons, painted yellow, were built on the northern slopes of Bray Head. Steel wires ran from pylon to pylon and from those wires hung the passenger gondolas. The new aerial chairlift could carry 300

passengers an hour in each direction, up and down Bray Head.

But as Feargal Quinn remembers, since the gondolas were open to the elements, the chairlift was very weather dependent, including the wind. He also says it cost one shilling and sixpence to go up and a shilling to come down.

He and his sister Eilagh were regular visitors to the attraction in the 1950s.

The new device soon proved its popularity, with queues forming at the foot of Bray Head as early as 10am during the summer months; many people went up to the Eagle's Nest for morning coffee, while others went to the viewing point on Bray Head that had been built for Queen Victoria's golden jubilee in 1887.

The evening dances at the Eagle's Nest were always popular, even though the dancers, clad in all their finery, had to make the ascent on the chairlift.

During the peak tourist season, Eamonn Quinn also organised trips to the chairlift for people who were spending a

■ Using the chairlift to deliver Coca Cola to the Eagle's Nest restaurant on Bray Head in 1963

The evening dances at the Eagle's Nest were popular, even though the dancers, clad in all their finery, had to make the ascent on the chairlift

holiday at Red Island. Those weekly excursions attracted up to 100 people at a time.

In 1970, I met my wife-to-be, Bernadette Quinn, and one of the first excursions we did was the ascent of Bray Head on the aerial chairlift.

Admittedly, the views were spectacular, but doing the trip in one of the open gondolas was slightly scary, even more so because it was all too evident the chairlift was coming to the end of its days. It closed down soon afterwards.

In recent years, says David Forde, the district administrator in Bray municipal district, there have been discussions from time to time about whether the chairlift should be reinstated. But those discussions have never gone any further and he says that if there were to be a new chairlift, it would have to be privately operated.

At least the original route of the chairlift is still clear of any developments, and David Forde suggests that if the chairlift was ever reinstated, it could go even higher, to the cross on the top of Bray Head,

built in 1950.

In the late 1960s, there were plans to build a similar structure in the Devil's Punch Bowl area near Killarney, while in the 1990s, there was much talk of a cablecar system linking Inisbiggle to Achill island in Co Mayo, but neither of those schemes ever came to anything.

Despite those setbacks, one aerial cablecar system is still going strong, linking the West Cork mainland to Dursey Island, opened in 1969.

I can testify from our own experiences that swinging high above the sound that separates Dursey Island from the mainland is pretty exhilarating! The service is run by Cork County Council and runs daily, with a 30-minute break for lunch. These days, there's a coffee dock in summer beside the cable-car landing area, essential because Dursey has no pubs, restaurants or shops.

Perhaps one of these fine days, Bray will get a modern cable car system to emulate the one in west Cork, and once more, Bray Head will become a top tourism attraction.

February 27, 2018

Hugh Oram

An Irishman's Diary

Capel Street is everything its "big brother", O'Connell Street, isn't – funky, irreverent, gloriously diverse and highly individualistic. It's the true heart of today's diversified Dublin.

It never started out that way, indeed when the street was created during the late 17th century, it was filled with fine houses, adorned by gardens to match, together with some Dutch Billy houses, posh homes for posh people.

A century later, Dublin's focus moved downriver, with the opening of the Custom House and the Wide Streets Commission decision to create what is now O'Connell Street.

Around that same time, Capel Street was reconstructed with two bay brick buildings, which give the street its present appearance, where no two buildings look the same.

Commerce arrived in the street, in the shape of apothecaries, jewellers and milliners, and during the 19th century, and people coming from continental Europe opened shops in the street. But many of the buildings decayed into tenements.

The architectural history of the street, as an architectural conservation area, is well documented by Dublin City Council. But the social side of the street is less well preserved.

Capel Street has an amazing collection of very individual retail outlets, selling everything from camping gear to pets, antiques to car accessories and hardware.

One of the oldest shops is undoubtedly McQuillan's hardware shop, built in 1867, long advertised as having "the finest display of tools in Ireland".

Just across the street is another renowned hardware shop, Lenehans.

Sex shops and charity shops help create a truly eclectic mix, along with vintage shops, a model shop, a pawnbroker, there since 1850, and a long-established men's fashion shop, Louis Copeland, but one thing you won't find there is a branch of a multinationally owned fashion chain or outlets belonging to one of the big supermarket groups, apart from a solitary Centra store. There's also Ladbrokes, so shiny looking it's a bit out of place.

In recent decades, multiculturalism has come to Capel Street in a big way. It now has some of the best Asian supermarkets in Dublin, a Brazilian one too, while that same diversity is evident in the restaurant sector. Korean barbecue restaurants, sushi restaurants and noodle establishments are popular and plentiful. Some excellent local eateries, too, are on the

■ **Tourists visiting Slattery's pub on Capel Street.**
PHOTOGRAPH: ALAN BETSON

66

Capel Street is the true heart of today's diversified Dublin

Capel Street "must" list, including Camerino, a local bakery and coffee shop, and just a few doors away, Brother Hubbard, cooking simple but interesting food.

Capel Street has some excellent pubs, including Jack Nealon's, founded in 1905, with a tremendous interior; J McNeill's, a traditional Dublin pub and traditional music venue; and the Boar's Head. Slattery's of course is well recognised for being one of the best live music spots in Dublin, a magnet for tourists.

Numbers 114 to 116 Capel Street demonstrate just how consistent Capel Street has been over the years in reinventing itself. These buildings originally housed the Dublin United Trades Council and the Labour League. In the mid-1930s, these building became the Torch Theatre, for a brief enough period, and then in much more recent times, housed an antiques firm.

Much of the street's architectural heritage does look decidedly shaky these days, but this ragged raffishness merely adds to the street's charms.

Strolling along the street, one cannot but be aware of the pulsating energy that comes from all this diversity.

Over the years, a great variety of characters have intensified this feeling, everyone from Peg Woffington, an early-18th-century actor brought up in Capel Street, who found fame on the London stage, to Gerald Davis, art gallery owner and Joyce scholar, who died in 2005.

He turned the family shop, which made rubber stamps, into an art gallery, and one of his many contributions to the gaiety of Capel Street, indeed the city, was appearing as Leopold Bloom come every Bloomsday. In recent years, nothing has symbolised diversity more than Pantibar, an iconic venue for the city's LGBTQ+ community, and which hosts the biggest street party of the year, Pride.

The street also has another essential resource for that same community, the Outhouse centre.

I was brought up in a relentlessly middle-class environment; Capel Street is a wonderful escape route from this conformity, which is precisely what you can't say about O'Connell Street.

April 3, 2018

Hugh Oram

An Irishman's Diary

Over the years, it's been inevitable that many of Dublin's streets and lanes have disappeared, in the name of progress.

But in recent decades, the largest-scale demolition of streets came when the Ilac Centre was being built. The land in the area had been acquired by the old Dublin Corporation over many years and its plans for redeveloping the site culminated in the construction of the Ilac centre, which opened in 1981. Around a dozen streets and lanes were demolished, including Coles Lane and Riddal's Row. One of the streets torn down was Little Denmark Street, where 2RN, the predecessor of RTÉ, began broadcasting in 1926. Four markets were wiped out, the Anglesea Market, famous for its second-hand clothes, shoes and furniture; the Norfolk Market; the Rotunda Market; and Taaffe's Market.

Today, only part of Chapel Lane and a little of Sampson's Lane remain, in severely truncated form, as a reminder of what once stood there.

When the other two Dublin city centre shopping centres were built subsequently, the Jervis Centre and the St Stephen's Green shopping centre, there was no big destruction of streetscapes. But building the St Stephen's Green centre entailed pulling down the Dandelion market off South King Street (where U2 played one of their first gigs), May's music shop, the Green cinema and Rice's pub.

Long before anyone had thought of shopping centres, when Busáras was built, probably the most controversial new building ever constructed in Ireland, the streetscape around it was much altered to make the new bus station an island site. It opened in 1953.

Much earlier than that, on the north side of the river Liffey, Oxmanton Green was a vast area of common pasturage that stretched from Blackhall Place as far as the Phoenix Park. It was much developed in the 17th and 18th centuries and part of it was given over to what has been the headquarters of the Law Society of Ireland in Blackhall Place since 1978. Today, there's nothing to be seen of this once vast green area.

Coming back to the city centre, Exchequer Street is one of the oldest streets in Dublin, going back to the 12th century, and until the late 18th century often called simply Chequer Street. It once ran from George's Street to Grafton Street. The way in which the street was used over the centuries changed dramatically; in the 18th century, it was notorious for its multitude of brothels, while in the 20th century it became the site of a telephone exchange. In the course of all these changes, many of the lanes off Exchequer Street were wiped off the map, including King's Head Court, Pennett's Lane and Trinity Place.

The Falcon Inn (Bleeding Horse) pub and Charlotte Street in 1972.
PHOTOGRAPH: DUBLIN CITY COUNCIL/COMEHERETOME.COM

Many of Dublin's streets and lanes have disappeared over the years

Elsewhere in the city centre, many other streets and lanes disappeared. High Street once had three lanes, each called Ram's Lane; all have long since vanished. Canon Street, off Bride Street, was once the city's shortest street, with one building, Rutledge's pub. When Bride Street was widened in the early 1960s, the pub and the street vanished.

The present Wood Quay bears no resemblance to what existed before the 1980s, when it had one of the most important Viking sites in Europe.

Close to the Grand Canal, Northumberland Street was a short-lived thoroughfare in the 19th century that linked Charlemont Street with Upper Leeson Street. Today, the only stretch of what was once Northumberland Street is that very short stretch of street where Upper Leeson Street swings round into Sussex Road, renowned for places like O'Brien's pub and the Canal Bank café.

In the 1980s, a short street at Kelly's Corner called Charlotte Street disappeared, to make way for a hotel and a big office block. The street officially ceased to exist in 1992. Fortunately, the Bleeding Horse pub survived this change.

It was the same story in the suburbs. Mount Brown lost its Cutthroat Lane, and Murdering Lane too, while in more recent times, Inchicore lost Keogh Square in the late 1960s

In Stillorgan, the village was bypassed and today, you can still see the turn into what is now the Old Dublin Road, close to Oatlands College; this sharp bend was once a bend on the old Stillorgan Road. The most recent loss of a thoroughfare in the city centre has been the Leinster Market, a pedestrian-paved passageway, once well kept, that is now barred to the public and is filled with waste bins and rubbish. It ran from D'Olier Street to Hawkins Street. It used to open out onto that once great centre of entertainment, the old Theatre Royal. As long ago as 1861, the Leinster Market had been described as a "quaint, narrow passage with very little light, even in its open parts".

Change is inevitable as the city progresses, but fortunately we've managed to hang on to most of our main streets.

April 18, 2018

Hugh Oram

An Irishman's Diary

On a glorious sunny afternoon recently, I strolled around Howth harbour and it felt just like being on the south coast of France, lovely and warm and packed with people sitting outside enjoying their food outside the many restaurants on the West Pier.

These days, the West Pier has close on a dozen restaurants and an equal number of fish shops, even an art studio, all intertwined with the mechanics of a working fishing harbour, trawler repairs, net sales and all the other paraphernalia needed by fishing crews, adding to the authenticity.

Needless to remark, all these restaurant and fish shop developments have brought the pun brigade out, as with Nicky's Plaice.

The West Pier is also excellent for walking, and the East Pier even better.

The history of the harbour itself goes back a long way, over 200 years. Construction on the east pier started in 1807, but after the collapse of part of that new pier, the great Scottish civil engineer John Rennie took over.

Ironically, the granite used to build much of the piers in Howth came from Dalkey quarry, which also supplied the same stone for the construction of its arch rival, what is now Dún Laoghaire harbour. The lighthouse at the end of the East Pier in Howth was built in 1817 and the adjacent lighthouse keeper's house in 1821.

One of the historical oddities of Howth Harbour are the set of footprints at the end of the West Pier. King George IV visited Howth harbour on August 12th, 1821; he was described at the time as being in high spirits, in other words, gloriously drunk. A local stonemason carved the king's footsteps on the pier, and they are still there today.

Howth harbour was built the wrong way round, so that it began to silt up very quickly. It had a brief tenure as the Dublin terminal for packet ships, but the traffic soon moved to Dún Laoghaire.

In more recent years, Howth harbour has seen much development of its marina, so the harbour is packed with yachts, adjacent to Howth Yacht Club.

A new middle pier was built for the fishing fleet, and the developments in recent decades within the harbour for trawlers have meant that Howth is now the biggest fishing port on the east coast.

The harbour is also noted for its RNLI lifeboat station, built in 1983.

Two lifeboats are on station there, an all-weather class boat

Howth pier and marina
PHOTOGRAPH: iStock

> "

A local stonemason carved the king's footsteps on the pier, and they are still there today

and a D Class boat, the smallest in the fleet, but the real workhorse.

There are all kinds of other historical curiosities around the harbour, such as the old mariners' church on the West Pier, once used by Scottish Presbyterian fishermen docking in Howth.

Between the Harbour Road and the harbour, the monument to all those lost at sea is a reminder of how treacherous the seas and the currents can be around Howth, while there's also the modern, totem-like monument close to the entrance to the West Pier.

If you stand on either of the piers at Howth and look towards Howth itself, much of the skyline remains thankfully undeveloped, while St Mary's Abbey dates from nearly 1,000 years ago.

One thing that struck me on my recent visit to Howth was how clean and tidy the harbour and the village itself were, with little sign of litter. Even the seagulls seemed quite magnanimous, well behaved even, taking it easy!

In and around Howth, there are lots of walks, as well as trips to Ireland's Eye. On a calm summer's day, Ireland's Eye looks so tempting. Two ferry companies operate on the West Pier, running trips to Ireland's Eye. One of them, Mark Doyle's Island Ferries, uses a unique boat, the MV *Little Flower*, which is the oldest passenger boat used in Ireland, going all the way back to 1921 but still in perfect condition.

On land, the Martello tower, on the way up to Howth village, is now a vintage radio museum, packed with old radio sets, much nostalgia on the bygone stars of radio, and Morse code as well. Howth also has the national transport museum.

On the Dart coming back to Dublin, there were so many foreign tourists I hardly heard a word of English spoken.

Once the harbour in Kingstown, now Dún Laoghaire, drew away most of Howth's maritime trade, but these days, the tourism barometer has swung in the other direction, in favour of Howth. The piers in Dún Laoghaire were also badly damaged in Storm Emma last March, whereas Howth largely escaped its ravages.

June 20, 2018

Hugh Oram

An Irishman's Diary

What I miss most about the old-style corner grocery shops, which have now all but disappeared, is having a chat with the person behind the counter, someone inevitably well-tuned into local gossip.

Modern supermarkets are all very convenient, but you don't get into discourses on neighbourhood foibles and follies at the checkout or in the bagging area.

Most social and commercial trends, good and bad, that have come to Ireland over the years have originated in the US. After the first supermarket opened, in New York, in 1930, it took nearly 30 years for the idea to cross the Atlantic.

A long-vanished supermarket chain, H Williams, opened Ireland's first supermarket, in Henry Street, Dublin, in 1959.

Supermarkets then swept the country during the 1960s.

Until then, refrigeration and convenience foods did not exist, so housewives had to shop daily in their local grocery store, giving their orders to the person behind the counter. Most items were sold loose; the deluge of packaging that bedevils present-day supermarket shopping did not exist. Tins full of biscuits, sides of bacon, weighing scales and big old-fashioned cash registers were usual sights.

Practically every item on sale was grown or produced locally, here in Ireland. Nothing had chalked up countless air miles to reach a supermarket shelf. No-one had ever heard of a ready meal or avocados.

Orders could be delivered, by bicycle or van, and long before the advent of credit and debit cards, customers could buy groceries on tick and pay at the end of the month.

With better-off houses, maids would go to the grocers or the shop would send a messenger boy to make a note of what was wanted.

Two chains of grocery shops dominated the retail scene, Findlaters and Leverett & Frye; Findlater's had shops all over the greater Dublin area, from Crumlin Cross to Foxrock, while Leverett & Frye shops were spread across the country, far beyond Dublin.

Customers discussed endlessly which chain was the more high falutin'.

On one infamous occasion in 1923, the Christmas windows of Findlater's shop in Upper Baggot Street, Dublin, which is now a Tesco branch, were broken by six DMP policemen, who helped themselves to the festive turkeys and ham.

The manager was too drunk to do anything and merely locked up the shop at its usual time that evening and went home.

Findlater's shops, trading for close on 90 years, were late in turning to self-service,

Most items were sold loose; the deluge of packaging that bedevils supermarket shopping now did not exist

although by the late 1960s, it had 10 self-service outlets. At the end of the 1960s, it made a disastrous decision to concentrate on a home delivery service, which failed within a year. The last of the Findlater's shops closed down in 1969.

Leverett & Frye's general manager, Michael Wogan, had a son called Terry, who became a renowned broadcaster. Michael Wogan had progressed from being manager of the chain's Limerick shop to the man in charge of all its shops in Ireland.

Another renowned store chain was Lipton's, which at the beginning of the 1960s, had 60 shops in Ireland, including one in Grafton Street, Dublin.

But by 1970, all its shops had closed down, such was the speed with which supermarkets were advancing.

Another long-forgotten chain, Blanchardstown Mills, sold most groceries in loose form.

The mid-1960s also saw the demise of the Monument Creameries, started in 1919, and which grew to 33 outlets in Dublin.

It was famed for its fresh dairy and bakery products, long before products were refrigerated or chilled.

Many customers were fascinated by the sight of assistants in its shops cutting one-pound chunks from huge blocks of butter, using wooden paddles.

Among countless small grocery shops that did well until the 1960s was the Wee Stores in Pembroke Lane, just off Upper Baggot Street, Dublin, taken over in 1941 by John Harrison and his wife Mary Catherine. They sold every conceivable kind of grocery item and much of it was locally produced. The tomatoes came from a neighbour's greenhouse just across the lane.

Mary Catherine was from from Co Monaghan and one of the regulars in the shop, who often came in for a chat, was a certain Patrick Kavanagh, who lived nearby.

Today, that shop is still in the same family, but is now the First Editions antiquarian bookshop.

The revolution in grocery retailing, instore and online, has been one of the most profound changes in Irish life over the past 50 years, in the process banishing the chit-chat at the counter.

July 24, 2018

Hugh Oram

An Irishman's Diary

Reginald Gray had a remarkable and very bohemian career as an artist, mainly in Paris, and his work is still highly regarded today. Yet his upbringing was decidedly middle class, in Blackrock, Co Dublin.

The family home was comfortable; his father had a management job in the Guinness brewery. Reginald himself, born in 1930, started off along the conventional educational route, beginning with a local national school, All Saints, and progressing to the old technical institute in Blackrock.

After a short period at the National College of Art & Design, his career took an unconventional swerve; he remained unfettered for the rest of his life. At the age of 19,

he joined a small group of Dublin artists in the Dublin Atelier group and he was much inspired by the work of a then contemporary French painter, Bernard Buffet. He was also taken under the art tuition wing of Cecil Ffrench Salkeld, whose daughter Beatrice married Brendan Behan in 1955.

Studio
When the two got married in the Church of the Sacred Heart in Donnybrook at the ungodly hour of 7.30am, Gray was the best man. By the time Gray was in his early 20s, he had his own studio on Leeson Street.

Some of his early artistic forays were into theatrical set design and the first set and costume designs he did were for a UCD production of *The*

King's Threshold by WB Yeats. The lead part in the play was given to a young actor and poet called John Jordan; Gray painted his portrait, which now hangs in the Dublin Writers' Museum. It was his first portrait in the long series of celebrity portraits he did over the years.

Gray moved on to doing set design for the Pike Theatre, including for the highly controversial production in 1957 of *The Rose Tattoo* by Tennessee Williams. Allegations that a condom had been dropped on the stage led to highly charged reverberations that lasted for years, but shortly after that particular production, Gray had decided he'd had enough of Dublin's small, often closely intertwined artistic set, and left for London.

One of the famed portraits he produced in London, in 1960, was of Francis Bacon, the Dublin-born painter. It now hangs in the National Portrait Gallery in London. But by 1963, Gray was on the move again; he had got married in London in December, 1958, but by 1963, the marriage was failing, so he decided to move to France.

■ Reginald Gray was taken under the art tuition wing of Cecil Ffrench Salkeld, whose daughter Beatrice married Brendan Behan (above) in 1955. PHOTOGRAPH: THE IRISH TIMES

One of the famed portraits he produced in London, in 1960, was of Francis Bacon

He had planned to settle in Paris, but en route, he stopped off in Rouen, where he spent about a year. The sales of his paintings weren't good there, so he became a pavement artist and also got a lot of work as an extra in the mostly operatic productions of the Théâtre des Arts de Rouen. Eventually, he made it to Paris, in 1964, and went to live in l'Académie de Feu, on the rue Delambre in Montparnasse, where he lived for three years, sharing accommodation with about 15 sculpture students. After three years at the academy, Gray moved on, living in various left bank ateliers.

Fashion photography
Then came another big work change, when he became a copy editor at the old *International Herald Tribune* newspaper. He often sketched portraits of personalities being interviewed, including Jean-Paul Sartre, Jacques Brel and Alberto Giacometti.

He switched career again, moving into fashion photography and then became a cameraman, filming some of the Paris fashion collections. In 1975, he also directed the first of his two

feature films.

Gray had a decade-long break in his Paris sojourn, when he lived in a château 80km north of Paris, where he brought up his second daughter and his son. But throughout his career, he kept painting portraits, very poetic in style, still highly regarded today.

His subjects included writers such as Brendan Behan, Samuel Beckett, Günther Grass, Sean O' Casey, Harold Pinter and Ted Hughes, other personalities like Garech de Brún and Yves St Laurent, as well as actors such as Juliette Binoche and Helena Bonham Carter. He even produced the unlikely portrait of a French banker. He was always contemporary in his choice of subjects; in 2008, he painted a portrait of Tracey Emin.

He reached the apex of his artistic career in the 1990s and was honoured by Unesco in Paris with a large retrospective exhibition of his work. The quality of Gray's considerable artistic output continues to be well recognised. He died in 2013, aged 82, survived by his three children and his second partner, Doina, whose portrait he produced in 2004.

August 13, 2018

Hugh Oram

An Irishman's Diary

PL Travers, the Australian-born writer who created the character of Mary Poppins, had close connections with Ireland and lived at Upper Leeson Street, on Dublin's southside, for several years in the late 1960s and early 1970s.

She was born in 1899, at Maryborough in Queensland, as Helen Lyndon Goff. Her father, Travers, was of Irish descent. Her mother, Margaret, had Scottish origins and was the sister of a previous premier of Queensland. Her father was a very unsuccessful bank manager, and his career was blighted by chronic alcoholism. He died when Helen was just seven.

She, her sisters and their mother moved to New South Wales, where a great-aunt supported them in considerable style.

As a child, Helen had a rich fantasy life and loved both fairy tales and animals; she often imagined herself as a hen. She was a precocious reader, of such works as Gibbon's *The Decline and Fall of the Roman Empire*. The editor who put her first poem into print was Rupert Murdoch's father.

From writing, she turned to acting and dancing, but she found family disapproval stultifying and Australia conservative and stodgy, so at the age of 24, she sailed to London. She created a new identity for herself, as Pamela Lyndon Travers, using her father's first name as her surname.

In London, she was very conscious of her Irish background, and in 1925 she sent some poems to George Russell (AE), editor of the *Irish Statesman*. He started publishing her work and he remained a friend and supporter until his death in 1935. Her association with AE drew her to Dublin and in 1939, over a decade after she had first come to Dublin, she adopted a young Irish boy called Camillus. But she flatly refused to take his twin brother and years later, when Camillus ran into him in a pub in London, it was a shocking experience, as he had been told nothing of his family background.

Travers was also friendly with WB Yeats and other Irish literary figures; these encounters enhanced her love of Irish mythology and storytelling.

Her first published book, in 1934, related her Russian travel experiences, but that same year, while recovering from pleurisy at a remote cottage in Sussex, AE suggested that she should write a story about witches. It evolved into her first book about Mary Poppins, the governess with magical powers, who had a parrot-head umbrella for transport, and an uncanny

■PL Travers: the Australian-born writer who created the character of Mary Poppins had close connections with Ireland

AE suggested that she should write a story about witches. It evolved into her first book about Mary Poppins

ability to organise tea parties on the ceiling.

In writing the book, Travers drew extensively on her own childhood experiences and fantasies, as well as her subsequent encounters with Irish mysticism.

When it came out in 1934, it was an instant success and she wrote a further seven titles in the series, the last of which was published in 1988.

Very private and even more prickly, she never married and although she had some relationships with men, her overwhelming preference was for women, and she had a long-time roommate, Madge Burnard, whom her friends considered to be Travers's romantic partner. Her private life always remained just that, totally closed off. During her lifetime, Travers went to enormous trouble to ensure that people couldn't access her personal history, the reason why she used initials in her name.

In the late 1960s, she decided to move to Dublin, to the house at 69 Upper Leeson Street that had once been her father's home. It's a fine mid-19th-century terrace house, still there, with no indication that the famous author once lived there.

But her mythological perceptions of Ireland, dating from the late 1920s, didn't fit at all into how she found modern Ireland, so her stay here was comparatively brief. Most of the rest of her life was spent in London.

She had also spent time in the 1960s as a writer in residence at various American universities in an unsuccessful bid to reclaim her serious literary reputation.

Walt Disney negotiated with Travers for nearly 15 years for the rights to Mary Poppins and the film emerged in 1964. Travers was very unhappy with many aspects of the production over which she and Disney had many strong disagreements. At the premiere, she wept. But selling the rights had made her seriously wealthy.

Disney's remake of Mary Poppins is due for release in December. The fantastical character of Mary Poppins has become a legend not only with countless readers, but within the entertainment industry itself. As for PL Travers herself, she lived for nearly the entire 20th century, until 1996.

October 23, 2018

Hugh Oram

An Irishman's Diary

For more than two centuries, Ireland has had observatories closely watching the night sky.

The first was Dunsink in Castleknock, Dublin, opened in 1785. It was where Sir William Rowan Hamilton, one of Ireland's foremost mathematicians and astronomers, professor of astronomy at Trinity College and Ireland's Royal Astronomer, lived and worked. It was also the place where the time standard for Ireland was set until 1916.

Originally, Dunsink was part of Trinity College Dublin, but it was bought for the State in 1947 and is now part of the Dublin Institute for Advanced Studies.

It has free open nights through the winter; if the skies are clear, visitors can see many celestial sights through the historic Grubb telescope.

Armagh Observatory is four years younger than Dunsink and it is a modern research institute with some 25 astronomers; the surrounding Astropark's attractions include scale-models of the solar system.

During the 19th century, two of the key observatories in Ireland were run by talented amateurs. In 1830, Col Edward Joshua Cooper set up an observatory at Markree Castle, just south of Sligo. For several years, it had the largest telescope in the world, which in the late 1930s ended up in a Jesuit seminary in Hong Kong. The castle is now a luxury hotel.

In the 1840s, the third Earl of Rosse built a huge telescope in the grounds of Birr Castle in Co Offaly. It enabled his lordship to see further into space than anyone had previously managed and one of his major discoveries was the spiral nature of some nebulas, today known to be spiral galaxies. Today, Birr Castle has an interactive science centre, where people can see 19th-century astronomical equipment.

The tradition of amateur observatories continues strongly to the present day.

The last observatory set up in 19th-century Ireland was the Crawford Observatory at University College, Cork, which dates from 1880.

More recent times this century have seen a second observatory in Cork. The observatory at the historic Blackrock Castle was set up in 2007, as part of the Cork Institute of Technology. The castle also has two planetariums, which put on many live shows for around 60, 000 visitors a year. They can even send an email to the International Space Station.

Also in Co Cork, Schull has a

■ **Dunsink Observatory in Dublin.** PHOTOGRAPH: ERIC LUKE

> **Dunsink has free open nights through the winter; if the skies are clear, visitors can see many celestial sights through the historic Grubb telescope**

planetarium, which was opened in 1989, thanks to the generosity of a German industrialist, Josef Menke, and his family.

The newest planetarium, together with a maritime museum, is in the old coastguard station at Greencastle on the Inishowen peninsula in Co Donegal; it opened in 1994.

Clair McSweeney, centre manager at Blackrock Castle observatory and planetarium, says that we have a very deep astronomical heritage in Ireland, one that is very easy to tap into.

She adds: "Astronomy is one of the most inclusive and beautiful of sciences and it's our job to unlock it".

Ireland also once had a great reputation for making astronomical telescopes.

Thomas Grubb was a Quaker from Co Waterford, a self-taught mechanic with a great interest in astronomy; he started making telescopes at his first factory and observatory, beside Charlemont Bridge on the Grand Canal in Dublin. In the mid-1860s, when the Grubb firm won an order for a colossal telescope for Melbourne Observatory, it had to move to a new and larger factory nearby, in what is now Observatory Lane in Rathmines.

The Grubb firm moved to England during the first World War, so the name of Observatory Lane is the only remnant of Dublin's one-time astronomical telescope maker. The firm then went into liquidation but was revived by Sir Charles Parsons, youngest son of the third Earl of Rosse, surviving until 1985.

Given the scale and depth of Ireland's astronomical heritage, it's hardly surprising that Astronomy Ireland claims to be the most popular astronomy club in the world.

There's just one cloud on the horizon: worsening light pollution, a growing problem in many parts of the world. A mere 5 per cent of the country now has pristine night skies, unpolluted by artificial light. The aggregated lights of Dublin are now so so bright that they can be seen from space. For people living in urban areas, the night skies are so blocked off by lights that the stars are barely visible.

December 12, 2018

Hugh Oram

An Irishman's Diary

Few if any public parks in Dublin have had such a long and convoluted history as Ranelagh Gardens in south Dublin, which also gave their name to the district.

It all goes back to Willsbrook House, built in the early 18th century, and which had close connections with the Church of Ireland.

A dramatic change of ownership came in 1768, when the house came into the possession of William Hollister, a harpsichord maker. His grand plan was to turn the gardens of Willsbrook House, which then stretched almost as far as Northbrook Road, into a grand centre of entertainment. Hollister named the gardens after Lord Ranelagh from Co Wicklow. After they opened in 1769, the gentry of Dublin flocked to this newly opened feature to enjoy all kinds of frivolities, carnivals and balls.

What really put Ranelagh Gardens on the map was the first balloon ascent in Ireland, organised by Richard Crosbie on January 19th, 1785. The balloon was extravagantly decorated, including depictions of Minerva and Mercury, while Crosbie himself was exotically dressed, including with a silk coat and red Morocco leather boots. Around 30,000 people turned up in the Ranelagh Gardens to see the balloon soar aloft, a remarkable event for its time, comparable to space travel in the modern age. Crosbie had planned to cross the Irish Sea but in the event, got no further than Clontarf.

Today, Crosbie, scientist and showman, is commemorated by a statue in Ranelagh Gardens, while his ascent from Ranelagh Gardens has been replicated in modern style in 2010, as can be seen on YouTube.

Shortly afterwards, in 1787, as the newly opened Rotunda Gardens at the far end of the city centre began to draw the fashionable set, Hollister decided to close the gardens. They were soon reopened by another entrepreneur, but any time he organised a spectacular event in the Ranelagh Gardens, heavy rain stopped the fun.

By then, the gardens had given their name to the newly developing village of Ranelagh, which otherwise would have been called Cullenswood. A further change to the use of Willsbrook House and its gardens came in 1788, when a group of Carmelite nuns moved in. It was an enclosed order, so the Ranelagh Gardens remained sealed off to the public for close on 200 years.

In 1975, the land was sold for building and the nuns retreated to Malahide. AIB was said at the time to have been interest-

Ranelagh Gardens in 1986.
PHOTOGRAPH: DUBLIN CITY PHOTOGRAPHIC COLLECTION

> **After the gardens opened in 1769, the gentry of Dublin flocked to this newly opened feature to enjoy all kinds of frivolities**

ed in Ranelagh Gardens for its new bank centre, before it decided to build its new headquarters on the Merrion Road in Ballsbridge, which it has only recently left.

Lots of apartments and houses were built on part of the site at Ranelagh Gardens after the old convent was demolished.

All this construction meant that the size of Ranelagh Gardens shrank drastically to one hectare, around a quarter of their original size.

The gardens were taken over by what is now Dublin City Council, which is still responsible for their upkeep.

Susan Roundtree, an architectural historian, who has lived in Ranelagh since 1984 and who has written extensively about the area, says that the council has overseen various developments in Ranelagh Gardens, including a new children's playground in 2017, which was very controversial with local residents when first mooted. The council itself plans to improve seating in the park during 2019 by replacing the park benches; it wants to continue improving its biodiversity, as well as enhancing the island in the pond.

The park is also often used for community events, including the annual Ranelagh Arts Festival.

The underground Swan river, once an open river, flows beneath the park, but has no connection to the large pond that is a comparatively new feature of Ranelagh Gardens.

The island in the pond has a "no fishing" sign, but the pond has long been fishless. The main entrance to the park is through a spectacular arch beneath the Luas Green line.

In addition to the Crosbie statue, the park also has a memorial cross to the nuns who kept the gardens shut off from the public for so long.

As for the future, Susan Roundtree can't see any reason why the park can't stay as it is, a little green oasis that, even in Ranelagh, isn't always known about.

She also says that the name of Ranelagh has spread around the world, as far as Buenos Aires, New York and Tasmania, and in London, too, while in the 16th arrondissement of Paris, three streets are named after Ranelagh. Paris too has its own Jardin du Ranelagh.

January 3, 2019

Hugh Oram

An Irishman's Diary

We may be going through a golden age for whiskey distilling, especially in this part of Ireland, but that's nothing new.

Back in the 18th century, Ireland had over a thousand licensed distilleries, so many in fact that in 1758 the minimum capacity of stills was set at 200 gallons, to reduce the proliferation of small whiskey-making operations, many of them home based.

Some of the great names in the whiskey business date back to the late 18th century, with Jameson, founded in Dublin in 1780, and Power's, also established in Dublin, in 1791. Power's originated the concept of Baby Powers and its former distillery lives on as the National College of Art and Design.

Even when Jameson and Powers came into being, the art of distilling had been actively practised in Ireland for some four centuries, although whiskey distilling dates back the best part of 1,500 years.

The origins of distilling were in Asia and from there, it was developed by the Moors, who used an alembic apparatus to distill the essence of plants and flowers, to make the likes of rose water.

The art of distillation was brought to Ireland by monks, probably from the Moors in Spain, and they adapted the alembic concept to create the pot still so renowned in Irish whiskey.

The first written reference to whiskey came in the Red Book of Ossory, in 1324, 170 years before the first written records were made of whisky in Scotland, in the form of primitive excise returns.

Here in Ireland, we not only developed a huge number of distilleries, but also a thriving illegal industry, in the shape of poitín.

By the early 19th century, consumption of whiskey, both legal and illegal, had become a huge problem, creating fertile ground for Fr Theobald Mathew, who founded the temperance movement in Cork in 1838.

Like all such movements, it surged quickly, then fell back. Within a short while, Fr Mathew had signed up 150,000 adherents and for a few short years, his preachings had a dramatic effect on whiskey consumption.

Yet throughout the 19th century, many fine distilleries were built, such as Persse's on Nuns Island in Galway.

Derelict buildings, once distilleries, can still be seen throughout Ireland. Towns and cities all over Ireland lost their distilleries, and still today partial ruins at least can often be seen.

Drogheda was once almost on a par with Dublin in terms of whiskey distillation, while Belfast and Derry were also important distilling centres.

The Powerscourt Distillery in Co Wicklow.
PHOTOGRAPH: CYRIL BYRNE

Back in the 18th century, Ireland had over a thousand licensed distilleries

The catalogue of lost distilleries is elegiac for anyone interested in the history of Irish whiskey, yet too often, little material or indeed whiskey was left for future generations. In the case of Persse's distillery in Galway, little survived except for the very fine mirrors it installed in pubs in the west of Ireland.

Irish distillers also created a spectacular "own goal". Aeneas Coffey, a former excise man, adapted the traditional pot still so that it could produce whiskey far more economically and quickly.

In the main, distilleries in Ireland didn't take up the idea, but Scottish distillers adopted it with enthusiasm, allowing them to gain a worldwide lead over Irish whiskey, which they've never lost, although Ireland has made up much of the leeway in recent years, with whiskey often considered to have a much smoother taste than whisky.

Today Scotland has close on 130 distilleries, while in our new golden age of whiskey distilling, we now have just over 20.

Some of the newer distilleries, like those in Dublin, Dingle and Ballykeefe in Kilkenny, have made a distinctive mark, while among the latest of the new distilleries are those on the Powerscourt estate in Co Wicklow and on the Slane Castle estate in Co Meath.

The new distillery at St James's Gate, Dublin, is due to have its first whiskey ready in 2022.

The Echlinville distillery in Co Down was the first new distillery in the North for over 130 years.

A further 20 or so distilleries, including four in the North, are either planned or in development.

Some of the new distilleries are also producing gin, another drink that has also been having a huge revival.

Long-established brands have also undergone much refreshment, such as Tullamore Dew, which combines the three strands of Irish whiskey-making: grain, pot still and malt.

By the early 1980s, Ireland was down to two distilleries, Bushmills, the oldest licensed distillery in the world, and Midleton in Cork.

The turnaround since then, by both foreign-owned and Irish-owned distilleries, has been remarkable.

February 18, 2019

Hugh Oram

An Irishman's Diary

For countless centuries, all the flour consumed in Ireland was ground in mills all over the country, although nowadays nearly all the flour we use is imported.

The long history of mills and milling, water and wind-driven, the original green energy, has been been preserved, thanks to the dedication of one man, William Hogg, a noted industrial archaeologist. He did a huge amount of work documenting the mills of Ireland, once used not just for producing flour, but for many other purposes, too, such as sawmilling and textile manufacturing.

Going one step further, he set up the Mills and Millers of Ireland Society in 2001, to document and help preserve Ireland's old mills. Appropriately, he is now life president.

The society has about 80 members, one-third from the North, with the remainder from this part of the country. Many visits to mill sites are organised, and this year's programme concentrates on distilleries, beginning with the Midleton distillery in Co Cork. Usually, about 40 people turn up for each visit.

The society's website lists 35 locations all over Ireland. Some are water-driven flour mills that have been restored, a far cry from the heyday of Irish milling, around 200 years ago, when Ireland had over 7,000 mills.

Back in the 1940s, there were over 900 working mills in Ireland.

Throughout Ireland, there are still the remains of some 660 old grain mills.

Some of the old mills have been meticulously restored, like Martry Mill near Kells in Co Meath, grinding grain since 1641. It has been in the Tallon family since 1859 and is still producing flour. During the first and second World Wars, this mill was working 24 hours a day.

The Tallons are very involved in the Mills and Millers Society, but James Tallon doesn't see water mills being restored to the functioning level of Martry Mill in the future.

Ballindud Mill, on the outskirts of Waterford city, which dates back to the time of the knights templar, with a mill race that is over six kilometres long, was reconstructed around 1978 by the late Paddy Griffin.

The Finnerty's Mills, near Loughrea in Co Galway, also water powered, have also been meticulously restored and have a museum.

Craanford Mill near Gorey in Co Wexford is over 400 years old, but was restored to full working order in the 1990s.

Fancroft Mill, on the borders of Offaly and Tipperary,

■ Newmills corn and flax mills in Letterkenny, Co Donegal

Back in the 1940s, there were over 900 working mills in Ireland

derives its name from an anglicisation of Fionn Choradh, the white water.

In addition to mills once used for producing flour, other mills also have fascinating histories, like Bealick Mill, near Macroom in Co Cork, which in 1899 saw its water power used for the first public electricity-generating station in Ireland.

The society's list of mills includes windmills that have been restored, including the two at Skerries in north Co Dublin, Elphin in Co Roscommon, the Blennerville windmill, near Tralee, and Ballycopeland windmill in Co Down.

Two of the most intriguing mills are Patterson's spade mill in Co Antrim and the Wellbrook beetling mill in Co Tyrone, complementing mill history at the Ulster Folk Museum.

Other old mills have been converted to other uses. Near Navan, the Old Mill House at Rosnaree was once a mill, parts of which dated back to the 10th century, and which finally stopped milling in 1932. Barbara Heise says that they restored the mill using traditional methods, but that they use geothermal heat produced from the mill stream. The many visitors who stay are often most attracted by its sheela na gig.

In Co Kilkenny, an 18th-century mill was converted into the Grennan craft school, while Nicholas Mosse has his pottery in an restored mill in the same county.

Mullins Mill, also in Co Kilkenny, has a craft centre, while Belmont Mill in Co Offaly now has artists' studios.

The Foxford woollen mills in Co Mayo are renowned, together with the Kerry woollen mills in Beaufort.

These days, we only have one industrial flour mill left, in Portarlington in Co Laois, and according to Dermot Doherty, of the Irish Bread Bakers' Association, about 80 per cent of the flour we use is imported from the UK, a situation that will create its own set of problems after Brexit. But in Co Wexford, the Kavanagh brothers, Andrew and Ray, are building the first new flour mill in Ireland since the 1970s.

To paraphrase the advertising slogan of a well-known Dublin bakery, the history is in the milling.

April 26, 2019

Hugh Oram

An Irishman's Diary

Few streets in Ireland have changed as drastically as Grafton Street, Dublin, during the past 40 years. But what was once a street full of interesting locally owned shops has become an identikit Main Street, with some 40 multinational retailers, whose shops are replicated in similar main thoroughfares in numerous other countries.

I first got to know Grafton Street well in the mid-1960s, when I worked for a publishing firm there. The street was chaotic, full of traffic fumes, as cars and double-decker buses hurtled down it from the direction of St Stephen's Green.

Directly opposite the place where I worked was a branch of Liptons, a long-deceased supermarket chain, where I could buy food for my lunch.

Grafton Street is old, having been upgraded from a country lane in 1707.

It was created by Joshua Dawson, a developer and politician, who also created Dawson Street. Dawson named Grafton Street after Henry Fitzroy, the first Duke of Grafton.

In 1758, Whyte's Academy was founded where Bewley's, since 1927, is now trading. Whyte's had the likes of Thomas Moore and the Duke of Wellington for pupils and kept going, in Grafton Street, until 1824.

Hodges Figgis, the renowned booksellers, had its beginnings in Grafton Street in 1797 and it remained there for just over a century.

Its shop at 104 Grafton Street was a great centre of knowledge in the city. In 1920, it moved to Nassau Street, stayed there for 25 years before moving again to its present location in Dawson Street.

Today, Dubray Books trades in Grafton Street.

Many other renowned firms had their origins in Grafton Street, such as Switzers department store, whose one-time premises are now occupied by Brown Thomas. Another noted firm, Weir's the jewellers, at the corner of Grafton Street and Wicklow Street, has been there for 150 years.

As late as the 1980s, many of the shops in Grafton Street were locally owned, the likes of Louis Wine and his antiques shop, McConnell's fish and poultry shop, the Eblana Bookshop, FX Kelly, the men's outfitters, and Pia Bang, the women's fashion shop.

Shree was an interesting Indian fashion shop at Number 87. Callaghans was a noted outfitters on the street.

Combridges fine art shop was a fixture for years on the street, before moving to South William Street, where it succumbed to the recession in 2012.

Reflecting one of the fads of the time, the street had two bakery shops producing hot bread.

Grafton Street even had a reading room for the Church of Christ, Scientist, as well as an Arab information centre.

Trading names for local shops were sometimes quirky, like the Lunatic Fringe ladies' hairdressers.

The Peter Mark hairdressing salon at Number 74 is a rare surviving example of a shop that's lasted in the street for

■ Dublin's Grafton Street

What was once a street full of interesting locally owned shops has become an identikit Main Street, with some 40 multinational retailers

well over 40 years.

Dunnes Stores has also survived in the street, as have the likes of Fox's, the cigar merchants.

Thankfully, despite turbulent times and threats of closure over the past 15 years, Bewley's has survived, its interior much refurbished, but its exterior untouched.

Grafton Street's flower sellers have also managed to survive, adding bright splashes of colour, while a legion of street artists have continued to entertain the public. The Diceman was a regular on the street during the 1980s and into the early 1990s.

One intriguing survivor from that time is outside Captain America's, happily still going strong. A small plaque notes that the Irish Writers' Co-Operative was founded in that restaurant in 1975.

But the relentless takeover of the street by multinational retailers began in 1977, when McDonald's took over what had been the old Mitchell's café.

In 1988, Marks & Spencer began trading in Grafton Street. In 1998, Boots took over the old Dublin pharmacy chain of Hayes, Conyngham & Robinson.

As more and more multinational retailers crept in, other long-established trading names in Grafton Street gave up the ghost, following the Grafton cartoon and newsreel cinema, which closed in 1973. Woolworth's, there since 1914, shut in 1984, as did West's the jewellers in 2010, after 290 years.

Another casualty, five years ago, was Thomas Cook, the travel agents at Number 118, Lower Grafton Street.

Grafton Arcade and Creation Arcade, two retailing curiosities, were redeveloped out of existence.

One big positive change had come to Grafton Street in 1982, when traffic was finally banned in favour of pedestrians. At that stage, around 40,000 pedestrians a day were using Grafton Street, long before it became a popular promenade for visiting tourists.

But one promise the old Dublin Corporation had given for Grafton Street in 1982 never materialised: a pedestrianised thoroughfare that was going to be lined with trees.

Back in the 1940s, after Leo Maguire had written a song called Dublin Saunter, first recorded by Noel Purcell, one line stuck in people's minds: "Grafton Street's a wonderland".

These days, as Grafton Street has become a relentless retailing hub for countless multinationals, I somehow doubt whether those words have much resonance today.

May 27, 2019

Hugh Oram

An Irishman's Diary

Many fine designs for buildings have been created in Dublin over the past two centuries, but there's just one snag: they were never built. Dublin has inspired many grand architectural plans that never materialised.

Undoubtedly, the most striking example of a building that was designed but never built was the John F Kennedy Memorial Hall at Beggar's Bush.

The very impressive architectural plans were published in 1965, showing a large hall capable of seating 2,000 and a smaller 500-seat hall.

After nearly a decade of wrangling, the scheme was abandoned in 1974 in favour of the UCD Great Hall in Earlsfort Terrace being converted into what is now the National Concert Hall.

Grandiose plans that never amounted to anything went back as far as the late 18th century, when an ambitious design was published for the eastern side of Parliament Square at Trinity College Dublin, but it never came to anything.

Railways

In the next century, as railways started to develop, an extravagant plan was drawn up to link what are now Connolly and Heuston stations.

Bridges were envisaged, spanning D'Olier Street and Westmoreland Street, leading to a double-deck colonnade for the railway, along the southern quays.

Later on, in 1872, a design for a new grand central railway station in the Dame Street area came to nothing, the same fate as the plan for a new central bus station in Temple Bar, more than a century later.

The same outcome befell a Catholic university in Clonliffe, Drumcondra. The foundation stone was laid in 1862, but that was as far as the scheme got.

In 1884, a huge new theatre, the Lyceum, at the corner of what is now Pearse Street and Tara Street never came to anything.

One of the most spectacular designs that failed to materialise was that for the Lane Gallery spanning the River Liffey, in 1912. In 1915, there was an even more far fetched scheme, for a transatlantic liner terminal at Blacksod Bay, Co Mayo, designed to supplant Liverpool; it found its final resting place on the drawing board.

As the State came into being, the Abercrombie Plan was touted as the solution to the ills of Dublin city centre. Among the buildings proposed was a new Catholic cathedral in Bolton Street and a new national theatre at the top of Parnell Square. That plan hung

■ Raymond McGrath's unbuilt design for the John F Kennedy Memorial Hall at Beggar's Bush in Dublin. Courtesy of Archiseek.com

Dublin has inspired many grand architectural plans that never materialised

around for the best part of 20 years before being shelved.

In much more recent decades, all kinds of lavish architectural plans came and went.

From the 1930s to the early 1970s, the Catholic Church was in favour of building a new cathedral for Dublin in the park it owned at Merrion Square, but nothing came of it. In the end, the church gave the park to the old Dublin Corporation, so that it could be opened up for public use.

Neither did anything come of the 1979 plans to build an official residence for the taoiseach and a State guest house in the Phoenix Park. Similarly, 20 years on from that debacle, a dazzling plan was drawn up to build a shimmering new headquarters, in Infirmary Road, close to the Phoenix Park, for what was then the Department of Arts, Heritage, the Gaeltacht and the Islands. This new dawn was yet another false promise.

So too were a 1998 plan to build a Millennium Mall, running all the way from Mary Street to the Carlton cinema in O'Connell Street, a 2001 plan for covered kiosks in O'Connell Street, a 2003 plan for a huge office block on Carlisle Pier in Dún Laoghaire, and a 2004 scheme for a 100-metre-high tower on the site of the old Player-Wills factory on the South Circular Road.

One of the most recent designs that fizzled out was that for U2's skyscraper, at the end of Sir John Rogerson's Quay, turning onto Britain Quay. The apartment skyscraper, over 120 metres tall, was to be topped with a recording studio. The design was released in 2007, just before the big economic crash, and it was all due to have been completed by 2011, at a cost of €200 million. We're still waiting!

Not long before U2's plans had been announced, a great residential and office tower block for George's Quay, overshadowing everything else in the city, got no further than an architect's out-tray.

Many of these schemes planned, but never built, were chronicled by Paul Clerkin of archiseek. com where there are 36 very full pages devoted to "unbuilt Dublin". With a certain sense of irony, Paul Clerkin is now living and working in Winnipeg.

September 9, 2019

An Irishman's Diary

Hugh Oram

DUBLIN'S BAGGOT Street is a most interesting architectural curiosity, with the two parts of the street dating from different periods. Lower Baggot Street is fundamentally Georgian, while Upper Baggot Street is mostly Victorian. These separate architectural styles live on, despite large-scale developments over the past three decades.

Lower Baggot Street has been home to many professional practices – mostly doctors and solicitors – for many years. A century ago, 126 Lower Baggot Street housed the Baggot Street private hospital, as it still does. The H. Williams grocery shop was flourishing in Lower Baggot street 100 years ago. Today Tesco is trading there, with the *Sunday Tribune* newspaper on its upper floors.

In the late 1960s, the Bank of Ireland caused great controversy when it proposed demolishing a whole row of Georgian houses, some of which had once housed the Lincoln & Nolan motor company, to build office blocks. Before Lincoln & Nolan, the premises had been occupied by Thomas Dennehy's coach-building works; the transition from horse-drawn to horseless carriages had been made in the earlier 20th century.

Despite widespread opposition to the destruction of this large section of the original Lower Baggot Street, the bank's offices were completed between 1968 and 1978, so minimalist in style as to lack any character. So much bronze manganese was used that it affected the world price of that commodity. Facing the bank in this part of Baggot Street is the renowned L'Ecrivain restaurant. Ironically, the bank itself is now seeking to move its headquarters elsewhere.

Just a little way along from the Bank of Ireland, at 63 Lower Baggot Street is the birthplace of the painter, Francis Bacon, whose chaotic studio now graces the Dublin City Gallery, the Hugh Lane, in Parnell Square.

The Convent of Mercy, a little further along, has seen many changes and extensions over the years since it opened as Catherine McAuley's first House of Mercy in 1831, but it still fits in well with the streetscape, complete with a sculpture of its founder facing on to Baggot Street. Catherine McAuley died here in 1841, from tuberculosis.

curious building, designed on the lines of a Greek temple, once graced the site – the First Church of Christ, Scientist, which lasted a mere 40 years from 1934, until it was redeveloped. Next door is the

The early Victorian façade of the Royal City of Dublin Hospital building on Upper Baggot Street

office block that housed the headquarters of the old Bord Fáilte; this was one of Dublin's very first modern office buildings, nearly 50 years ago.

One shop at the halfway point of Baggot Street is still fondly remembered – Parsons bookshop on the bridge over the Grand Canal, complete with its *Irish Times* sign above the door. It was once a great literary institution of this part of Dublin and some of its literary denizens repaired frequently to the Waterloo House pub in Upper Baggot Street, now modernised. Upper Baggot Street was once one of the favourite haunts of Patrick Kavanagh, who for many years, lived close by.

Upper Baggot Street has a whole litany of lost retail names. The cobblers' shop that stood near the bridge for many decades now sells mobile phones, while Mooney's pub on the opposite corner is now a bank. Shops such as Dunns, the fish merchants; Liptons; Findlaters; the Kylemore Bakery shop and the Monument Creamery are long gone.

Restaurants too, by their very nature ephemeral, have also vanished. In the 1960s, the Horseshoe Café at 24 Upper Baggot Street was a popular venue, while in more recent times, Kilmartin's restaurant, named after the bookie's shop that was once here, was a gregarious bistro. Today, restaurants include the long-established Langkawi Malaysian restaurant.

Kilmartin's itself has been replaced by a sandwich bar, one of a number of fast-food shops, coffee bars and sandwich shops

Road, long since replaced by modern office buildings, once stood the vast structure of the Episcopal church, a striking building, opened in 1835 and closed in 1945. In its latter days, it became an asylum for penitent women.

But some aspects of Upper Baggot Street remain, amid the flurry of new outlets. The original Royal City of Dublin Hospital building dates back to 1832; it is still in everyday use as a community hospital and its convoluted brick facade is undiminished by time. Another Upper Baggot Street institution is Weir's hardware shop, which has been trading here for many decades. As long ago as 1900, Weir's was renowned as an ironmonger's. In those days, it also had a bicycle factory on the premises. Around 150 years ago, when this part of Baggot Street was built, most of the buildings were private residences for the well-to-do. Further back, around 1800, this street was known simply as "the road to Blackrock".

As for the name of Baggot Street, it comes from Robert, Lord Bagod, who was given the Manor of Rath in the 13th century. His great dwelling, Baggot Rath Castle, once stood at what is now the junction of Upper Baggot Street and Waterloo Road. It's hard to imagine now, with the flood of traffic sweeping round the corner here, that this very spot was also once the setting for a great battle, in 1649, between the forces of the Lord Lieutenant of Ireland, the Duke of Ormonde, and a Cromwellian army.

Personally, I never fail to be fascinated by the numerous historical insights evident in Baggot Street. It's a great place for observing the results of the sweeping social changes Ireland has experienced in the

January, 2020 (unused)

Lightning Source UK Ltd.
Milton Keynes UK
UKHW031836120220
358614UK00003B/6